DON'T QUIT YOUR DAY JOB

Acclaimed Authors and the Day Jobs They Quit

Edited by Sonny Brewer

First Published in 2010
M P Publishing Limited
12 Strathallan Crescent
Douglas
Isle of Man
IM2 4NR
www.mppublishing.co.uk

Library of Congress Cataloging-in-Publication Data

Don't Quit Your Day Job Acclaimed Authors and the Day Jobs they Quit
Edited by Sonny Brewer

ISBN: 978-1-84982-108-7 (hardcover : alk paper)
1. Southern States - Social life and customs
2. Short Stories, American - Southern States. 1. Brewer, Sonny

Manufactured in the United States of America
10 9 8 7 6 5 4 3 2 1

Cover design by Barry Moser
Book design by Maria Smith

DON'T QUIT YOUR DAY JOB
Acclaimed Authors and the Day Jobs They Quit

Edited by
Sonny Brewer

Contributors
Howard Bahr
Rick Bragg
Larry Brown
Pat Conroy
Connie May Fowler
Tom Franklin
Tim Gautreaux
William Gay
John Grisham
Winston Groom
Silas House
Suzanne Hudson
Joshilyn Jackson
Barb Johnson
Cassandra King
Janis Owens
Michelle Richmond
Clay Risen
George Singleton
Matthew Teague
Daniel Wallace
Brad Watson
Steve Yarbrough

This book is dedicated to my dear friend John Evans.

Acknowledgments

I wish to thank:

My family, again, and always first—Diana, my wife; Emily, my daughter; John Luke, my son (who also gets a shout-out for the title); and Dylan, my son. I couldn't hit a lick at a snake, as my grandfather would say, without them near.

John Evans, whose misunderstanding of my answer to his question of what I'm working on next, led to this book.

The writers, my friends, who threw in here.

Booksellers by name everywhere in the world. And libraries.

Caroline Carter, my agent.

And, you, the Reader. Without you, all of us in this book would still be clinging, white-knuckled, to our day jobs.

Table of Contents

Introduction

by Sonny Brewer

When my stepfather died in a car wreck on a Mississippi back road, it was 1963. He was home on a weekend pass from Air Force guerrilla warfare training in the Everglades, bound for Vietnam, a twenty-two-year enlisted man at that point. He left my mama with his seven children, her three, and their one. I was fourteen, my oldest stepbrother was fifteen, and we stair-stepped back to one-and-a-half. Mama was thirty-two.

The next year for her must have been, as William Gay once said to me on a late-night stroll down Beale Street in Memphis, a dress rehearsal for hell. I can only dimly imagine how a woman of thirty-two must have felt to look around her house and see eleven pairs of eyes desperate for some word of what comes next.

I remember when she almost broke.

But, like the strong country woman she is—who could run a circle saw, drive nails, sew together a dress or a shirt, fill up the oven with two dozen biscuits—she didn't let it take her all the way down. She bit down on the pain of it and drew a good breath to redden her blood and add some gristle to her heart, and called a come-to-Jesus meeting around the kitchen table.

"You young'uns, here's how this is going to work," she said to us bigger ones. "I can keep food on the table. I can keep a roof over our heads. I can keep clothes on your backs. That's it. Y'all have to help me. You four oldest boys, go get a job. You are going to want

1

some kind of car before long. That'll be yours to get. And yours to keep gas in. If you want a Coke and a hamburger, you'll have to buy that, too. Y'all are on the football team. You'll have to buy your own letter sweater."

She laid it out, and she laid it down.

And Jimmy and Butch and Frankie and me, we stood up and were counted.

When I spied that old '47 Ford under the trees behind Russell's skating rink, I had the fifty dollars it took to buy it. I was head hamburger cook and chief chicken fryer at Woodie's Drive-In in Millport, Alabama. (I could pick up a whole chicken and knife it into two wings, two breasts, two thighs and two legs in less than thirty seconds.) I did not have four hundred and fifty dollars in my ammo box at home when a '56 Chevy caught my eye, but by then I was busting tires, pumping gas and wiping windshields, and changing oil at Ravis Ayers' Mutual gas station, and my boss thought enough of my work to front me the money and take it out of my check.

Mama co-signed a loan with me at Pacific Finance so I could roll into Tuscaloosa in a standard-shift '65 Chevy Bel Air. It had an eight-track player and was plenty good enough for a freshman at the University of Alabama. (The speakers went out and I got some home stereo box speakers and wired them up and attached them to the window shelf behind the rear seat. My Scottish frugality still wins over good taste, sometimes.) My stepfather had left all eleven of us kids entitlement to four years of college on the GI Dependents Bill.

Even with a monthly check coming in to pay for it, I didn't like college. Hey, I had been "somebody" back at Kennedy High School, where if I didn't know every single one of the 247 students in grades one through twelve, I knew their older siblings or cousins. I was on the starting football team. My girlfriend in the tenth grade was a senior who was head cheerleader. I had pull with the teachers and the principal, and worked it.

I had no influence at the university. I hardly knew anyone. I had no money after the $135 monthly check was spent—usually by the middle of the month. I was not an athlete. I did not belong to a fraternity. I did not have a girlfriend. I wanted to go home. To Lamar County and to trade school in Vernon to take up the study of welding.

And then along came an English comp class. And a teacher who marked one of my papers with an A+ and (I swear I am not making this up), "You are sweetness and light." All for filling up five or six sheets of notebook paper with a description of the campus bell tower, Denny Chimes. Sitting cross-legged on the grassy quad, pleasantly distracted now and again by pretty girls, the words came easy into my head like a cool drink of water on an Alabama August afternoon.

When I tore the pages from my notebook, folded them longwise, wrote my name and course number for the teacher, I didn't think a thing about it. Just another assignment, if a hell of a lot easier to complete than, say, some Statistics 101 homework. But then the professor handed back our papers, and when she put mine down on my desk, she tapped it with her index finger, made long eye contact with me and nodded, but didn't say a word. I looked down and saw my grade in red ink and two things happened. One, I fell in love with the teacher. Two, I am not now a welder. (At least two or three times a year, however, I still wish I could weld. And I might even learn the skill at the community college here in town; if I wait until I'm 62 in a couple of years, tuition will be free.)

I changed my major to journalism at the next semester. I moved in with my pretty professor, who taught me never to forget that I was Somebody. Okay. Now I've veered off into the dreamy world of fiction. But it is a fact, like slack in an old Ford truck steering wheel, that I was set upon a road that had Writing up ahead, my destination.

A damn circuitous route it's been.

Before I sold *The Poet of Tolstoy Park* to Random House, I was an electronics technician in the US Navy, a six-night-a-week singer in a honky tonk band, owned a tire store, sold cars, built houses, helped to found a weekly newspaper, edited a magazine, sold real estate, published a magazine, managed a coffee house, wrote in-house for a Fortune 500 company, and owned a bookstore. So my most recent day job was shelving and selling books and hosting book signings and readings at Over the Transom Books in Fairhope, Alabama, when it came to me to decide: Quit my day job? Or, pass on invitations to read from my book in bookstores all over the South, even out in California at Book Passages, turn down The Georgia Center for the Book, and such, and such.

I quit my day job.

Years earlier, Bill Butterworth, my pal who writes as W.E.B. Griffin, told me through thick cigar smoke on a barstool at The Magnolia Bar & Grille here in Fairhope, and in his kitchen, and at his desk, and riding in his Cadillac, "Do not quit your day job."

Bill said he would help me to the degree he was able, to break into book writing. "But first, finish my carport." I was a carpenter back in those days. (The best day job I ever had, as I think about it now.) And I did finish his carport. It still stands today. And he did guide me some. Bill suggested I try selling houses instead of building them, a nice segue to an easier day job without the obligation to clock in every day. Sell a house, get a fat commission check, and hang out for a spell in a hammock thinking up a plot line. I trusted Bill's advice, and got a real estate sales license, but I hated the work. When I found myself sales manager of a condominium project down at Gulf Shores, sitting in a portable building, with palm trees hauled in and stuck in the dunes beside a big sign with a painting of the castle I'd be selling, I lost it and quit that job, on a day when I'd sold two units to a man from Texas driving a drop-top Beemer.

Bill also gave me writing advice that I still quote. Like, it's okay to say little white church in the vale and stop there so you don't take it away from the reader, who knows of a little white church that is dear to them. "Don't tell me a damn thing about the cross-shaped knocker on the door unless it's going to be ripped loose and used as a murder weapon." Made sense to me. Still, I wouldn't listen to Bill on his other big piece of advice. Given the shot, finally, to do something as a book writer, and not a bookseller, I quit my day job.

You know, this little town I live in is perched on a bluff overlooking Mobile Bay, not far from the city of Mobile. I think of what Eugene Walter once wrote: "Down in Mobile, they're all crazy, because the Gulf Coast is the kingdom of monkeys, the land of clowns, ghosts and musicians, and Mobile is sweet lunacy's county seat." So we're told not to quit our day jobs and what do we do? Crazy-up and quit.

When I thought up this anthology idea (actually it was handed to me in a misunderstanding...but, hold that thought a minute), and pitched it to the writers whose names are in here, I said something like, "Tell me how those day jobs you quit inform your art these years later."

Rick Bragg said to me, "Oh, drop the pretentious literary bullshit. The pick-and-shovel work I did informed me there was an easier way to make a damn living." But read his essay in this book for a twist.

Back to the handoff: I was on my way to give a talk in Brookhaven, Mississippi, and had a flat in Jackson. The tire store said they'd have to get a tire for me first thing in the morning from their warehouse, so I stayed the night with my friend John Evans. When he closed his Lemuria Bookstore, we got together for a cheeseburger at the Bulldog. He leaned in closer, and asked above the din, "So, what are you working on?" I said I had about four chapters of a memoir called Forty Hats: The Day Jobs in a Writer's Life. John didn't hear the "memoir" part. "That's a damn good idea," he said. "Does it have to be living writers? I think it would be cool if you'd ask Richard Howorth to write about Larry Brown when he was fire chief." Richard Howorth founded Square Books in Oxford, Mississippi, and was a close friend of Larry Brown, who died in 2004. Richard had served two terms as mayor. He knew Larry when Larry was the town fire chief, an ex-Marine, before he was Larry Brown, acclaimed author of six novels and two short story collections, an autobiography and a collection of essays.

I don't know what else John might have said. I wasn't listening. I was going a thousand miles an hour down the road toward a new book idea. Not a memoir, an anthology. I'd ask Rick Bragg to write about busting rocks with a sledgehammer; I'd ask William Gay to write about hanging sheetrock in the hills of Tennessee; I'd ask Winston Groom to write about being a soldier on the battlefield in Vietnam; I'd ask Tom Franklin to write about wearing a HazMat suit and working at a grit factory; I'd ask John Grisham to write about being a lawyer; I'd ask, I'd ask, I'd ask...

Next day I kept my cell phone hot in my hand, on the charger as I rolled on my new tire toward Brookhaven. To a person, each writer got it immediately. Each one wanted to throw in, to be included, to tell readers about their day jobs. When I asked William to write about hanging sheetrock, he said no, he'd write about working at the pinball machine factory. What he wrote about was dipping boat paddles. The authors took the idea and ran with it. I knew we were on to something. A book that would be a picture of work in America. Untold sums of people have worked at all the jobs these writers have. And here were the best storytellers in the country giving voice to the dynamics of that work, of trading their time to get coffee and rent and keep a car going.

As we fished around for a title for the book, after being told the one I liked—("The Railroad as Art" from Howard Bahr's essay) would cause the book to be shelved with art books and mistaken for a handbook on steam engine paintings, John Luke, my teenage son, said to me, "Why don't you just call it, *Don't Quit Your Day Job: Southern Writers and the Day Jobs They Quit.*"

Badabing! I loved the seesaw irony of it, and the simple truth of it. Right at deadline, I was told to take out Southern, for that would keep it off the shelves of three-quarters of the country's bookstores. And I knuckled on that one, too. Tim Gautreaux told me his short story collection, *Welding With Children*, is often stuck on the shelves with industrial arts books. Steve Yarbrough's collection, *Veneer*, is put with the plywood books. Winston Groom told me to just let readers discover, once they're in, that they are in the South with the writers in this collection.

And I'm okay with that. The book will speak to you, no matter where in the country you live. For this reason: Work is universal. Somebody today might've punched a time clock in Tennessee to dip new-made boat paddles into vats of hot lacquer. Or in Maine. Maybe in Colorado, where people love to paddle kayaks and canoes on beautiful rivers and lakes. There are mail carriers in every state in the union. There are waitresses, and schoolteachers, and dump truck drivers, and lawyers, and pizza deliverers, and manure muckers from sea to shining sea.

And right now some of them are thinking of picking up one last check.

If there is a writer among them, just waiting to be discovered in a full bloom of genius, he will someday jump at the chance to write about all that hard work, and the day he quit his day job.

Foreword

by Ian Robertson

Warren Wilson College, a liberal arts college just east of Asheville, NC, is one of seven work colleges in America. Simply put, a work college requires all resident students to work. Freshmen, sophomores, juniors, and seniors do real work for several hours every week (we require fifteen), work of the type that can be called day jobs. The students are plumbers, electricians, janitors, cooks, and dish washers. They are doing all the things it takes to run a campus and, in this case, maybe also a village.

As Dean of Work at Warren Wilson, I get the chance every August to address the incoming freshmen and transfer students. The students are a sea of faces in front of me. "Welcome to a college that works," I tell them. Right away I tell them we expect them to work and to take responsibility for the work they do, to become engaged members of our college community. I tell them that in 1894, twenty-five young boys came into this valley and helped to establish Warren Wilson, not merely by enrolling in classes, but also helping to build the buildings, and to grow the crops, and pitching in on chores to support the student community. I tell the new students that after more than a hundred years we still do things the same way. So, these young people, many for the first time, go to work. They will work and study for four years. They will get a degree, and they will have learned the value of work.

Sometime later on during the first semester, I ask students to reflect on their first eight weeks of work at the college. As you can imagine, some have been working in jobs they don't particularly like. I tell them there are rewards for efforts that seem tough. To put things into perspective, I take out a letter, one from the college archives. "Here's a letter," I tell the students, "that describes a boy who walked seventy miles barefoot without money or a change of clothing, hoping by some chance he could get into school. There happened to be a vacancy and he was welcomed into the College." Then I ask the students, "How many of you walked here? I presume you all drove here or flew," I say, expecting silence.

But once, from the back of the room, came a voice, "No, I bicycled."

I looked up and asked, "Oh. How long did it take you?"

He replied, "Just over two weeks." It was my turn to be silent.

"So where did you come from?" I guessed close by, maybe ten or fifteen miles.

"Maine," he replied.

Silence from me again. "From Maine?" I wasn't quite sure what my next question would be. I took a look at him and said, "Well, what did you bring with you on that bicycle?"

And he said, "Important things."

Now, I, along with staff and faculty and other students, have helped a lot of people move into their rooms on the weekends when students first arrive. We take carloads of personal belongings up into rooms, many bags, lots of possessions. So I was interested in what was important to him, when the load had to be brought in by bicycle.

"Well, I brought pictures of my family, a journal. I brought a musical instrument. I brought clothes. Maybe most important, I knew why I was coming to college. I brought that."

I looked at the students gathered in the seminar, and I asked them if work, the real work of the last eight weeks, had helped them understand why *they* were at college. It's always a good discussion. The talk covers important points, moving past complaints about, say, being assigned to the trash-collecting crew.

We talk about the responsibilities of work. I want them to understand that no work is ever wasted, that something is gained intrinsically from focused effort. And, finally, I like to close our session by pointing out the joy of work, and the pride of work. I say to the students, "The work you do is hard, but it's also a creative effort, not unlike any artist." I tell them they should be proud of all the work they do.

"And when artists believe what they have created is finished," I say, "they step back and sign it." I tell students to step back from whatever they have done, whether they have buffed and cleaned a floor, raised a litter of pigs, washed a stack of dishes, or joined a piece of copper pipe. I tell them to step back and sign it. There's a deep satisfaction in knowing a job has been accomplished well, and there's also satisfaction in taking credit for the good job you've done.

The writers in this book, even if they are no longer at some day job, are still working. They've "graduated," as it were, to making a living interpreting their experiences, creating art from words. And when they look at what they have created, and sign their name, it may be the best payday of all.

Ian Robertson
Dean of Work
Warren Wilson College, Asheville, NC

Railroad As Art[1]

by *Howard Bahr*

Author's Preface; or, Bad News for the Young

In the Church, the Preface introduces the canon of the Holy
Eucharist which means that the sermon is over, *Deo Gratias*, and
the congregation may bestir itself once more. In literature, however,
the preface usually means that the sermon is just beginning, and
so it is, *viz.*

Writers—the artist species, I mean—are, as a general rule, a
likeable and friendly lot. They are rarely competitive in the way
scholarly writers, for example, are inclined to be. A scholar may
well be an artist in his own kind, but he and his brethren dwell in
communities and struggle with that "Publish or Perish" nonsense
while, in the creative realm, there is only solitude and thus only
Perish. Artists don't get tenure[2], nor can they rest on their laurels.
What they *have* written doesn't count; what they are *going* to write
is all that matters. For a brief while after publication, a writer
on tour may hear, "I love your work." How quickly the universal
question becomes, "What are you working on now?" Writers write
and write and write, publish if they are lucky, then perish anyhow,
for that is the nature of the craft. A writer is in competition only

---

[1] The footnotes in this essay are dedicated to David Foster Wallace, who said it was okay
to use them.
[2] Unless, obviously, they are part of the academic system, which is good luck. An artist
who scorns the academy on general principle is biting a historically generous hand.

with himself, and even when he harbors jealousy of another's success[3], it is always short-lived and rarely personal. Writers, in their solitude, are forever drowning in the troubled waters of self-doubt, and out yonder in the dark they hear the cries of their fellows. For companionship, then, if for no other reason, writers are likely to share a lifeboat when they find one.

My Persona and I believe this present volume to be a welcome lifeboat indeed. Everyone aboard this leaky craft is good company in a storm.

Regarding Persona: almost every writer has one. He creates it for much the same reason that a doctor or a soldier uses black humor to shield him from the grim realities of his trade. Persona is the mask a writer wears to readings and signings, the photo he sends to newspapers and conference coordinators, the little dress-up part of himself that he presents to audiences and to an indifferent Universe to prove that he is not *really* drowning, or, if he is, he doesn't really care. Thus the artist's Persona—bumpkin, academician, comedian, Southern belle or gentleman, rogue motorcyclist, mother-of-three, cynic, chest-thumping primitive—is always more or less ironic. A sympathetic audience understands this and plays along good naturedly. As for the Universe... well, the Universe always knows the truth, but no matter. Though God wrote the number one best seller of all time, He is, apparently, not much of a reader and therefore has never been a target demographic.

I believe that Persona is most valuable when it is worn modestly. Trouble arises, I think, when a writer, especially a novelist, makes the unhappy mistake of confusing his Persona with who he really is. This alone is bad enough; things grow worse when the novelist loads his Persona onto his work, thereby entering the shadowland of egoism. At a reading, the egoist often spends more time talking about himself than he does about the work that brought him there. The egocentric novelist burdens his work with acknowledgments and thanks to his editors and his loving, patient wife and the old

---

[3]The artist should be granted this flaw. When a novel about some silly Masonic conspiracy sells a million copies in its first week, and the person who wrote it already has a movie deal, the beleaguered artist carrying his $175 royalty check to the bank should be allowed to feel cranky. And anyhow, he gets over it in short order.

Choctaw woman who taught him "the ways of corn," and so on. He tacks on introductions, historical notes, prefaces, forewords, afterwords, appendices, and other apparatus that have their places in certain contexts, but are deadly to the novel which exists in its own dimension. A novel ought to be sacrosanct and left to stand in its own space, safe from intrusion, especially by the author. Addenda leave the story not a living thing but a self-conscious artifact squeezed out of its creator's unique intellectual journey, all this in an effort to convince the reader that the writer's unique intellectual journey really does matter. Nowhere is this delusion better demonstrated than in some authors' biographical sketches or, even more telling, in the roster of contributors to a literary journal, always composed by the writer himself but cast in the third person as if by some admiring sycophant. We learn that so-and-so "has sold mail-order shoes and raised goats and was last seen picking blueberries in New Hampshire while drinking corn whiskey and wearing his grandfather's original Big Mac overalls," or that such-and-such is "finishing a novel while living with fifteen cats and an African hedgehog in a villa by the Somme," or that a certain poet "loves macramé and tries to teach trees to talk in her spare time." All jolly, all eccentric, but, in the end, merely silly and pathetic, for such baubles ignore two irrefutable facts. First, an artist's talent is not the result of something *he* has done; rather, it is a gift of which the artist is no more than a steward, an instrument. Second, the intelligent reader will play along with Persona just for fun, but in the deep chambers of his heart, he does not care about an author's aberrations, current or otherwise. He does not care about an author's unique intellectual journey. In fact, he does not care about the *author* at all. What the genuine reader cares about is the *story*, and he would prefer that the author keep his self-trumpeting ass out of it. This is what I think, and here is my advice to the young: The *work* is all that matters, so let it stand by itself in a self-contained fictional dream, and offer nothing that distracts from the story, which, in the end, is the whole purpose of your struggling.

Author's Foreword; or, More Bad News for the Young

Many young writers, putting the yellow-wheeled phaeton before the horse, believe that Persona is what they must first achieve if they are to master the craft[4]. They read Camus and Joyce; they let their beards grow and don't do their laundry; they gather in bookstore coffee shops and drink espresso out of little cups and tap-tap-tap on their wireless laptops and talk about ideas. Am I being unfair? Perhaps. I don't know if young people read Camus anymore. I never did read him, though I enjoy saying his name: Ca-moo! Ca-moo! In any event, their Persona sinks its shallow roots in *ideas*, that old plowed ground where no one really knows what anybody else is talking about[5]. Hear what John Evans, a wise bookseller, saith: "I am astonished by the number of would-be writers who come around here thinking that an *idea* is enough." Well spoken, this implication that ideas alone are not sufficient to make a writer. What then? Nothing wrong with ideas, of course; a writer must have intellectual ammunition, if only to know where others have gone before him. Ca-moo! But what else? What is the essential soil from which a writer of the artist kind grows?

Here's the juice, children: If you want to be a writer, if you want to create a Persona and a body of work that is woven in the golden thread of Truth, then you must, before anything else, go out into the world and do some serious looking around. Ideas without experience tend to make a writer, especially a young one, smug and disagreeable, like a person who expects to be taken up in the Rapture. To paraphrase Mr. William Faulkner (who had the benefit of genius), a would-be writer, a nascent artist (and a scholar, too), must descend from the ivory tower (or the MFA program) now and then and participate in the streets and alleyways. He must listen to the way people talk, and watch what they do, and in the process get his hands dirty, get his heart broken, sin a little or a lot, get shot at maybe, find himself afraid, and come to know

---

[4] This, of course, is a delusion. No one, without benefit of genius, ever masters the craft. No one ever figures it out, which is one of the hard truths that leave the writer swimming alone in troubled waters.

[5] As an example, does anyone know what Deconstructionism really means, and if anyone does, what possible difference could it make?

what being lonely and tired and angry really means. He must learn that passion, if it is real, has consequences, and one of them may well be the grave. There is no other route to being an artist, here endeth the lesson.

Having said this, I reiterate my gratitude for the project represented by this volume, whereby I can at last violate my own doctrine and do something I have always wanted: that is, write about Myself with a clear mandate. After Beth Fennelly, Stuart Bloodworth, Inman Majors, George Thatcher, Marly Youmans, and several hundred others, Myself is my most favorite author and therefore one of my most favorite subjects to write about. Thus I offer up a compendium of personal experiences to illustrate my remarks in the paragraph above. I make this sacrifice, not for any personal gain, but to serve and instruct the innocent, which I have always believed to be among life's higher callings.

To begin, let us compose, in the highest traditions of the egoist, a suitably reverent, obsequious, third-person

Biographical Sketch of the Author: 1946-68

Howard Bahr was born Howard Leslie[6] Hereford[7] in the once thriving railroad and lumber town of Meridian, Mississippi, which, after years of civic pride and progress, exists now only as a crowded strip of indistinguishable motel and fast-food franchises along Interstate 20. Leslie's birthplace on 7th Street, a ramshackle old house in the Queen Anne style, has long since vanished along with all its neighbors, replaced by a parking lot accommodating the numerous and ever-growing congregation of the nearby First Baptist Church. This may disappoint tourists who hope to visit a literary shrine; on the other hand, it relieves the community of a fiscal burden, and the parking lot is always open for viewing.

---

[6] Howard Bahr has, from infancy, despised his middle name, especially in its childish diminutive form, "Les." He was only permitted to go by the name Howard after he enrolled in the University of Mississippi.

[7] The Hereford name originated in Normandy, invaded England, emigrated to Virginia, owned slaves, grew cotton, participated in a successful revolution and an unsuccessful Confederacy, and exists today among romantic and impractical descendents, both black and white. It is a good name, and the author wishes he could get it back.

Leslie was eleven years old and living in Dallas, Texas, when Sputnik, to the world's astonishment, went up into space and stayed there. In the general hysteria that followed, Leslie hungered to join the ranks of science, a tragic delusion, as it turned out. His stepfather, Mr. C.F. Bahr—The Old Man, scion of brick-headed Kraut immigrants to Southern Illinois—thought this an improvement over the boy's previous ambition to be a game warden, so, at Christmas, 1957, along with the usual plastic soldiers, cap pistols, and *faux* automatic weapons, the future author and prize-winning novelist received a Gilbert Chemistry Set. Leslie loved the test tubes, the little beakers, the mysterious chemicals, the pictures on the box of men in lab coats. Eager to learn, he sought out physics, chemistry, and astronomy in the family's doughty 1949 *Britannica*, a beautiful set of leathern volumes with pages that smelled of England. Young Leslie puzzled over these subjects. Like Belshazzar, he saw the writing but could not shew the interpretation thereof, and his heart was humbled, and so on. Moreover, his initial studies revealed that mathematics in exotic variations seemed to figure in every scientific discipline. This was discouraging. Leslie was already in the sixth grade and had not progressed much beyond whole numbers and multiplication up to, but not including, "times twelve," nor had anyone reason to expect he ever would. Leslie learned a hard lesson: Before one could become a scientist, one had to learn math. As a result, Leslie dropped science like a bad habit and used his Gilbert Chemistry Set to make explosive devices and stink-bombs for himself and his schoolmates.

The Old Man was disappointed in his stepson's failure at math. In a series of lectures, the Old Man implied that, were Leslie of *his* Teutonic blood and sinew, instead of the impractical, romantic, and hopelessly English Herefords and Lanes, he would be able to solve any number of logarithms and the like. As Leslie stood at attention before The Old Man (who did not allow parade-rest), that gentleman pointed out how the boy would find mathematics essential for success, and he would have to learn it if he wanted to *amount* to something. The Old Man said that if young Leslie

Hereford wanted to *succeed*, he must *buckle down* in math under his stepfather's direction. Thus, in addition to regular school work, Leslie was given arithmetic problems to "solve" at home. The Old Man meant well, and, as it turned out, he was sagacious. Leslie never learned math, and, as a result, he has never amounted to much of anything.

Back to the *Britannica*. That marvel offered other treasures for the inquisitive mind. Under "Locomotives," for example, the young inquirer could view the innards of a steam engine, while a peek at the illustrations under "Belgian Congo" revealed actual naked breasts more satisfying than those modestly tucked into brassieres in the Sears-Roebuck catalog. In the *Britannica*, Leslie learned that the people of French Indo-China, which would have a different name when he visited there a few years later, wore cone-shaped hats of straw and carried human waste, which they called "night soil," in baskets hung from a yoke. Fascinating! Guided by these revelations, Leslie decided to become an historical writer. This was his next tragic delusion.

His first book was given the working title *A History of the U.S. Air Force*. In preparation, the boy author-historian laid out some vivid, if historically confused, illustrations for inclusion in the volume: B-29s and B-36s (Whatever happened to the B-36, that ungainly goose with its "gun blisters" and drooping wings?) passing over in anachronistic formations, dropping strings of high explosive on Nazi armor down below. In every picture, the German tankers suicidally display huge swastika flags from their turrets and send streams of red-crayon tracers arcing aloft. A few years later, when "Les" Bahr watched Puff the Magic Dragon hose red mini-gun tracers through the Asian night, he found they looked just as he had drawn them. Much later, he would wonder how many dead lads, their names now stark and perpetuate in black marble, drew similar boyish fantasies of war on manila paper in their 1950s classrooms?

When the illustrations were completed to his satisfaction, Leslie Hereford turned at last to the text. He wrote, in pencil, a single sentence on ruled notebook paper: *The U.S. Air Force has never been stopped except by other planes and big guns.* It was an airtight thesis, and Leslie was encouraged. Unfortunately, his insight into the subject was exhausted, and a second sentence failed to appear. As would often happen with later works, he was drawn up short, as if a *fliegerabwehrkanone* had drilled the cockpit. From this experience, young Leslie Hereford learned another hard lesson: Before one could write about a thing, he must first know something about it.

The Old Man was a traffic agent on the Illinois Central Railroad—"Main Line of Mid-America"—a fine company of which The Old Man was determined to be vice president one day. In 1962, the *pater familias* was assigned to St. Louis, several steps up the ladder on the corporate pile. Leslie finished high school across the river in Belleville, Illinois, where he finally took the name Bahr for convenience sake and because it would be a useful disguise in a predominately German community. In high school, Leslie Bahr had an English teacher who praised his writing. This English teacher was a small, diffident man who always wore a bow tie and never raised his voice. In World War II, he was a bombardier until his silver B-17 was nailed by a *fliegerabwehrkanone.* He parachuted into the arms of a battalion of Kraut infantry and was a POW for months. Another teacher, Mr. William Hall, did not seem to care for Leslie; indeed, he may not even have known who Leslie was. Mr. Hall, who was bald and always wore a drab business suit and wire-rimmed glasses, taught American History, a subject in which he had participated personally in a tragic way: He had lost all his money in the Great Depression. Poor Mister Hall could not speak of that period without breaking into tears, a disadvantage for an instructor in a classroom full of hooligans. In their adolescent cruelty, Leslie and his fellow hooligans called Mr. Hall "Weeping Willy." At the time of this writing, Howard Bahr wishes he could apologize to that gentleman, but too late, for the old history teacher is dust now. One hopes that he laid up treasures for himself in heaven, where neither rust nor moth corrupt, etc.

Leslie first began experimenting in the short story genre in typing class his junior year. The students had a textbook from which they were supposed to copy exercises, business letters, invoices, things of that nature. Leslie, finding the text stultifying and of little virtue, improved the time by banging out, on the old Royal Standard to which he was assigned, heroic stories featuring him and his friends. They were brave woodsmen—game wardens and government hunters and so on. They all lived in a little town in the high Appalachians, and they all had girlfriends modeled on the ones they had in school, or wished they had. The stories were immature, which is to say, corny and pathetic. Nevertheless, they possessed a certain energy, for they were written under duress. Character development, plot, point of view, all the elements of fiction had to be puzzled out while the bespectacled old-maid typing teacher, hands clasped behind her back, inspected the other students' work. Leslie failed typing that year, along with algebra and Latin[8]. What did he pass? Who knows?

Somehow, Leslie Bahr managed to finish high school with the immortal Class of '64. The Old Man had a summer job lined up for him. Leslie was to be a messenger boy in the IC yards in East St. Louis, and then, in the fall, he would go off to college. This was contrary to the young writer's own plan, however. Though he had always been attracted to the craft of railroading, Leslie thought it would be a better idea to join the Marines instead. He was only seventeen, however, and to accomplish his goal, he had to have a parent's approval. The Old Man, an Infantryman in World War II, greeted his proposal with slander and violent denunciation. Marines were glory-hunters and cannon fodder! Leslie Bahr would not be a Marine! He would go to college! He would finally learn math and *amount* to something!

The truth was, Leslie Bahr was not ready to amount to something. He wanted to expand his knowledge of the world and have some control over his own destiny, or so he argued at the time. That was bullshit, of course: All he really wanted was to escape The Old Man and his god damned lectures. Out of kindness, his mother, who knew him better, took him down to the recruiting station in the St. Clair County courthouse and saw him enlisted in

---

[8] While the author never mastered algebra, he has, over the years, memorized a number of Latin phrases. He would recommend this course to any young person who, like the author himself, wishes to appear smarter than he really is.

the Navy in June, 1964. The recruiter, a Chief Boilerman, wanted to know why "Hereford" was on the applicant's birth certificate if his name was "Bahr." Leslie's mother explained that "Bahr" was easier to spell, and the recruiter, who needed to meet his monthly quota, was satisfied.

After boot camp and gunnery school—a dreamlike transition from a world he had hardly come to know into another he could hardly have imagined—Leslie and his teenaged comrades, who called him "Les," voyaged in antique rusting ships to the former French colony of Indo-China, steaming in and out like extras in a prodigious war movie, landing battalions of doomed boys whose fathers and stepfathers had allowed them to join the USMC. Les Bahr saw many people, mostly fishermen, in cone-shaped straw hats, but not a single one ever took a shot at him. Les Bahr was not traumatized by the war—indeed, he had been worse traumatized by long division and fractions—so Howard Bahr, in these later years, cannot excuse his erratic, often sociopathic behavior on those grounds. After all, an amphibious landing, a shore bombardment, or a picket boat watch were as pie compared to the Ia Drang Valley, Dak To, Hamburger Hill, Hue City (Semper Fi!), or the Tet Offensive.

On his voyages across the Pacific and through the Combat Zone (where he and his comrades got free postage on their letters to the homefolks and to the girlfriends who, in their girls' wisdom, had long since attached themselves to various draft-deferred college-boy sons of bitches whose prospects shone like diamonds in the broad fields of Tomorrow), Les became a fairly proficient sailor. Somewhere along the line, he stumbled upon Ann Tyler's early novels. He fell in love with Ann Tyler's jacket photograph and would have married her if he could. Other women writers he would have married were Rosanna Warren and Susan Minot[9] after he met them years later at the William Faulkner house in Oxford, Mississippi, where, under the name Howard Bahr, he was curator and a famous, much-beloved (if largely fraudulent) Faulkner

[9] Note to historians: Miss Minot is the person who broke Mr. Faulkner's reading glasses in the library. She didn't mean to. Curator Bahr was quick to forgive her, and he believes that History should do the same.

scholar. Unhappily, Howard Bahr's credentials impressed neither these elegant girls nor any other chick who happened by during his long tenure at Rowan Oak. In any event, Les Bahr, the young sailor, read *The Tin Can Tree* and *If Morning Ever Comes* a dozen times, and Guy Owen's *The Ballad of the Flim Flam Man*[10] at least three times, and through those novels he learned for the first time what Southern writing was. In addition, like his shipmates—indeed, like every other serviceman in that tumultuous era—Les devoured all three hundred and fifty four Louis L'Amour paperback westerns, which taught him how *not* to craft plot, scene, and dialogue. From L'Amour, Les also learned about the concept of Formula Writing, whereby an author could become famous by writing the same story over and over, changing only the characters' names. Howard Bahr would later identify this technique in the work of other writers, all of whom are too rich to mention. Howard Bahr does not think there is anything wrong with a writer being rich, except that he is not.

In November, 1966, in the shipyards at Portland, Oregon, Les wrote his first novel manuscript, in longhand, with a ballpoint pen, on typing paper stolen from the ship's office. It was a gloomy, fog-enshrouded narrative (anticipating *Cold Mountain*[11] by thirty years) of three Mississippi boys adrift after the Civil War who, in the winter of 1865, happen onto a town in the Missouri Ozarks. All the characters are traumatized, and, in the end, most of them are killed in a bank robbery. The manuscript was eagerly read by all Les's pals in the gunnery division of *USS Fort Marion*, LSD 22. These lads, all L'Amour scholars of course, pronounced Les's work equal to the great Western author who, in his prefaces, always assured the reader that if he mentioned a waterhole, the waterhole was there, and the water was good to drink, etc., etc., bullshit, bullshit. Tragically, the Missouri manuscript was lost when Les's rented room on Second Street in Pass Christian, Mississippi, was inundated by Hurricane Camille in 1969.

---

[10] While on R&R in Hong Kong, Les watched the movie of *The Flim Flam Man* with Chinese subtitles in a cheap movie house full of drunken English soldiers. It was a silly experience.

[11] *Cold Mountain* appeared in the same month as Howard Bahr's *The Black Flower* and steamrolled it off the charts. Mr. Bahr forgives the author of this book and hopes History will do the same.

So far, both Leslie and Les had written out of pure compulsion, informed only by some vague interior blueprint of what the world should be like and what their places in it should be. In the midst of this adolescent floundering, however, other forces were at work. Experience was beginning to accumulate, and with it attendant images and emotions that the author Howard Bahr would draw on for his highly acclaimed, prize-winning, and feverishly depressing novels of relentless violence in which all the characters are traumatized.

–USS *Calvert*, APA 32, on an amphib exercise off Coronado Strand. Seaman 1/C Bahr goes topside just after dawn to discover the water like a sheet of plate glass, unruffled by any landward breeze. A fog has crept in, obscuring the horizon, so that sky and water are of the same ochre hue and no demarcation between them. The ships at anchor have turned with the tide. Their boat booms are deployed, anchor chains stretched. They seem suspended in a silent universe without boundaries or definition; weightless ships floating in air. Presently, the bosuns' musical call for "Sweepers" pipes from every ship, and the watches turn out. None of them can tell the color of the sky.[12]

—Crossing the Pacific in November, 1965, outbound from Pearl with a battalion of Marines who still carry M-14 rifles. *Calvert* has received a dozen M2 .50 cal. machine guns still packed in Cosmoline; an old Marine gunnery sergeant has shown the gun division how to assemble them, check the head space, deal with the new barrel spring, and so on, while the shipfitters jury-rig mounts to shoot them from. Now all that is laid aside for the night, and the old ship steams at peace through the calm water. While elements of the First Cavalry Division are fighting for their lives in the Ia Drang Valley, Seaman 1/C Bahr is off-watch, asleep in his warm rack, dreaming perhaps of Kathy H–, his once high school sweetheart who is now engaged to a draft-deferred college-boy son of a bitch. So it goes. Suddenly, Les is rudely wakened in the red-lantern-tinted dark by Gunner's Mate 2/C Howe, a Korean War man, who was a Wyoming cowboy in another life. *Bahr*, says Howe. *Get your ass up.* Les obeys without question. He struggles

---

[12]This is known as a "literary allusion." All the high-toned writers use them.

24

into his dungarees and boondockers, his pea coat and itchy wool watch cap. He follows the old cowboy through compartments crammed with sleeping men, then up a ladder into the chill, moist night air. They go forward and climb the ladder to the gun tub and stand beside the shrouded 3-inch gun. The bow gently rises and falls. *What the fuck?* inquires Les in the usual tiresome, profane vernacular of the serviceman. *Be quiet*, says Howe. *Be quiet and wait*, he says, and lights a cigarette. The bow light is haloed with sea-damp; the silence is vast and palpable. There is the smell of the bitter, vacant hour; of the salt that clings to every surface; of the grease and the mildewed canvas cover of the gun. Above are the Northern constellations and a spray of uncountable stars and the Milky Way's white road through heaven. Les has seen all this before, but this is different. He has traveled from the comfort of dreams to this great silence and dark, and he and the older gunner seem the planet's final inhabitants, cast adrift on a ghost ship steaming into eternal night. This is Ur-time, God's hour, that parcel He reserves for Himself when he closes His hand on the axle of the world and feels the vibration of souls. The hour owns that bitter, vacant smell, true enough, and it has weight and presence, but it has no correlation to the luminous numerals on Les Bahr's wristwatch, nor to the strokes of the watch bell. Time is, for just a while yet, God's own, and the laws of mortals do not apply.

Then, all at once, God removes His hand, and the axle turns again. Anyone abroad at such an hour can feel it; those asleep can sense it in their dreams. Time belongs once more to the country of men.

The two sailors in the gun tub know it as a blush at the edge of the world, a rift in the darkness as though a gap were opening between night and day. Les Bahr is nineteen years old, callow and ignorant, but he understands, dimly, that he is witness to something extraordinary. How many days have opened thus since the world began, and how many men, on their lonely night watches, have been privy to the miracle? No matter: Les Bahr feels that he is the first. He believes that no man has ever sailed, as he is sailing, into the maw of a new day, a region of promise so musical, so beautiful, that it defies even his own youth's imaginings. Every dream he ever owned is waiting beyond that pink line at the world's edge.

It happens quickly now. The pink turns to red, the rift widens, the sky is scored with salmon rays and rays of orange like the spokes of a great carnival wheel. Fleeting clouds appear, all tinted with the color of the sun. The shroud of night falls away, and the red ball of the sun himself, like the rim of a molten coin, emerges from the deep: Helios and his flaming chariot rising from the mysterious bourne of Tomorrow, setting the sea alight.

The bow light is invisible now, for the sun has leapt full and round, and the eastern sky is blue, and the trifling lights of men are humbled. Colors are born anew: the haze gray of the deck, the darker gray of bollards and cleats, the black of the anchor chains and pelican hooks. The water is a deep green, and from its depths, flying fish leap in silver flashes.

The new sun paints Gunner Howe's broad, creased, weathered cowboy's face as he flicks his cigarette away. He looks old now, though he is only in his late thirties, and a trifle embarrassed. He shrugs. *I thought you needed to see that*, he says. Then he turns and disappears below, leaving Les Bahr alone in the morning to contemplate the nature of men. The young sailor is sleepy and hungry and homesick, but he lingers still, watching the day grow around him. He knows something has happened. He has changed somehow. What he does not understand just yet is that he is seeing connections among the tangled threads of a stunningly indifferent universe.

–*Fort Marion*, LSD 22, night steaming in the combat zone, no lights topside and no stars, no moon. The stern watch listens to the shush-shush-shush of the screws in the water, a sound so mesmerizing and surreal that it partakes more of silence than of sound. The ship's wake is a glittering arrow pointing homeward, if there be such a place: an arrow so straight and true that the ship might have been guided by GPS, but GPS does not exist and will not for a generation; instead, there is only a tired boy, the helmsman in the pilot house, whose gaze is fixed on the yellow dial of the compass repeater. He needs make few corrections in this calm sea. *Fort Marion's* blunt bow cleaves the water, and in the bow wave a pale luminescence: phosphorous, churned up by the ship's passage. Gunner's Mate 3/C Bahr and his gun crew, minds blurred from the long watches, lean in silence over the steel rim of the gun tub and see fantastic shapes and apparitions in the glow: loved ones' faces, drowned men beckoning, maidens reaching with delicate fingers, the lamps of cities long hidden by the sea. To walk about the decks is to enter a Stygian universe where the hand cannot be seen before the face, but the tiny red coal of a watch-stander's forbidden cigarette burns bright on a ship half-mile to port.

Once, in this stupefying dark, in the last hour of night before a landing, GM3 Bahr, just off watch and moving aft, comes unexpected on a fearsome tableau: a UDT team readying itself to be carried ashore, amphibious phantoms moving without sound but for the clanking of their accoutrements and cumbersome air tanks, and the racking of bolts in their Stoner submachine guns. Then the gurgle of an approaching diesel engine, the momentary blinding flash of a searchlight, and a sinister black Coast Guard gunboat comes alongside to take the frogmen away, away, away into a darkness even deeper. Meanwhile, the horizon is lit with flash and thunder: the destroyers and cruisers on the gun line are sending HE toward the beach in advance of the UDT. The shells pass overhead, whispering Death.

Later, in the gray light of that same dawn, Les squats behind a .30 caliber machine gun mounted on the bouncing sternsheet of a Papa boat. The gun is merely decoration since there are no targets out here. It is raining, of course, and the boat crew is soaked and shivering. They wear life jackets and steel pots. On the sternsheet also is young Billy Balk, a boatswain's mate, the best helmsman in *Fort Marion*. It was he who, not long before, steered them through the treacherous San Bernardino Straits. Billy Balk believes that, in a drunken rage a few weeks ago, he murdered a knife-wielding Filipino pimp in the back alleys of Olangapo. No one else believes this, but Billy does, and it has distracted his mind. Now, with cold rain dripping off his helmet, Billy Balk is redeemed. He points here and there, saying *Holy shit, look at that!* The two sailors know to pay attention, no matter how miserable they are, for around them, in panoramic Technicolor, is one of history's last old-time World War II-style amphibious invasions[13] unfolding across the troubled waters of the Gulf of Tonkin: a concert of ships and helicopters and hundreds of landing craft grinding shoreward, each one loaded to the gunwales with frightened, seasick boys whose fathers and stepfathers allowed them to join the USMC. Semper Fi.

—Steaming combat-dark on a mission in the South China Sea under a bright moon, and from the pilot house of *Fort Marion*, Les and his watch mates behold a vision cross their bow: the white hospital ship *Repose* festooned with lights, passing silent with its great red crosses and its cargo of pain across the glittering wake of the moon. Once, in Da Nang, Les visited this beautiful ship to call on a comrade who was injured in a terrible fall, from wingwall to well deck, in *Fort Marion*. The passageways below were green and white, filled with light. In the wards, wounded soldiers and Marines read, played cards, wrote letters. But not all. Some of the wards were dim, the shapes lying in the steel bunks still and ghostly, traveling the thin line between life and death. One does not have to walk that line himself to understand how easy it is to misstep.

* * *

These vignettes illustrate but a fraction of Les Bahr's adventures from age seventeen until, at twenty-one, he descended the gangway of a Navy ship-of-war for the last time. Together with the earlier accounts of intellectual confusion and experimentation, they will serve, perhaps, to illustrate the species and depth of experience necessary for the preparation of an artist. The young writer will no doubt protest that he cannot duplicate experiences of this nature in the modern world. This is nonsense and merely an excuse to

---

[13] Operation Ballistic Arch, November, 1967. You can look it up. *Fort Marion* was actually operating in North Vietnamese waters above the DMZ, hoping to draw fire from the shore batteries on Tiger Island so that F4 Phantoms could swoop down and destroy them in a scene representative of Leslie's colorful drawings in art class. Tragically, nothing came of it.

remain in graduate school. The object is not to duplicate Bahr's experiences, but to duplicate their *quality and intensity*. The young writer must accomplish this in his own context of time by seeking out endeavors that remove him from his mother's bosom and the safety and comfort of the student union. He must place himself in harm's way, a little.

In this brief Biographical Sketch, we have seen Bahr move beyond the parameters of home and family. Presumably, the future author matured along the way; after all, one hears much about boys (and girls, too, now) "growing up" in the service. Indeed, on the day he carried his seabag down *Fort Marion's* rickety gangway, Les Bahr seemed to have weathered nicely. He had a tattoo now and a collection of memories: sordid, tragic, painful, funny[14]. He wore a set of tailored dress blues decorated with his Gunner's Mate rating, a service stripe, a ship's patch, three ribbons, a mount captain's badge, and liberty cuffs from Hong Kong. His cap was set at a jaunty angle, and his neckerchief was tied in the salty "San Diego Roll" style. However, it was an illusion, for Les Bahr was still the same callow ass he had been when, as a Seaman Apprentice, he ascended *Calvert's* gangway three years before. He wore the emblems of experience only and not of maturity. All he had seen and done was not ready to apply itself to art. That would come later.

In due season, Les Bahr, as Howard Bahr, did become something of a writer. His main ambition in that regard was to solicit the attentions of young, braless, loft-dwelling artist girls. After bitter experience, he learned that this was only another tragic delusion, for women who buy novels, and underline passages, and come to readings, etc., are good and sweet and kind, but they all wear bras, live in the best part of town, and are married, happily, to rich husbands. They invite their writer to parties, which he attends on the chance that he might meet an artist girl there. News flash: Artist girls are not invited to these affairs. Moreover, the hosts want their writer to be cheerful. They do not want him to sulk in a corner. They do not want to be reminded of the lesson their writer

---

[14] There were many funny incidents, but they do not translate well into the language of civilians.

has long since learned: that art, like Vietnam, is lovely from the air—glamorous, exotic, mysterious—but down under the canopy, by the brown waters where the snakes live, it is a real bitch.

Now Howard Bahr reclaims his own narrative as he contemplates the next stage of experience, which he calls:

The Railroad as Art; or, Everyman's Existentialism

I was discharged from the Navy on the 153rd anniversary of the Battle of New Orleans. I went straightway, by airplane and Trailways Bus, to Gulfport, Mississippi, where my aunt and uncle lived. The Old Man, closing in on his Americabn Dream, had moved his family to Chicago, the home office of the Illinois Central Railroad, nine hundred miles to the north. This was not enough distance, but, since I did not care to live in Mexico, it would have to do.

I no longer wanted to be a scientist or a game warden or an historical writer. My single desire, borne over a thousand nights of shipboard dreaming, was to be a railroad man. I had not been ready before, but I was ready now, and I began at once to pursue this high purpose. My seabag was still unpacked when, on a wintry morning, I caught an L&N passenger train to Mobile and took a battery of tests and a physical examination. The L&N officials informed me that my eyesight was too bad for railroad work. It was sufficient for the Land of Cone-Shaped Hats, but not for "The Old Reliable," and there you have it. On the long train ride back through the early winter dark, my heart was heavy: here was only another tragic delusion, and I supposed I was doomed to go to college and amount to something. When I got off the train at Gulfport, however, I looked across the nighttime tracks and beheld a collection of red-brick buildings in such woeful disrepair that they could only be railroad structures. Next day, I discovered that these decrepit hovels marked the southern terminus of the Gulfport District of the Illinois Central. With trepidation, and steeled for disappointment, I entered the dim, dusty, wonderfully mysterious grotto of the IC yard office. A man came to the scarred board-and-batten counter, a sleepy and disheveled gentleman with a kind, if sardonic, face. I would come to know him as Gary Brown, the day trick operator. *Can I hep you?* he said.

I want to be a railroad man, I replied, *but the L&N won't take me.*

A second man, Charlie Stringer, the chief clerk, stepped up. He was smiling like the tom cat does when the goldfish flips out of the bowl. Charlie Stringer put out his hand. *Come on in,* he said, and, with a flourish, opened the counter gate, a piece of green-painted plywood, a humble entrance to a world that, once entered, would forever be the traveler's own. Two days later, I was a yard clerk assigned to banana traffic on the same railroad of which The Old Man was about to become vice president.[15] Some might sense a whiff of paternalism here, but The Old Man never knew until I called my mother several weeks later. This was a choice I made for myself, and a world I shaped for myself right under The Old Man's nose.

Once, not long ago, I read a book about existentialism, but could not make much out of it. Nevertheless, I thought it would be awfully clever if I could draw a parallel between railroading and existentialism. A man is free to make his choices in an attempt to find meaning in a world that is essentially absurd. He is responsible for the choices he makes, and this leads to anxiety and alienation and despair. This lean definition applies sufficiently to railroading so that I might look back and claim it as my first experience with Railroad as Art.

I was on the job about a month when, in a warm twilight, I carried some waybills over to the L&N depot. On my way back, I was jumped by three drunk, angry young black men who did not introduce themselves. They seemed to know *me*, however, for they addressed me as *You white motherfucker.* They knocked me on the side of the head, tore my shirt off, and ripped away my Episcopal War Service Cross which, next day, I searched for but never found. Their attack, and their remarks, were silly and meaningless enough to satisfy Kafka himself. One lad had a full

---

[15] Sadly, Mr. C.F. Bahr never finished his quest. He worked so hard, and struggled so manfully to amount to something, that he died of a heart attack in 1971, age fifty-two. May he rest in peace.

bottle of Four Roses whiskey, which he brandished menacingly, though he did not use it as a weapon—it *was* full, after all. I said, *Come on, motherfuckers*[16]. I did not fight well, as I might have had I been allowed to join the USMC, but I fought sufficiently, so that by-and-bye they stumbled on their way—bored, probably. I hope they came to a good end, but it is doubtful. Oddly, I was not afraid during this absurd encounter: it all seemed to be happening to someone else—the Other—while Myself stood aside and took notes. I had observed this phenomenon in Vietnam, and out at sea as well, during the times we were in peril. The Other would serve me years later when I set out to write about traumatized characters in impossibly violent situations.

I loved my job on the IC. I loved the good men and women who worked there, and even the mean and cranky ones. I loved the sounds and smells, and, as the complexities of the craft began to come together in my mind, I cherished the confidence I gained. I became a railroad man. I used to ride the switch engine on my days off, and the boys taught me to do trainmen's work. Liability would forbid that today, but I had the advantage of a less rigid time so that I could learn in the old-fashioned way. In November, '68, I followed my friend David Herrington[17] over to Mobile and worked as a brakeman on the Alabama, Tennessee, and Northern. On the road, however, I lost my confidence and deserted back to the IC in time to reclaim my seniority. David would do the same directly, but not for the same reasons. In any event, back in Gulfport, I supposed I had found my place, my craft, for the rest of my days. A tragic delusion.

When Hurricane Camille lashed out of the Gulf on Sunday, August 17th, 1969, I was working second trick, reporting for duty at three in the afternoon while the storm was building. Joining me were my Aunt Helen (whom we called "Sister," of course, and who, thirty-five years later, would succumb to Hurricane Katrina), my uncle Bill Gleaton, my twelve-year-old cousin David Gleaton,

[16] This epithet originated in Vietnam among black servicemen. It was so vile and disgusting that we white boys adopted it with enthusiasm

[17] In the early spring of 1970, David would be killed while switching a woodyard at Sumrall, Mississippi. May he rest in peace.

my widowed grandmother Rita Lane, and "Spooky" the big red dog—along with Charlie Stringer and Ted Harrelson, the agent—in the old nineteenth-century brick freight house[18]. About four PM, I fought my way, in my '63 Ford Pinto, up to John Quincy Avenue (now Martin Luther King, Jr. Blvd.) and checked the last trains to leave Gulfport: five extras taking all our cars north out of harm's way. I was supposed to record the car numbers of all these trains hauling ass over the crossing, but after the second one passed, I could no longer see anything, not even a freight train, for the blinding rain and wind. As a result, I was told later, cars were scattered and lost all up and down the railroad. I do not think this was true, but merely folklore. Mythical or not, it remains a catastrophe that I may always claim as my own.

It was a long night. The wind howled and cried in frenzy, as though a thousand Maenads swirled about us, hungry for our flesh. Sheets of tin roofing the size of boxcars sailed through the air, and our automobiles, parked in a row outside the yard office, were battered to ruin before our sorrowful and astonished gaze. When the storm's eye passed over, Charlie Stringer and I went out under a little overhang by the southside door. Charlie said, *Les, did you go to church this mornin'?* I replied that I had not. Charlie thought a moment, then said, *Reckon we could find one open now?*

When the storm resumed, much of our building collapsed, save the yard office on the south end where we had taken refuge. There, a deluge of rain poured through the ceiling, though the spot where my grandmother sat praying her Rosary was dry all night. Was it because she was praying, or because she was lucky enough to find a dry place? Who knows? *Ave Maria!* As for me, I was not afraid. Once more, the Other did the work, while Myself recorded every image on the blank pages of my subconscious. When morning came, mockingly clear and cool, we walked out like survivors of a raid by my old English teacher's silver B-17s. We were dazed and unbelieving. We could not make what we saw fit what we remembered. I had never before seen the universe rearrange itself in such a fashion, and I would not forget the feeling.

---

[18] Today, liability issues would have forbidden them this haven.

After the storm, I helped my aunt and uncle get their affairs in order, then, in September, I ran away. I was in Jefferson City, Missouri, to check on a job with the Missouri Department of Game and Fish; at the hotel, I noticed a train register on the counter. Hah! Next day, instead of going to the Game and Fish, I went down to the division office of the Missouri Pacific Railroad. I said to the trainmaster, *I am a brakeman and a yard clerk and I have run away from Hurricane Camille.* The trainmaster, a young man in shirtsleeves and a loosened tie, put out his hand and said, *Come on in.* Thus I became a brakeman on the MoPac main line, Jeff City to Kansas City, Missouri. It was late September, a lovely, autumnal time when the leaves were changing and the moon lay full on the Missouri River beside which we traveled. I received high marks from the road conductors under whom I "broke in," for in theory, I really was a good brakeman, having been schooled by the IC switchman in Gulfport and the old, crotchety alcoholics on the AT&N. I knew how to pass signals and make couplings; I knew the safety rules, and—something that seemed to impress my conductors—I was not afraid to grab a fast-rolling car on the fly, clamber up the ladder, and set the hand brake. I could fasten a torpedo to the rails without getting off the caboose, and I made good coffee on a coal-burning stove. However, when I was no longer a "cub," when the time came for me to go on the extra board, I ran away. I lost my confidence, just as I had on the AT&N. I knew I was a dreamer, easily distracted. I knew I was clumsy. I grew afraid that I might get run over, or, worse, get somebody else run over. So, to save myself and others, I slipped away in the night. That is what I have always told myself. Perhaps the truth is simpler and less melodramatic. Perhaps I was afraid of the newness wearing off. Perhaps I knew enough about the railroad life that I feared being trapped by call board and seniority list. Perhaps I was prescient enough to know that the craft I loved was fast disappearing. Perhaps I was afraid of having so much control over my own mortality. Or perhaps I was merely lazy.

I had run away before—from The Old Man, from the prospect of college, from Swift Boat school in the Navy, from the AT&N,

from Hurricane Camille. I would run away again and again. I would desert the Mississippi National Guard in 1974, and I would vanish from three marriages, and I would quit the PhD program at Ole Miss in the eleventh hour, when only my dissertation remained. Running away seemed to be the answer to everything, even when no answer was needed. Details and excuses are irrelevant. Only redemption matters.

I went over to East St. Louis, where I had some ruffian friends. Also Kathy H—and her draft-dodging husband lived up the hill in Belleville. I visited her once, which was poor judgment. I tried to go to a junior college there, on the GI Bill, but after a few weeks was told, by an honest English instructor, that I was simply not ready for a liberal education. Whitman's *Song of Myself* had something to do with this. At the time, I could not seem to get past the twenty-eight young men bathing by the seashore and all so handsome, etc. Then I learned that the Southern Railway needed a yard clerk. I got the job because, even though I had failed typing in high school, I could still hunt-and-peck faster than my fellow applicants: a dozen or so black lads who wore afros and shark-tooth necklaces and pointy-toed shoes, who had never experienced a typewriter before. God bless them, and I pray they have done well.

I did not like the Southern Railway much. I don't remember why. I do remember being scared shitless most of the time while wandering about the vast, incomprehensible yard, marking two-hundred-car freight trains in snow and sleet and darkness. True, I got called for a daytime trick now and then, but these usually turned into sixteen-hour double-overs, which was more work than a sensitive person like myself could safely endure. Then I heard that the CB&Q was hiring.

Once Upon a Time on the CB&Q

The Chicago, Burlington, & Quincy was a big granger road, drawing its sustenance from the fertile plains of the Midwest. On the "Q," engines were called "motors" and cabooses "waycars" after the Western fashion. Both were striking in red-and-silver livery. Rolling stock were emblazoned with the motto "Route of the Zephyrs," a reminder to the traveling public that, on the "Q," passenger trains ran like the wind.

I had been two weeks working out of the East St. Louis yard office: a dingy, rambling affair of yellow clapboard hemmed in by an impossible maze of tracks and surmounted by the yard master's tower, a region as dim, mysterious, and inaccessible as the air controller's lair at Lambert Field. I was, as usual, on the second trick, three to eleven PM. My official job title was "Train Desk Clerk," though, in fact, the job had little to do with desks. Had the Sioux or Cheyenne been running the railroad, my title might have been "He Who Wanders The Yards By Night," a rendering more accurate and certainly more romantic.

Now, in those days, no person on any railroad endured more hardship than the trainman in yard service. He worked outside in all weathers and could be kept there for up to sixteen hours. He lived in a world of movement that demanded constant vigilance. To the engine foreman and his crew, even the temporary warmth and safety of a locomotive cab was luxury. The switchman was, in short, the standard against which every degree of suffering was measured. Such was my observation, anyhow. Yet, for all his trials, the switchman was fortunate in one respect: he rarely found himself alone. This morbid affliction was reserved for the lowly, unsung, much-despised, scorned, and vilified yard clerk, a functionary invisible in railroad folklore, a weary pilgrim for whom no songs nor poetry were ever written, no eulogies composed, no sympathy offered. The mythic fog of romance and glory that shrouds the reality of railroad life has never touched the yard clerk; he plods unnoticed through the lonely train yards of history, his pencil forever poised above a yellow yard-check pad, his lantern probing the eternal night for car numbers that, if morning ever came, would be as vanished and forgotten as himself.

Carmen sometimes went about their rounds in solitude, though more commonly they were accompanied by an oiler. Special Agents—the railroad detectives—stood lonely stake-outs and prowled about in the dark with only their sawed-off shotguns, brass knuckles, slapjacks, hold-out guns, .45 automatics, and radios for companions, but I would argue that railroad dicks were designed by Providence to be, like possums or foxes, nocturnal and solitary creatures who could find happiness in no other environment. The yard clerk, on the other hand, was by nature a social organism. His preferred habitat was one of light and warmth among his fellows, a convivium of musty papers, spittoons, coffee cups, ringing telephones and littered desks, rattling typewriters, tobacco smoke. Often that region beyond the grimy windows of the yard office assumed, for the clerk, an abstract quality, like an alternate universe. For example, the movement of a box car from its position deep in Track 29 to, say, the Rip Track a half-mile distant demanded, on the part of the switch crew, considerable physical labor, cunning, skill, and (for the conductor) the foresight of a chess master. For the yard clerk, the same operation was only a matter of moving a waybill from one slot to another, with less exertion than it took to light his pipe or fetch a cup of coffee. Cynical and elderly clerks, after years of service, were able to bid on daylight jobs that kept them thus sequestered. For those of us in the lower orders, however, the reality was different. For us, who always worked in the shadows, the moment arrived, sooner or later, when we had to close the office door behind us and guide our reluctant steps toward the *Terra Incognita* beyond the yard lights, that country of yawning boxcar doors, groaning brake cylinders, surly hobos, and the relentless and indifferent night.

So it was for me on a freezing, moonless, starless night in November, 1969. It was, in fact, Thanksgiving. A year previous, I had passed the same holiday in a caboose on the AT&N, rambling its old-timey way through the pine barrens of Alabama. This year, on my way to the CB&Q yard office, I took my Thanksgiving dinner alone in a greasy hamburger joint on Missouri Avenue, the grey skies spitting intermittent sleet, the streets awash in filthy melting snow. Later, I would think about that meal, about the surly fat waitress and the truck drivers and railroad men hunched over their plates, the cheesy Christmas lights over the bar, the neon Carling sign in the window, and the skeleton of an abandoned factory dimly glimpsed across the broad avenue. It was an image not of Rockwell, the mawkish sentimentalist, but of the realist Edward Hopper, who knew too much about solitude and desolation. Hopper did but a few railroad scenes—a solitary boxcar, a locomotive—but in these he captured the fundamental essence of the craft. Look at his watercolors, with their bleak shadows and empty streets, and you will catch a glimpse into the souls of those who took their dinner in that forgotten, long-vanished café on Thanksgiving, 1969.

That evening, late in the trick, I was compelled by the night yardmaster to journey down to the vast abyss of "A" Yard, the inbound yard, the yard that lay along the Mississippi River, a region where, after sundown, only clerks, trainmen, railroad police, and felons ever trod. My mission was to find a cut of Cotton Belt Railway boxcars set out for interchange by a Terminal Railroad switch engine for the train we called the Blue Comet[19]—a fast freight train, St. Louis to Chicago, with a manifest of automobile parts. The drag was hot and ran on a schedule like a passenger train's, but the cut was not in the usual interchange track. Panic! The cars were misplaced, not unusual in the days when flawed human beings did all the work. The cars needed to be found, and quickly, for the Blue Comet's departure time was nigh.

In my subsequent quest, I reached a part of the yard illumined by no lights save the dim, faintly sinister red and green eyes of the kerosene switch targets and the miserable circle cast by my lantern. A little way distant, I could see the loom and lighted arch of the Eads Bridge where it crossed the river. Between yard and river lay a gloomy stretch of willows that stirred the imagination of a sojourner like myself. What dark horrors lay in wait in that somber wood? What eyes were watching, what alien tongues plotting ambush? I had a pistol, of course. In East St. Louis, everyone, even little children, carried pistols. Mine was not the heavy and various artillery of the railroad detectives; it was a rickety old Colt

---

[19] This may not have been the name of the train, but it is close. We all believed it was important then; not so much now, I guess, since all those fast trains have rolled away into an eternal night from which they will not return.

Lightning, caliber .38 Short, serviceable enough, though in fact it was no more than a good-luck charm, like a rabbit's foot or a St. Michael medal, both of which I also had on my person. Of what use are pistols and medals against the phantoms of the mind? And anyhow, shooting people whom I could actually see has always run contrary to my temperament. But never mind. I was glad to have the piece. It rested comfortably in the pocket of my wool jacket along with the rabbit's foot, my pipe and tobacco and matches, and the list of wayward cars that were the object of my quest.

Presently, I found myself in a bleak midwinter landscape of scrub brush and willow groves, of little-used tracks where the occasional forlorn boxcar, wheels rusting, waited for someone to find it. In this wasteland, I discovered at last the cut of Cotton Belt cars, perhaps ten or a dozen, stretching away into a tangle of willows and swallowed by a comprehensive darkness that I knew I could not enter. I checked the numbers on the first two cars and was satisfied that the rest would be in their proper places. It was cowardly, perhaps, but all the finances of the CB&Q railroad could not have driven me into that shadowy dark tunnel of whispering trees. I cursed the Terminal switchmen who had delivered our cars to such a remote place, but I was proud to have found them, and by-and-bye, if I survived, I would be able to report their location. I moved away from the willow groves and warmed my hands at a switch target. I set my lantern on the ground and filled my pipe and lit it, for I was reluctant to leave right away. My pocket watch said that, if I dallied here, I would arrive back at the yard office just in time to go off duty. Besides, I could sense something happening around me, more important than the fear that tightened my innards: something I needed to know about. The Other, who usually helped me out, was already off duty. There was only Myself, and I was alone.

In fact, I had never in my life, not even at sea, been more alone, and I have never been so alone, not even in marriage, in the forty years hence. It was, I decided later, an actual existential experience, where one might search desperately for meaning, but in the end find only himself in utter solitude, with nothing but pipe and tobacco, pistol, lantern, and the delicate blue hands of a Hamilton watch to define reality and arbitrary time. The place where I stood was faintly illumined by some ambient light. I heard the gentle patter of sleet, the sound of traffic on the bridge, the creak of willow branches, the far-away melancholy echo of locomotive whistles. The place smelled of the stagnant water of ditches, of grease and oil, of rust and creosote, and over it all hung a whiff of decay—not of man, thank heaven: there is no smell in the earth like that. Between the rails lay a myriad of bleached and weathered bones: generations of raccoons, possums, dogs, kitty cats who had died under the implacable steel wheels. Some of the more recent relics clung yet to the stiff, ragged flesh and fur the creatures had worn in life, and from these pitiful remnants the smell arose. All manner of trash lay about—paper drinking cups, newspapers, whiskey bottles, rags. It was the kind of place one might expect to hear the croak of ravens, or find an old, yellowed telegram from Death caught in the brittle grass.

I stood a while yet, smoking nervously, my hand touching the butt of the pistol in my pocket. Directly, I picked up my lantern, a trainman's lantern from my IC days with its bail and guard and naked bulb, a device made for signaling and only tangentially useful for finding one's way. I threw the paltry light against a bank of weeds and picked out a pair of shining eyes: a cat, most likely, for the yard was full of them. The "Q" shopmen, for sport, would trap a cat now and then, and put her in an empty oil drum, and build a fire under her. The eyes blinked away, and I heard a slight movement die in the weeds, and felt more alone, if possible, than before. It was just then that the messenger came.

The sound was like a silk garment moving, a whisk-whisk-whisk out of place in the dismal nocturne of the yard. Stranger still, it came from above, and instinctively I turned the lantern that way and in the light captured the broad wings and outstretched talons of a Great Horned Owl descending, intent on some creature only he could see, a field mouse perhaps, stirred up by my presence. When the light caught him, the owl beat his wings frantically, trying to stop his descent. I ducked involuntarily, he brushed my face and sailed away, off into the willows, where I could hear him rustling his feathers in annoyance. For a fleet instant, I had looked into his glowing unblinking yellow eyes, and I see them yet in this distant, rainy Mississippi midnight where I write in the illusion of safety, and I wonder yet what news the owl brought from out the dark. If the universe has no meaning save that which we impose upon it, then I am free to name the bird as a messenger. The message itself remains unspoken, but there is time to hear it yet. There is always time to learn, to listen for the voices of those who speak in the night. This is what the artist knows. It is why he listens always, and watches. It is why he welcomes his fellows into the lifeboat, that they might listen together.[20]

Back to the Old IC, and Beyond

At length, I grew weary of the cold, the complexities of main-line railroading, and the annoying accents of Southern Illinois. In April, 1970, true to form, I ran away again, back to Gulfport where, miracle of miracles, I walked right into a full-time clerking job, second trick, of course. I stayed three years this time, until August, 1973, when I left the road forever and ran off to the University of Mississippi, where ideas lay in wait. For once, I was encouraged in my flight by a wise, if contentious, comrade: the switchman Frank Smith, who knew things deeply, and felt them deeply; whose mind seemed to have opened like a lotus flower since I had been away. Frank knew, had learned somehow, that the way to be an authentic person was to cast one's lines into the darkness, regardless of the cost, and he instilled in me, the reluctant neophyte, this hard wisdom. One night in the yards, he put into my hands a copy of *The Hamlet*, which I read with the astonishment of one who has wakened from a long dream. We read *Steppenwolf* and found something of ourselves there. We read *The Greening of America* and

---

[20] Later, when I read Loren Eiseley, I learned that he had a similar experience with an owl at the mouth of a cave in the West. Of the encounter, Eiseley says, "I remember the eyes best. I caught them in my flashlight the same instant that I rammed my nose into the dirt and covered my head." Reading this passage, I felt a shock of recognition and knew for the first time that I was connected, through experience, to something greater than I.

Future Shock and listened to James Taylor, Carly Simon, and Cat Stevens, the '70s' greatest poets. Around a fire in the North Yard, we talked of things neither of us had ever thought of before. One night, Frank drew his pistol from his back pocket—it was a Colt Peacemaker .22, which he still owns and still threatens me with from time to time—and drew the hammer back. *Time for you to go to college, my man*, he said. College or death: not even The Old Man had couched it in those terms. So it was that I loaded my red Volkswagen[21] and went off to Academia, this time with the intention of *learning* and not *amounting*. I bid farewell at last to a life that I had assumed, by way of delusion, would be mine forever. Though not all delusion this time, for under all the degrees and accolades I was able to fool people into awarding me over the years, I remain, in some fundamental way, a railroad man, all because I passed through that plywood gate in the IC yard office in the early winter of '68. At my beloved University of Mississippi, I came to learn that ideas were important, but they meant nothing, were mere empty utterances, without experience to shape them and make connections among them. Existentialism, nihilism, Augustinian grace, negative space, surrealism: when I met them in college, I recognized them as old friends. I had already met them out at sea, or on the railroads in perilous dark.

It would take what sailors call a "long glass," and a long glass indeed, to see back down the glittering wake, over the rim of time, to all the lights and shadows through which I have passed since the moment I first understood that I might, however humbly, call myself an artist. I am not even sure when that moment was. There might not have been a single moment at all, in fact, but a slow accumulation of moments: watching my aunt working at her easel; by the noontime bayou behind Beauvoir where I sat as a youth; listening to my grandfather speak of birds and insects and the moon as we walked to the post office summer nights. The Old Man's lectures in a 1950s bedroom may have stirred me more than

[21] The car in which, during an adventure in September, 1975, my friend Roy Finger, a promising artist recently graduated from the MFA program, was killed when we met a pickup head-on, just south of Holly Springs, Mississippi. His brush is stilled forever. May he rest in peace.

I knew. It may have happened when I stood with Gunner Howe, that good man, at the edge of dawn, or rode in a locomotive cab along a moonlit river. The moment may have come while Frank Smith and I spoke of books and, yes, ideas around a fire in the train yard. It may have been born as I listened to the old-time professors at the University, men I admired and wanted to be like and never could, who had plowed behind mules and been in wars. It may have come in some trial of loneliness in the little town in Tennessee where I taught for many years and was grievously unhappy and whence my first novel came, and my second, and my third. I have tried to pay attention, and I have tried to be a good steward of the gift. I have learned from war, solitude, peril, humor, guilt, shame, and the firm bonds of comradeship. I have learned from the Church and from the struggle that Faith demands. I have listened to humble men talk, and exalted men, and learned from them all; I know the names of birds and trees and constellations and have seen how they sometimes speak of who we are better than we can ourselves. At times, I have been a bad boy indeed—even a felon now and then—and that was all right, as it turned out, for one gains wisdom of a sort from poor judgment and an afternoon in jail. I never learned the ways of corn, but I know about Demeter and Persephone and how archetypes shape us even in our smug Presentness when we think we are so wise and have all the answers, yet still plant by the signs as the old ones did, and still fear the night and grow melancholy in the dying time of winter and rejoice at the resurrection of spring. For all these things, light and shadow, I am grateful, for they have made me an artist, a writer, I think. I hope so, anyhow. An artist and a sailor and a railroad man, each inextricable from the others. One could do worse, I reckon, with the time he is given.

The owl who came to me in the old "Q" yards is long gone now, with no one to mark his passing. His feathers and bones have turned to dust in some willow grove by the river; they have enriched the earth, fed the young shoots of grass, blossomed perhaps in the wild morning glories of that desolate place. Yet his message remains, waiting to be discovered. In this way, he, too, was an artist, marked by the Great Spirit to carry truth to them who would listen. May he rest in peace, and so might we all. Amen.

November 13 to December 22, '09
Jackson, Mississippi

Real Work

by Rick Bragg

All my life, I believe, I will feel that shock, that force, rush through my hands, feel it travel up my wrists and past my elbows and into the tensed muscles in my neck and face. I even dream about it, decades later, and wake with my hands shaking. I bring them to my face in the gloom of an early morning, fearing the worst, to find them still there, trembling but not twisted or truncated or misshapen. Sometimes when I am writing my fingers freeze above the keys and I think about it, how even this easy, mechanical thing would be impossible for me if the man in the khaki work clothes had missed even once. But he never missed. I pound home one more key, then another, clumsy fingers searching for the words, and know I will never be half the man he was. He swung that sledge at the end of the chisel I held in my unsteady hands, and he was dead solid perfect a thousand times, ten thousand, more. All I do is tap a damn key, and I rarely get it right the first time.

"What if you miss?" I asked him, just once.

"I won't miss, son," he replied.

I held that chisel for the first time when I was eleven, aiming it at the place where the black rubber of a big, dump truck tire joined the steel wheel. It took the force of a sledge to break that seal on a flat tire, and I did it, among other things, till I was eighteen, till

I finally straightened up, dropped that chisel in the dirt, and got myself a necktie job.

The man in khakis, my uncle Edward Fair, gave me work all of my young life, but it was hard, dirty, sometimes dangerous work, and I forgot to thank him, across those years, for the money I made. I wasted it on rolling death traps and peroxide blondes, on honky tonks and rum and cokes and pearl snap button shirts—actually, I guess I didn't waste a damn dime. But along the way he gave me some free advice, and I have thanked him, many times, for that.

Hang some of those tools on the wall, he told me, some of those chainsaws or chisels or big yard forks that would hold seventy pounds of rock in a single scoop. Hang 'em up high so you can see 'em real good, he told me, after you finally get yourself an easy job, and every time you feel like griping, take a long, hard look.

I never did hang a sledgehammer on the wall, but I do think about what he told me, when I start feeling sorry for myself, and sometimes I am a little ashamed and sometimes I laugh out loud.

Those of us who write for a living want the rest of the world to think it's real, real hard. We invent myths about it, to make it seem like man's work. I have always loved the stories about fighting writers, carousing writers, whiskey-drinking, bull-fighting, foxhole-diving, swordfish-catching, señorita-romancing, big game-hunting, husband-defying writers, and tell myself that is where I belong, not with the fretting, pencil-neck writers who need to see their therapist twice a week to connect with their inner child. But the toughest writer I ever met, I ever heard of, would have lasted about a week on my Uncle Ed's crew.

It makes the fans of such writers angry, to hear that their storied writers would not match up against a plain ol' redneck. But really. How long do you think Mailer would have lasted against a roofer with a tire iron?

I have never considered myself a tough man, within the fraternity of working men, but I know I am one when I stray outside it. I owe my uncle for that toughness, for what there is in me. But mostly what I got from my Uncle Ed was perspective, enough of it, one shovelful at a time, to realize how good I have it now, how easy it is—at its hardest—to do what I do.

My Uncle Ed was his own boss. He ran a bulldozer and a front-end loader, at the heart of his operation, cutting roads, clearing lots, grading for construction. I have seen him knock the top off a mountain, or dig a lake, in the space of an afternoon.

He needed us, my brothers and me, for the pick and shovel work, for the tight places the machines could not get into. We dug water lines, ran chainsaws, loaded pulpwood by hand, for minimum wage.

The first job I had with the crew was cleaning the mud and roots from bulldozer tracks when I was about ten years old. The giant yellow machines would growl and churn through the red clay, unstoppable, until their tracks got all gummed and choked up with a debris. The operators would stop them, impatient, and I would gouge and hack at them until the tracks were free.

It paid nearly nothing, not even minimum wage, but it was my way into that fraternity, a circle of men in training where you settled your disagreements with your fists, or a broken-off tree limb, or whatever you could find in the dirt.

And the best that could ever happen to you, I once believed, was to be the man on the machine.

We would have resented my uncle, sitting up on that big machine, so high and mighty, if he had not on a regular basis crawled down there in the muck and dust with us, and put us to shame. He could do more, faster, than most of the young men on his crew. The shameful part was that he outworked us on damaged legs. A car had crushed him below the waist when he was still a teenager himself, and his legs were held together with steel rods. It was hard to complain, much, when a man with a built-up shoe was kicking your ass, was loading more rock, digging more dirt, piling up more pulpwood.

But still, it was hateful work. It did not teach me character, just toughness, taught me that I could stoop lower and strain harder than most people were willing to.

The worst of it was the pulpwooding. I had never met a pulpwooder who had all his fingers and toes, but it had to be done, when we cleared land for houses or roads. To leave the pulpwood piled on the land would be like burning money on the ground.

We did not fell the trees. The bulldozers did that, knocking the pines down into a morass of stumps, trunks and interlocking limbs. We waded into it the best we could, big chainsaws bucking in our hands, and took off the limbs, then cut the pulpwood into logs.

The biggest problem was the footing. The trees were slick with mud, and piled atop one another, limbs twisted back under thousands of pounds of pressure. At best, a tree would just come alive as you straddled or stood on it, bucking, heaving or twisting, rolling you underneath.

At worst, a limb as long as a transfer truck and as big around as your waist would just whip free, suddenly, and bash your brains out.

I was hit so hard, routinely, that I had to think a minute to remember my name. Once, working near my brother, Sam, a limb sent me crashing into him, my saw buzzing, and I came within inches of opening him up like a fish.

You worked at a run, because every minute the big machines idled nearby, unable to get at the dirt under your feet and under your trees, money was trickling away. You did not stop except for a few seconds, to wipe the bits of bark from your eyes. You did not even stop for the snakes.

Despite what the timber companies want you to believe, not very much lives in a pine barren except rats and snakes. Old growth timber, a true forest, is home to all kinds of living things, but more and more of Alabama is under pines, planted to control erosion after clear-cutting, and nothing warm and fuzzy likes to live in the gummy, sappy, acid-rich world of pines.

The rats flee, when the trees come down, but the snakes just get belligerent. I don't know how many dozens of rattlers I faced down in that mess of limbs and roots and mud, but usually with the same outcome.

The problem is, you can't hear a warning, can't hear them rattle over the noise of your saw. You just see a movement, a limb that writhes more than it should, and you hold out the saw or swing it in a slow arc, and the snake can't resist. It strikes out at the whirring teeth, and its head disappears in a spray of red.

Once the pulpwood is cut you pile and burn the limbs, so the trucks can get into the woods close to you, and you start loading the logs by hand. The skinny ones are light, and you throw them around, and the fat ones—hundreds of pounds apiece—are light, too, because you are tougher than anybody else, and you pick up pine logs that weigh more than you, and heave them onto the trucks.

At the end of the day you look barely human, specked head to toe with bark, sap in your hair, grime in every crease of your skin. You don't make enough that day to replace the shirt and pants you ruin in the trees.

The next day might be easy. You may just have to haul some dirt, may just have to coax the old Chevy dump truck up the side of a mountain, and hope its bald tires and brakes will last till you get back down again. Or it may be twelve hours on the end of a shovel handle, or pick.

I had a friend once who was always after me to go to the weight room with him, and I would laugh out loud every time.

The most ridiculous work was on the end of a yard fork. It was about half a man long, with thick iron tines. It looked like a giant salad fork. With it, you scooped up the rocks, roots and mud clods that were raked or dragged on landscapes, and either piled it into a wheelbarrow or heaved it over the side of a dump truck.

It was ridiculous because of the height of the truck. I was not tall enough, and the fork was not long enough, to allow me to successfully heave the load of rocks or clods over the side. I had to get a running start and jump, hoping the sheer force of it would carry me high enough, with my fifty-pound load, so that I could heave it over the side of the truck. If you could leap high enough, your load cleared the lip of the truck and you banged, hard, into the iron bed.

If you did not, you banged hard into the iron bed, and fifty pounds of rock and mud clods showered your head.

At the end of those days, you felt like you had been drawn and quartered.

But this is just whining, I know. It did not kill me, though it killed others.

I know that not just any fool can be a writer. But I also know that not just any fool could get that yard fork over the lip of that truck.

I know which makes me prouder, now.

A Late Start in Mississippi

by Larry Brown

I've only been writing for about twelve years. I didn't start until I was twenty-nine. I figure most people who write start a lot younger than that. Most people who want to make something out of their lives probably take control of them a lot earlier than that.

I live at a little place called Yocona in North Mississippi, in Lafayette County, an area whose history and people have already been well documented by Mr. Faulkner, a writer I hold great respect for. Some comparisons have been made by reviewers holding my work up to his, and this is something I didn't want that I knew was going to happen anyway. I also knew there wouldn't be anything I could do about it. There's already been a good bit written about the handing down of some sort of symbolic literary torch. People just naturally expect a lot out of me as a writer because I was born in Oxford. But I try not to worry much about it, and just go on and do my work.

One of the questions about human nature that interests me most is how people bear up under monstrous calamity, all the terrible things that can befall them, war, poverty, desperation. As a writer, it bothers me to be accused of brutality, of cruelty, of hardheartedness, of a lack of compassion. Only a few reviewers of my work have lodged these complaints. But more than a few seem to register a certain uneasy feeling, and I wonder if this is because I make them look a little too deeply into my characters' lives. Maybe

I make them know more than they want to about the poor, or the unfortunate, or the alcoholic. But a sensible writer writes what he or she knows best, and draws on the material that's closest, and the lives that are observed. I try to write as close as I can to the heart of the matter. I write out of experience and imagination, toward blind faith and hope.

Flannery O'Connor, who I'm happy to admit is one of my idols, said that a writer didn't need to have much happen to him after age twenty-one. She said by that time, there was plenty to write about. And even though I'd had plenty of material for a long time, just like everybody else, I didn't know that I needed it or was ever going to want to use it until I was almost thirty. When I was twenty-nine, I stopped and looked at my life and wondered if I was ever going to do anything with it. I had been a firefighter for six years, and on my off days I had set out pine trees, done carpentry work, cleaned carpets, cut pulpwood, deadened timber, you name it. I'd built those chain-link fences for Sears & Roebuck, and painted houses, and I'd hauled hay. I knew what it was like to pick up heavy bales and stack them on a truck all day under the sun, and then unload it and stack it in some hot old barn full of red wasps. I had done all these things to support my wife and my two little boys, to make ends meet. When I was in high school I never gave a thought to more education. I did poorly in school, especially English, and I paid so little attention to that course that I was obliged to attend summer school after my senior year just to get my diploma. I loved reading, and had all my life, but I didn't see how English was going to help me get a job after I got out of school, which was all I wanted to do.

But standing just short of thirty I suddenly realized that if I didn't find something else to do with my life, I was never going to amount to anything. When I had gotten married, I hadn't looked too far into the future. I guess what I thought for most of my life was that I'd just let one day take care of the next. I'd made it that way okay for a long time, had some good times, some beautiful babies. But those babies were going to grow up. They were going to want things, and I wanted things to be better for them than they had been for me. I didn't want mine to start out like I did, working in a factory.

The proposition of writing came on me slowly. I had been wondering how this process evolved, how these books and stories came to be written. I knew that people sat down and wrote them, but it seemed almost impossible that people could actually do something like that. I wondered what it took to be a writer, and I wondered if just anybody could do it. I wondered if it might be like learning how to build houses, or lay brick, or even fight fires, for that matter. I knew that some writers made a lot of money. I was a big fan of Stephen King, and I knew that his books sold well. The main question was, could a person teach himself how to do it by doing it? It seemed a logical question to me. I had absolutely no idea of the odds against me when I decided to try it.

My wife had an old portable Smith-Corona electric, and I went out and bought a box of typing paper and sat down in our bedroom one night and started writing a novel. It was about a man-eating bear in Yellowstone National Park, a place I'd never been to, and it had a lot of sex in it. I thought sex sold, because of the Harold Robbins novels I'd read. I was wrong. Nobody in New York wanted it. I know because I almost wore that novel out sending it around. It took me five months to write it and I couldn't understand why nobody wanted it. The main reason they didn't want it, I know now, is because it was horrible. You would not believe how horrible. Just imagine. It was 327 single-spaced pages of sex and man-eating.

That was my first acquaintance with a thing called the Apprenticeship Period, but it got me hooked on writing, on telling a story, putting down words on paper. After that I decided I'd try my hand at short fiction, so I wrote a few horrible short stories. Nobody wanted them either. Nobody would even write anything on a rejection slip. I decided pretty quick that nobody in New York knew his ass from a hole in the ground about fiction, but I decided that I would forge gamely on, in spite of them. I was working at a place called Comanche Pottery on my days off then. We poured liquid plaster into rubber molds shaped like pottery, Indian heads, leopards, and elephants, let them harden, then stripped the molds off. One night the whole place burned down and I was out of a part-time job for a while, but that was okay. It gave me more time to write.

Also during this time I tried to sell some stuff to *Outdoor Life*, some nonfiction pieces about things I'd seen and done while I was hunting. The first person who ever showed me any kindness was a girl who worked there named Jeannie Jagels. She wrote me a letter back about one of my early efforts, telling me why they couldn't publish it, telling me, gently and kindly, why it wasn't good enough. She was the first saint I met in the publishing business, and the publishing business is full of saints. Later on she turned another story of mine over to a guy named Rich LaRocco, who was a field editor for *Outdoor Life*. He read my piece, which was pretty horrible and illogical, and used a lot of words in a lot of ways they didn't need to be used, and he wrote a cryptic note: "Write the way you'd write a letter to a friend." Mr. LaRocco will probably never know how much good that little piece of advice did me. What it did was cause me to look at my own work and actually try to evaluate it with an objective eye, which was something I'd never done before. I'd always thought I'd just send it off and they'd buy it and publish it. Up to that point it had never occurred to me that I still had a lot to learn.

I decided that it might be a good idea to go to the library and find some books on writing and start learning more about my craft. So that's what I did. I checked out books on writing by the armload and read them from cover to cover. I also started reading work by better writers. I had been reading Faulkner since I was about sixteen, but not with any regularity or sense of purpose. I started rereading him and other novelists, and I started reading the collections of short stories that appear every year, books like the *O. Henry Awards* and the *Pushcart Prize* and the *Best American Short Stories*. I began to see how weak and pitiful my own work was, and it was a depressing thing to see. I saw that there was a great gulf between what I was writing and what I wanted to write. But I still had the belief that if I hung in there long enough and wrote enough, I would eventually learn how. So I started another novel. This one was about a couple of old boys in Tennessee who were going to plant a big patch of marijuana and make a lot of money. It had a lot of sex in it, too, but I'm a slow learner. I think that one took about seven months, and when I finished it I knew it was a lot better than the first one, and I sent it off knowing it would be a hit. The same thing happened, nobody wanted it. I sent it out enough times to realize that it wasn't going to be taken, and after a while I shelved it, and chalked it up to experience, and apprenticeship. I did that for years, and I kept writing, and reading.

It was only later that I learned to write about what I knew, which was Mississippi. I wasted a lot of time writing about things I didn't know anything about, instead of using my natural home and the landscape that creates the lives that are lived here, and the characters who live in my fiction. I didn't think too much about the dirt roads, or the vast forests and the creeks and rivers that run through them. I didn't know back then that I would eventually learn to listen to people talking and look at their lives or wonder what caused them to do the things they did.

You don't know when you start out that there's plenty of life around you, no matter where you live. It took me years to follow Miss Flannery's advice, or anybody else's. I didn't know how rich I was with material. I didn't know how many characters I could summon out of my imagination and Lafayette County and put them into a place other people would recognize without ever seeing it. I guess I didn't think there was anything here worth writing about, but you don't know a lot of things when you start. You don't know that what's inside the heart of a human is the only story you have to tell, or the vast millions of acres of imagination that door opens when you find it. You don't know that you can make a story out of absolutely anything, or that the things you know best are the easiest things to tell. What you *know*. But nobody can tell you this stuff. You have to find out, slowly and painfully, over a long period of time and failure. You write, and fail, and you write, and you fail. The main thing is that you don't give up hope and stop writing. You learn to reach back into your memory and take what you see around you and combine it with your imagination and you learn to build your stories and novels out of that and make it all real. And once you can do that, the reader will follow you as far as you care to take him.

I see stories around me constantly now, but I didn't use to. I can see a story now just driving down the road, or watching some people fishing, or cutting up in a beer joint, or working in a field. Loggers and housewives and children and drunks and farmers and mailmen and lawyers and widowed old ladies and mechanics and cowboys and bums and preachers, every one of them has a story, and I know now that the little place I live in is full of stories. I know what the woods look like in winter, and how a hawk sails over the grass looking for rabbits in the spring, and how the rain marches across the land at the end of a dry spell in summer, and the way the leaves on the ridges start turning brown in the fall. All these things are worth writing about because they're a part of my life, and I never tire of looking at them. I don't think I'll ever tire of writing about them. There's too much beauty in the world that I know, about ten miles out of Oxford, Mississippi.

In the early years I read a lot of essays on writing by fiction writers. The things they had to say about their own early careers could be tremendously heartening. I knew that I was a late starter and I figured the answer to that was to write even more, as much as possible, every chance I had, and compress the years of learning into a shorter period of years. That's what I did. My children were small then, and whenever I was home I could usually lock myself away in a room, sometimes for ten or twelve hours, sometimes for as much as five or six thousand words.

By that time I had realized there wasn't going to be any money made any time soon off writing, but I decided to go on anyway, for as long as it took. Two other things had happened to me. One was that I was enjoying what I was doing enormously, and the other was that I was teaching myself, without knowing it, to become a better reader. I had started reading the best writing by the best writers, and I began to find out it was what they called literature. I couldn't write it yet, but at least I knew what it was. I finally knew what I was aiming for. And that was Mr. Faulkner's advice all along: read all you can by the best writers. What he meant was read literature, and maybe that's still the best advice young writers can get.

It took me a long time to understand what literature was, and why it was so hard to write, and what it could do to you once you understood it. For me, very simply it meant that I could meet people on the page who were as real as the people I knew in my own life. They *were* real people, as far as I was concerned, not just characters. Even though they were only words on paper, they were as real to me as my wife and children. And when I saw that, it was like a curtain fell away from my eyes. I saw that the greatest rewards that could be had from the printed page came from literature, and that to be able to write it was the highest form of the art of writing.

From that time on that's what I've tried to write, and in the past few years I've been lucky enough to see some of my stories published in literary magazines. I've seen that distant dream come true, a book with my name on it. It hasn't been easy and I doubt if it ever will be. I don't think it was meant to be easy. I think that from the first it was meant to be hard for the few people who came along and wanted to write it, because the standards are so high and the rewards so great, in my case, making readers look into the hearts of the people I've chosen to write about.

All of my work comes out of Mississippi, out of the dirt roads and the woods and the fields I drive my truck by. The people who live in this land are the people I've known best throughout my life, and together with the country we live in, they form a vast well that will never run dry.

Deacon Summer

by Pat Conroy

When I finished my dreadful plebe year at The Citadel, the *News and Courier* presented me with a fifty-dollar award for excellence in reporting for the school's newspaper, *The Brigadier*. It was the first time I ever got paid for my writing, and the first time I ever held a fifty-dollar check that actually belonged to me. I took a long train to Omaha, Nebraska, where my father was stationed at Offutt Air Force Base. I had sent an application to register black voters in Mississippi. It was 1964, and I thought I would be a participant in the events later known in history as Freedom Summer.

My appointment with Freedom Summer never came to pass because I encountered the unalterable opposition of my strong-willed Georgia-born mother, who was not about to let her oldest son drive black sharecroppers to the county seat to register to vote for the first time in their lives. My mother believed in everything about the Civil Rights Movement, the only Southern white woman I met in my childhood who could make that claim. My brother Jim would later say, "There was a lot wrong with our childhoods, but we were raised in the South by two people who weren't racists."

"Let me go register folks in Mississippi, Mom," I said. "It seems like a good thing to do, and I'll bet I meet some interesting people."

My mother said, "You'll meet some folks who'd shotgun you off a porch as easy as clean their toenails. I've hidden that South from you, son. You and I are related to that South and it's in our blood. That's why I kept you from visiting the folks in Alabama. I didn't want you to hear what you'd hear and see what you'd see. I raised seven kids and not a one of you uses that horrible word 'nigger' because I'd kill you if you did."

"You were a little strict on that one, Mom," I agreed.

"When my mother up and left her family in middle of the Depression, my brother and sisters and I starved. Starved—there's no other word you can use. A black farmer and his wife took pity on us and fed us. You can't tell me anything about poor. I was raised colored," she said.

"Then let me go to Mississippi, Mom," I said. "It'll be an adventure."

"Pat, listen to me. You don't know the Deep South like I do. Mississippi isn't like Georgia or the Carolinas. You've never seen hate like a Mississippi white boy can hate. They'd kill you in a minute. We'll find you something around here."

The following day, my mother announced at breakfast that I had a job interview in downtown Omaha. Since my father refused to let me get my driver's license ("It'll get you in trouble, son"), my mother told me about making the call to the Catholic Social Justice Center to inquire about a job for her college-age son. She had talked to a very nice priest and he was interested in meeting me for a discussion about what I might do for the church that summer. My mother waited out in the car, entertaining my smallest brothers, as I entered the modest offices of Father James Stewart.

Father Stewart came out of his office and invited me in and motioned for me to sit in a chair in front of his desk. He struggled with a natural diffidence that I found most attractive after my year in the barracks.

"Your mother told me you wanted to go to Mississippi," he said. "To register black voters."

"Yes, Father," I said.

"Why?"

"It's what I believe in, Father," I answered.

"Why do you believe that? Your mother said you were from the South. She has a heavy Southern accent."

"My mother's something, Father," I said. "She's really something."

"How did you plan to get to the training camp in Ohio?"

"I was going to hitchhike, Father," I said.

"Mr. Conroy," he said, "would you take me with you?"

"Sure. When do you want to go?"

Father Stewart leaned back in his seat and said, "Alas, Omaha's got problems of its own. Huge problems. Did you know we have a large black ghetto here?"

"I didn't know you even had one black person in town. I don't know one thing about this town."

"I'm the pastor of Holy Family Parish on Izard Street, located in the center of the ghetto. We've been trying to do outreach programs that will meet the real needs of our parishioners, but I'm not sure we've been very successful. We also have a large Indian population that we've had trouble reaching at all."

"Why's that?" I asked.

"For one thing, we don't know where the people in our parish live or even who they are. I mean, we know the ones that come to our church, but the church has not made great strides getting black converts. We've been trying to get a census of our parish for the last two years . . . it's been difficult. The area's very rough and the men we hire to take the census always quit."

"Why?"

"They're afraid of being killed," he said. "The Near North Side is a very rough area."

"Could I bring my mother in to hear this?" I asked him.

"Why?"

"Mississippi suddenly sounds a lot safer."

"Yes, but please, let me tell you about my offer. I can give you free room and board. I can't say the work won't be dangerous, but it'll be satisfying. I have three young men from the seminary who'll be spending their Deacon Summers at my parish. Two nuns will be doing social work. I can offer you a strong sense of community and can assure you that you'll be doing work that will make the Near North Side a better place. We can offer you. . ."

I interrupted him, saying, "I can't take a salary, Father. I come from the weirdest family on earth, and my father won't let any of us have a paying job."

"That's what your mother said. I find it strange. May I ask why?"

"It's a long story, but my father's something of an asshole, Father. Pardon my French," I said. "The Depression made him weird."

"Then consider yourself hired, Mr. Conroy," Father Stewart said. "If you always work for nothing, you'll never have trouble getting a job in America. That I promise."

So, I moved my meager belongings into a dormitory-like room below Holy Family Church in the worst neighborhood of Omaha to begin another summer of my life without a paycheck. The three deacons were out in the field, I was told by Father Larry Burbach as he showed me my room and instructed me how to conduct a census of a parish.

"It's just like the times of Caesar Augustus," Father Burbach said, showing me a map of the parish. "When Joseph and Mary had to return to Bethlehem. Since we don't know who lives here, we don't know their needs. We're happy to have you here. From this street to this street. From this street in the north and this one in the south. That's our parish. We're small, but there are a lot of folks living in this area. It's very poor. Be careful. You ever lived in a high-crime area before?"

"No, Father," I said. "I grew up on bases."

"You're living in one now. Poverty makes people desperate. It hurts people's souls," he said. "Go out now and be back for dinner at six and to meet everyone else on the team."

Conducting a census in the Near North Side in Omaha provided fabulous legwork and drama to tuck away in the secret archives of a would-be novelist. I began the census in the southeast quadrant of the parish and worked my way up to the corner of the northeast quadrant. I stumbled into my first whores and pimps that initial day out on the streets. The pimp was dressed with such flamboyance that I laughed when I saw him getting out of his high-priced car.

"What you laughing at, white boy?" he demanded.

"Sorry, sir. I've never seen anybody dress like you do," I replied.

"What the hell you doing here, white boy?" he barked.

"I'm working for the Catholic church on Izard Street," I said. "I'm taking a census. Gotta ask everybody some questions."

"Get your ass out of here. I got me some girls working in there."

"Working at what?" I asked, taking out my pen and pad.

"Put that shit away. You crazy? What you think they're doing? Look at me. Doesn't that tell you something?"

"No, sir, it doesn't tell me anything."

"These threads don't give you no clue, white boy?" he asked.

"You own a clothing store?" I guessed, and he howled with laughter.

"They're working girls, dummy. Get it? They're whores." But he pronounced the word 'hoes.'

"Hoes?" I repeated.

"Yeh. Hoes."

"Oh, whores," I said, finally getting it and writing it down in my notebook.

"Don't write that down, white boy. You crazy as hell."

"I've got to. I'm taking a census," I said. "Sir, where're you from?"

"Fuck you. You ain't my mama," he said.

"Your accent. I know your accent."

"I'm from South Carolina," he said.

"So am I."

"Go on! Don't feed me that shit."

"I go to The Citadel in Charleston."

"Bullshit. Bullshit. Bullshit," he said. "I grew up over near Burke High School."

"That's a Gullah accent."

"Come on in here, Citadel," he said in complete surprise. Then he softened and said, "I want you to meet my girls."

For the whole first month I crossed and re-crossed the crowded streets of Holy Family parish until I had knocked on every door of every dwelling and wrote down the name of every inhabitant who lived within the mean borders of that blighted parish. I watched men and women shoot heroin into their veins as their children looked on. Young mothers with desperate eyes would open their doors, all of them thinking I was a bill collector or warrant server, all showing infinite relief when I told them I worked for a church who wanted to do them some good. Because I liked to listen, stories flooded out of them when I began to ask questions. The entire history of the world played itself out over and over again in the ghetto of the Near North Side, and I heard variations on that grand, contrapuntal theme in every household I entered. Every day, I gorged myself on the extraordinary stories of perfect strangers. When I entered a house where trouble had nested, I wrote it down and reported it at the next meal in the rectory.

Around the great mahogany table, nine of us gathered to eat at every meal. Father Stewart sat at one end of the table and Father Burbach anchored the other. Two Sisters of Mercy, showily named Redemptoris and Juvenal, faced the three deacons I roomed with in the basement. This was their "Deacon Summer," the last summer they would spend as ordinary men who lacked the power to turn wafers of bread into God. I have rarely met three finer men: George Shoemaker, Tom Ward, and Tom Sellentin. A small-boned, mysterious social worker named Jerry Millencamp sat to the left of Father Stewart and a sweet-faced Irish woman named Milli, who fed us like a race of heroes, ruled the kitchen and environs.

It was the finest year to be a Roman Catholic in the history of the church, and it would never be like that again in my lifetime. The papacy of John XXIII had brought fermentation and pizzazz to the task of being Catholic in the world, his call for a second Vatican Council sending shockwaves through the church that still register in high figures on the theological Richter scale. The pope transformed the church from its medieval trappings and institutional lethargy into the most engaging place a human soul could find itself. Though I can still recite long passages of the Baltimore Catechism from memory, that summer in Omaha changed my relationship with God and the church forever. At the dinner table of Holy Family Church, I listened as six men and two women argued brilliantly about the direction the church was heading and what our roles as practicing Catholics should be to bear witness to God and promote justice in the world—the conversation around that table crackled and sparked with well-informed passion and faith-rooted zeal. To me, it seemed far more related to Pentecostal fires than dinner table chat. The three deacons were frisky and ready to rumble with the intellectual Father Stewart, the dry-witted Father Burbach, and the saintly Jerry Millencamp. I learned of Kierkegaard and Hume that summer, heard the names of Peguy and Claudel for the first time when the subject of French Catholics arose, and listened to debates over the merits of Thomas Merton, Dorothy Day, and Catholic activists around the globe. It was a joy to watch the Deacons challenge the priests on every issue and watch the priests handle them with both delight and patience.

Some of the nuns of my youth could have held down jobs as gargoyles along the eaves of Notre Dame Cathedral, but Redemptoris and Juvenal made me fall in love with the entire order of the Sacred Heart. Redemptoris was short and compact while Juvenal was tall and ample and rosy. Juvenal was raised on a Midwestern farm and she gave me, at the end of our time together, a photograph—which I still have—of her and her seven sisters standing around their elderly mother and father. All eight daughters had entered the convent. The two nuns provided me with distant warning signals about the coming of the women's movement in the future, and the liberation of nuns themselves from the patriarchal stranglehold of the church, the priests and deacons cheering them on. I had never been at a table where no idea was too revolutionary to utter aloud or too reactionary for consideration. No idea was safe from scrutiny or criticism, and I felt like I was spending a summer at the best college in the world. Sister Juvenal gave me a copy of Laurence Durrell's *The Alexandria Quartet*, and I spent my reading summer navigating through the baroque glooms of Durrell's Egypt. Father Stewart took me to an auditorium to hear Malcolm X address the citizens of Omaha. He remains the greatest public speaker I have heard in my lifetime. The three deacons took me to see *Lawrence of Arabia* when it opened in the city. The musical score of that movie became the background music of my Deacon Summer, and

I cannot hear that theme song without being parachuted back into the city limits of Omaha and my days knocking on strange doors that were answered by rough customers.

The food prepared by that sweet-faced, self-effacing Millie came from the kitchen in mouth-watering profusion. The corn of Nebraska made me feel differently about the poor ears pulled from the soil of lesser states. We ate it creamed and fried and boiled and stewed. Our cook displayed a small genius with vegetables; I remember platefuls of tomatoes laid out like playing cards, and cucumbers bathing in good vinegar and lima beans smoking as they were brought to the table, heads of cauliflower toupéed with a cheese sauce, green beans and turnip greens flavored with nuggets of ham, rutabagas and nutmegged squashes of all varieties. The breads were homemade and the butter was fresh, its creamy taste and texture speaking well of Nebraska herds. The steaks and roasts and chops that followed were beautifully prepared, and her desserts were sensational cakes and puddings and cookies that often came out warm from the oven.

At each meal, I would love the moment that the shy cook would step out to listen to the final stanzas of the day's conversation draw to a conclusion. She loved it when the two nuns challenged the priests about the role of the sisterhood in the church. Redemptoris and Juvenal wanted to be ordained as priests and nothing less. That was revolutionary talk in the staider precincts of Catholics in those days. The two priests seemed to agree with the nuns, and it fell to the three deacons to make the case for the traditional church stance on women. But nothing was forbidden at that dinner table; there were no taboos or sacred cows or shibboleths that could not be thrown out for discussion.

Deacon Summer handed me an invaluable gift at that same dinner table. That voluble and articulate gaggle of priest and nuns forced me into the conversation whether I wanted to be or not, whether I was conversant or not. They demanded to hear my thoughts and opinions on every conceivable topic, and they insisted I give them a report from the streets each day, about the people I met while taking the census. I simply told the stories that the invisible people of their parish told me. Because they were poor and desperate and mostly black, the stories were often dramatic and tragic and grim. If I found homes where children were happy, Redemptoris and Juvenal would bring food to that home. If I found a woman desperate for money to pay the rent, Father Stewart would send the nuns over with money. If I found someone sick, Stewart would find a Catholic doctor who would make house calls. When I found a dead man in his bed, Stewart sent the ambulance to his apartment. That summer I learned that extreme poverty had its own smell and taste. In most apartments I grew accustomed to the aromas of shit and urine and the putrescence of uncollected garbage. Every story I told that summer was a tragic one and hopelessness strangled the carotid artery that fed into the Near North Side. I was seeing things each day that I had not imagined possible. But when I brought a new story to the table, a nun or priest or deacon would follow in my wake bearing tidings of great goodwill. These people took the phrase Catholic social action seriously, and they tried to right every injustice I brought to dinner with me. If I found a hungry child in the morning I knew its belly would be full that night. If I found a sick mother, she would have medicine on her bedside table on the same day.

By July, I had nearly completed my census of the whole parish when I knocked on the door of Yunca Matkovich. Many of the neighbors had warned me about approaching Yunca, using words like addled, schizophrenic, and crazy as hell to describe her. Though I had become accustomed to people answering their doors holding revolvers in their hands, I had never encountered anyone like Yunca Matkovich. I knocked several times and got no reply.

"Mrs. Matkovich?" I yelled.

"Go away, nigger," she screamed at me from inside her house. It was one hundred degrees in the shade. Omaha, Nebraska, in the summertime felt like a lost acre of the Mojave Desert.

"Yoohoo, Mrs. Matkovich?" I called out again, worried that the black children who trailed me around on my daily route would get their feelings hurt.

"You get away from my door, nigger, or I'll call the cops," she shouted again.

"I work for Holy Family Catholic Church," I said. "I'm the whitest white boy this neighborhood ever saw."

She cracked the door and I saw a milky-eyed, foul-smelling, pitiful old lady staring at me blankly. "How can I be sure you're not a nigger?" she snarled at me.

"We could get an affidavit from my mother," I suggested, then added, "but I'd be careful using that particular word in this neighborhood, ma'am."

"Let me touch your hair," she demanded.

When she stepped out on the porch and I had to guide her hand to the top of my head, I realized that Yunca was blind. She gave off the body odor of something dead, and the smells coming from her house were repulsive.

"Are you in trouble, ma'am?" I asked.

"Not for long. I will die soon," she said, speaking in a deep Eastern European accent.

"May I come in and ask you some questions? I'm taking a census for Holy Family Church."

"Please, sit down in my living room," she said.

When I sat in an armchair, roaches scattered across the floor, and I had to compose myself to keep from gagging. She had been born in Poland, she told me, then filled out the details of a most unlucky life. Six months ago, she had gone completely blind. She'd never seen a doctor because she couldn't afford one since someone had begun stealing her social security checks. I tried to turn on a lamp but there was no electricity. Excusing myself, I walked back into the kitchen and saw a loaf of bread covered with roaches and a jar of peanut butter but could find no other food in the house. Opening the door off the kitchen, I saw the outline of a sink and a commode in the lightless room. The toilet was broken and excrement was everywhere. But something else was wrong in that room, terribly wrong. I looked at the black walls, aware only of a secret abhorrence of something staring back at me. I felt a movement in the impenetrable blackness of those walls; then slowly, as my eyes adjusted, I processed the scene with a horror coming over me that I'd never felt before when I realized that I was looking not at a color, but a billion-footed colony of roaches. The walls and ceilings and floors were encased with a satanic covering of insects. I'm a Southern boy and I know my roaches, but I'd never seen anything like the infestation I faced in the house of Yunca Matkovich. I shut the door and returned to the living room. Taking her by the hands I said, "Yunca, listen to me. I will help you. You can count on me. I work for the nicest people in the world. Please let us in when I come back."

"What's your name?" she asked.

"Pat Conroy," I said.

"Ah! The Irish. I always hated the Irish. Bad as the niggers."

"Hey, Yunca, you're gonna love my Irish ass," I said, going through her front door and leaving her house in a dead sprint. I was running at full speed down Izard Street when I spotted Sisters Redemptoris and Juvenal coming out of a house call on one of the side streets.

"Sisters!" I screamed as I ran to their sides.

"You look like you've seen a ghost, Pat," Juvenal said.

"You're sweating hard, Pat," said Redemptoris. Sweat had become a joke between us because both nuns sweated profusely in the penquin-esque, medieval habits they wore in the most torrid heat of a city on the Great Plains.

"I just found hell," I said. "You've got to come right now. It's an emergency, Sisters."

"After all you've seen this summer, I can't wait to see what you call an emergency."

Both nuns agreed wholeheartedly I had brought them to a dire situation. Poor Sister Juvenal threw up when I showed her the roach nightmare in the bathroom. When she tried to wash her mouth out with water, she discovered that the city water had been turned off, too. Sister Redemptoris took charge, sat poor Juvenal in a chair, and fanned her face.

"Pat, run back to Holy Family. Tell Father Stewart the situation. Tell him to give the deacons some money to get Yunca Matkovich's water and electricity turned back on. Tell him to give you some money. Buy Yunca some food, the basics. Buys lots of cleaning fluid. Lots of it."

"A TON of cleaning fluid," Juvenal agreed.

"Then go to the hardware store and buy one of those thingamajigs that kills lots of bugs. You know, the kind with the handle that you push in."

"Make that big, too," Juvenal agreed. "No can of Raid this time."

"Get back here as fast as you can, Pat," Redemptoris said. "The Sacred Heart Sisters are depending on you."

"Have I ever let the Sisters of Sacred Heart down?" I asked, making a muscle with my left arm.

"Never," Redemptoris said.

"Have I ever let down the only two nuns who didn't beat me to a pulp?"

"Not once," said Juvenal. "You've been our hero from the beginning."

"And I'll be your hero again," I said, leaving the house in a run.

I returned in less than two hours, and those two glorious nuns and I spent a long day of hard labor expunging the many layers of dirt from the sad, abused house. Father Stewart brought Yunca to his house, and the sweet-faced cook took her into Father Stewart's bedroom and gave her a bath and washed her hair and gave her one of her own dresses. George Shoemaker got the lights turned on and the two Toms restored the water to her residence. The entire Holy Family team roared into action, and Father Stewart set up a physical for Yunca with a Catholic doctor on the following day, when they scheduled an operation for Yunca's cataracts.

After we had cleaned for three hours, the two sisters approached me with odd smiles on their faces.

Redemptoris said, "We've come up with a plan, Pat."

"I don't like that smile on your face, Redemptoris," I said. "By the way, it's hard to take two people seriously who go by the silly names of Redemptoris and Juvenal."

"They are ridiculous names," Sister Juvenal agreed sadly.

"We've voted and you were a unanimous selection, Pat," Redemptoris said. "We've voted that you get to clean the bathroom." Both nuns collapsed, giggling so hard they had to hold the walls to steady themselves.

"Monster nuns," I said. "This is why you were hunted down like dogs during the Spanish Civil War. Why you were tortured then burned at the stake during the Protestant Reformation. Why you populate the nightmares of Catholic children everywhere."

"We just think you're the right man for the job, Pat," Redemptoris said, still laughing.

"Just what the doctor ordered," Juvenal said. "Pat, we haven't told you the worst part. We're going to lock you in there."

I said, "Brides of Satan."

I took a flashlight in with me, and the arc of light caused the roaches to stir into unspeakable life. I was wearing a tee shirt and blue jeans, sweat socks and Converse All-Stars. The walls were alive with cockroaches, and my presence didn't seem to bother them. I laid the flashlight in the sink, then lifted the spray gun and aimed it at the far wall. When I shot the first stream of poison into their midst, the room exploded with a pandemonium of wings and legs and carapaces clicking against each other like shaken chiclets. The entire room fled at once, but there were no exits. Roaches were all over me as I sprayed with my eyes closed, roaches covering my body in their panic to escape. I sprayed and sprayed and sprayed, occasionally running my hands through my hair to clean out the dead bugs. I sprayed until the gun was empty, then knocked on the door for Redemptoris and Juvenal to let me out. Walking out of the room into the backyard, I vomited. The nuns took roaches out of that room by the trash-barrelful. That night, the deacons took me to the emergency room of a Catholic hospital—I had poisoned myself with the same repellant I'd slaughtered a nation of cockroaches with.

It took us two full days to make Yunca's house habitable, and the next day Sister Redemptoris said, "We apologize, Pat. Neither of us wanted anything to do with that bathroom, but we didn't want to kill you, either."

"Locking you in there was a big mistake," Juvenal said. "We didn't give any thought to ventilation. Will you ever forgive us?"

"Of course not. If there is a God, both of you will roast in hell," I said. "Being in that room with cockroaches raining down on my head was the worst day of my life—and unlike you sheltered sisters, I've had me a few."

"Did we tell you we found the attic?" Sister Juvenal said, falling into Redemptoris' arms. "We took another vote. You won again."

"Hell is too good for you women," I said, moving toward the door they were pointing to as we inched our way through the accumulated waste of Yunca's house.

* * *

When Father Stewart made charts of all the data I had gathered in my census of his parish, almost every woman I'd interviewed volunteered that the need for reliable day care outstripped every other problem they had, except for the lack of money. A woman told me that it terrified her to leave her children alone, but how else were they going to eat if she didn't walk to the store to buy groceries?

"If day care is the problem, let's give them day care," Father Stewart said during evening meal.

"It's got to be on a limited scale at first," Father Burbach said. "This could get out of hand in a hurry."

"How do we know anyone will come?" Tom Ward asked. "One thing we found in the census is how few Catholics live in the Near North Side."

"George, why don't you write up a proposal and we'll get Pat to take a flyer into the neighborhood. Pat, will you be in charge of the recreation program?"

"Only if I get to boss Redemptoris and Juvenal around, Father," I said.

"You're not still bitter about the roaches?" Father Burbach said.

"I certainly am, Father," I said. "How will we feed these kids? If we invite them here we have to feed them."

"Confiscate the deacons' salaries," Juvenal suggested.

"Sell the nuns into slavery," I said.

"Sell Conroy into slavery," Father Burbach said.

"But this is serious," said Tom Sellentin, the earnest deacon.

"And expensive," Tom Vaughan, the funny deacon, said.

George, the blond deacon, said, "But important. Day care's important. It's what the community most wants."

I visited a bakery shop and told the owner about Holy Family's new day care facility, and he promised that we could use all the bread and pastries that he couldn't sell. The dairy promised free milk, and a grocery store donated soft drinks and Twinkies. I remember the businessmen of Omaha for their high-spirited generosity; not one refused me or sent me out empty-handed from his office. The daycare center opened with five children in attendance, but there were eighty at week's end. I was umpiring a softball game when Father Stewart came up to me between innings and said, "Look at this, Pat. Look around you."

Eighty black children—some playing chess, some building blocks, and some reading with Redemptoris and Juvenal—spread across the campus of Holy Family Church. I could tell that the sight of these happy children thrilled Father Stewart.

"If Christ came back today, Pat, where do you think he would go? What would he do?"

"He sure wouldn't come to Omaha, Nebraska," I said. "This place is really hot and I'm Southern."

"Would he live among the rich or the poor?" asked Father Stewart.

"The rich, if he was smart," I said.

"I think he'd come to a place like this. Or some other Near North Side. I think the poor would make him happy, and so would the children of the poor. We've finally gotten the neighborhood to come to this church. Can't you feel Christ's presence here?"

"No, Father," I answered. "Not with Redemptoris and Juvenal around."

Father Stewart never grew accustomed to my humor—I don't think I made him laugh once during the summer.

At the end of the summer, there was a great Midwestern gathering of the Catholic Church responding to the brief and shining papacy of John XXIII. I was as excited to be a Catholic that summer as I would have been to be a Boston Celtic. Catholic social action was one of the great overriding themes of the conference, and Father Stewart had spent several weeks polishing the keynote speech he would deliver.

In a great hall, I nearly burst with pride as Father Stewart described the work we had done at Holy Family that summer with little money but great energy and an abiding passion. His shyness made his oratory flat and matter-of-fact, but Father Stewart's decency lent credence to his message. He talked about the field work of the deacons and the nuns as Juvenal blew me a kiss from where she was sitting on the dais. The success of the day care program was the centerpiece of his speech, and he told of plans to increase its size and importance in reaching out to the community.

At the end of his speech, he caught me flat-footed and surprised by calling out my name and asking me to stand up. My awkwardness at this stage of my youth was not exactly pathological, but it could near that in a crowd. Since no one in the Midwest knew who I was, I decided to sit it out and just tell Father Stewart I had missed his speech, but the perfidious Juvenal rose and pointed me out. I stood up and blushed one of those blushes that boys do when you become aware that gallons of blood streaming through your body at all times can rush headlong to your face. I looked like a sugar beet staring up at Father Stewart.

"Ladies and gentlemen, I wanted you to see what Catholic action looks like in the flesh. Pat Conroy came out of nowhere to ask if he could help us this summer. He conducted a census in the toughest part of this town. He coached an Indian baseball team that he recruited off the streets. He ran the recreation program for the day care center and was responsible for getting businesses to donate food. He did everything we asked him and he did it for free. But, Pat, what the priests and the good sisters and the three deacons will remember most are the meals we ate together when all of us tried to get you to tell stories about the South."

I do not remember a single story I told about the South that summer, but I do remember the high quality of conversation at those dinners where God and poverty and politics and art were our daily bread. Each day I sat with six brilliant men and two dazzling and loving nuns in a paradise of conversation elevated to art form. I thought I had caught a glimpse of what it must have felt like to have walked beneath an olive grove with Socrates. For the rest of my life, my father would refer to my Deacon Summer as "the exact moment my oldest son turned into an asshole liberal," and he was right. The summer changed me in my bones and changed me for all time. When Father Stewart came to visit me at The Citadel the following year, he had me show him the poor people in Charleston. I took him on a tour of the black district, for he showed no interest at all in the showy mansions South of Broad. Because of my Deacon Summer, I still believe that people who dedicate their lives to easing the pain and grievous suffering and daily humiliation of the poor are the finest people who dwell among us. I have believed since my time in Omaha that the poor should inherit the earth.

When I went to say goodbye to Father Stewart, he heard my confession and gave me communion at the altar of Holy Trinity Parish. We embraced for a long time, then he said, "You've been worried that the plebe system ruined you. It didn't touch that wonderful boy in you."

Since I could not speak, he blessed me and handed me an envelope. On the train back to Charleston, I opened the letter and was surprised to find a check for fifty dollars. When I got back to The Citadel campus, I went to the small bank in Mark Clark Hall and opened up my first bank account with the two fifty-dollar checks. One I had earned for my writing; the other I had received for doing work I loved. It would take me years to discover that they were the same thing.

Connie May is Going to Win the Lottery this Week

by Connie May Fowler

As far as I can tell, no one in my family—not even a distant cousin or spinster aunt—ever had any money. Paternal? Maternal? Black? White? Native American? Doesn't matter. Generations upon generations of my people have remained poor as dirt since our DNA first crawled out of the swamp on the back of a tadpole.

The reasons why poverty clings with the ferocity of acid to my family make no sense. We are hard workers, all: sharecroppers, itinerant preachers, circus performers, street singers, writers . . .

Oh, wait. I spy a pattern. Even when we're able to get off the farm, we follow our bliss, but our bliss rarely intersects with any activity that has greater than a fifty-fifty chance of generating cash in amounts that would cease our endless hand-wringing. And that is why my retirement plan—the Bliss Plan—is totally dependent on me winning the lottery.

The job that I have held the longest is that of writer. In fact, I don't remember a time when I didn't write. I also don't remember a time when it provided a living wage.

Seriously. For illustrative purposes only, let's say I receive $100,000 for a book that takes me three years to complete (I'm being optimistic). My agent takes 15% of the $100,000, which leaves me with about $85,000. Various state and federal taxes extract another 30%. Now divide that number by three. I'm not a math whiz, but I'm pretty sure this means that my take-home pay for a job in which I reveal to the world my most painful truths, and get awards and fan mail for doing so, is $19,800. I know, I know; it's more than some people make but let's be honest: it stinks.

And because The Third Law of The Universe states, "There shall be only ten living writers at any given moment who actually get rich following their bliss and you're not one of them (and by the way, you're not going to win the lottery, either)," I have always worked other jobs.

Let me list some of them now in no particular order: bartender, waitress, maid, TV host, antique dealer, college professor, construction worker, actor, clothing store clerk, proofreader, door-to-door hawker of crap. Of the eleven stated professions, two provided no remuneration but I thought they might lead to something.

Currently, I'm an antique dealer and giver of how-to-write seminars. Thanks to the robust nature of the American economy, no one I know is buying nineteenth-century brooches, and folks these days will teach themselves how to write, thank you very much.

If there is a silver lining, I suppose it would be that I'm brilliantly maintaining the family tradition of, as my mother was so fond of saying, not having a pot to pee in or a window to throw it out of.

Writing is not for the faint of heart or the greedy. It is a mad act born of necessity. I must write. If I go too long without spinning a tale, I get all kinds of crazy. Thirty years ago, long before I penned my first novel, I was a poet. Faithful to the calling, I wrote every day, revised compulsively, and sent out pieces of my heart—SASE included—to strangers at literary magazines, occasionally getting published but mainly not.

As part of the dedication to my art, and in the wake of my mother's death, I decided to quit college, be a full-time poet, and see the world. As with the Bliss Plan, what could go wrong? I used my inheritance to fuel my dream: the $150 my mother left behind in her checking account.

I caught a ride with four guys—two of them I knew from a couple of classes we'd taken together and two were strangers. All four were from Saudi Arabia and on their way to Spokane, Washington, to sojourn with fellow countrymen. They were perfect gentlemen, only occasionally allowing me to pay for gas.

You're already suspecting, I'm sure, that this story has all the signs of being a sordid, tragic affair. And you're right. It was terrible. They dumped me in Spokane in a cold, wheezy apartment, picked up their buddies, and headed to Cuba via Mexico, where they thought Fidel would train them to be fighters so that they could return home and overthrow the Saudi royal family. What a plan!

Because this essay isn't about that little adventure, all I can tell you of their fate is that Cuba wouldn't allow the bozos into the country and I was stuck penniless 2,000 miles from home with winter fast approaching.

I'm from Florida. How could I have known that in Spokane pretty much everything—and I mean everything save bars and pizza joints—closes down for the winter and that if you don't have a job by, say, the end of August, you probably aren't going to get one?

My poetry wasn't going well. It was overwrought with abandonment issues and perpetual whining about the weather. But I had two things in my favor: The writing was preventing me from going totally berserk and the landlady felt sorry for me. That, and she wanted me to keep paying the rent on the tenement apartment, which was, by the way, chock full of disgruntled ghosts who routinely scared the bejeezus out of me.

My landlady hooked me up with a local construction crew. I swear. To this day I have no idea why the foreman hired me but I'm forever grateful that he did. I'll tell you right now, I'm not a hammer-n-nail gal. So you can imagine my relief when he put a trowel in my hand and taught me how to smear stucco mud on lath.

I was the only female on the crew and none of the males, except for the foreman, spoke to me. In fact, they didn't even look at me. When we broke for lunch, they sat on one side of the room and I sat on the other. This was a huge relief because even I could not imagine a conversation that included references to the Denver Broncos, that sweet piece of meat down at Lefty's, competitive puking, and Sylvia Plath.

The gig was minimum wage but it was enough to keep me in paper and typewriter ribbon. That's really all I wanted: just enough money to support my habit.

By my second day on the job, I knew something was terribly wrong. My eyes gleamed scarlet. Each time I blinked, it felt as if the undersides of my lids were lined with sandpaper. I feared I had pink eye and, in retrospect, this possibility may have fueled my co-workers' refusal to speak to me, and their insistence on maintaining a healthy distance.

On day three, my eyes began oozing toxic glue. In the cold air, the glue quickly dried, encasing my peepers in an amber crust. The foreman sent me to his doctor, who assured me I did not have pink eye, which was curable. I was, said the doctor, allergic to the stucco mud and he recommended that I immediately quit my job.

Easy for him to say. I didn't relish the idea—however romantic—of being a *homeless* poet. And the sending and resending of rejected poems required cash. My tenure as a construction worker had been so brief that I hadn't yet saved bus fare for the long trip back home across the broad continent. So, against doctor's orders, I did the only logical thing a girl in my situation could: I continued to smear stucco eight hours a day, five days a week, even as my condition grew rapidly worse.

My red-rimmed eyes swelled shut. I gazed at the world through a lens fading to black. The inflammation, oozing, and crusting blossomed anew, globular and hideous, with each arced stroke of the trowel. I worked—whether it was in construction or poetry—with a wet washrag in one hand, which I used to unglue my lids.

Fearing I was going to be a blind poet, I prepared. I watched—between hot washrag compressions—*The Miracle Worker*. I went to the library one cold evening—a fresh dusting of snow lighting my way—and checked out a manual on sign language, because I had become confused as to what actually happened when you lost your sight. I practiced walking around my apartment with my eyes closed, counting how many steps between the bed and the bathroom (twenty-three).

I kept my job through the winter and came home in the spring, a notebook bursting with not bad poetry. My eyes would not clear up for another four weeks, and when they did, I snagged a job as a waitress at Bennigan's. It was there that I ran into the University of Tampa provost; by luck or providence, the hostess seated him in my section. He told me to come to his office the following week and he'd reinstate my scholarship. I did and he did and the rest is history. My dream came true. I became the only thing I had ever really wanted to be in this life: a writer who, if things got dicey, had enough cash to get out of town.

As for my eyes, I can see just fine if I'm wearing my glasses but that is the result of age, not demon stucco mud.

My experience being doggedly committed to a nowhere job so that my higher calling of Artist/Writer could be fulfilled has served me well. I'm proud that for six months of my life I worked among people who wouldn't so much as say hello but who, when I quit, lined up and shook my hand, man by man. I earned their respect, not their friendship. And that was okay because I had sought neither.

Writing is a tough vocation made all the more difficult by changing delivery systems, archaic business models, and imploding economies. You write your heart out and some clown you don't even know takes a sucker punch at you in the media, and manners and tradition dictate that you remain silent.

But it's the best of jobs. In the early morning I sip my hot tea and browse the masters: Virginia Woolf, Gabriel Garcia Marquez, Flannery O'Conner, Zora Neale Hurston, William Faulkner. I might throw in some poets: Neruda, Eliot, Lorca, Ellison, Oliver, Dunne. Their words ferry me into my writer's skin. And then I begin. One word at a time—sentence by paragraph by chapter—I chase my bliss.

I know my retirement plan sucks, and that my next part-time job might entail picking up bottles along the highway. But that's okay. I don't need riches. All I need is time to write and a roof over my head. I have so many more stories to tell.

Delivering

by Tom Franklin

You're thirty-two years old and delivering pizzas.

Your manager is twenty-one.

Your co-deliverer, let's call him Dave, is late fifties and gray, bushy eyebrows and unshaven and untucked shirt with an explosion of gray hair at his unbuttoned collar. Always a Razorbacks cap, because this is Fayetteville, Arkansas. Dave doesn't like you because, among other things, you're a graduate student and he's a lifer.

You stand in the hot little back room of Pizza Hut folding pizza boxes out of brilliantly designed pieces of cardboard and watching the television monitor that gives the address of the next delivery. Whichever driver's at the monitor gets it. Next guy in gets the next delivery and so on. Sometimes they stack up, three, four, five addresses in a row, and you've noticed that Dave often takes ones lower down the line, out of order. You start to look for a pattern, and, after you've been delivering for a few weeks—

You're terrible at it, though. Delivering. This has to be said. You have no sense of direction. You wind up and down the nauseating mountains around Fayetteville with two, three, four pizzas cooling in their padded carrier on the seat beside you. You contemplate being a thirty-two year old grad student, that Dave hates you for it. He sees you as a young punk born with a silver spoon in his mouth, all that. Never mind that that's as far from the truth as you are from the present address clenched in your fingers, the wrongly

83

numbered mailboxes clicking past. Unaware of student loans, you paid for your own college, nine years for a BA in English, working at a warehouse (three months), at a factory that made sandblasting grit (four years), a chemical plant (three years), you worked first, second, third shifts, doubles, triples, you commuted. You did time in offices, gas stations, automotive repair shops, in a hospital morgue as well as delivering—but that's another story—for the Epicurean Dinner Club . . . You once took five classes while working eighty hours a week, got four A's and a B. And now, at last, you're where you were meant to be, in the Master of Fine Arts writing program at the University of Arkansas. You've met the woman you're going to marry, have made good friends, have never been happier. You've put your writing first, for the first time in your life, and you've realized that the series of jobs you worked in your twenties have provided you a writer's education, which differs from the academic one the University of Arkansas is giving you.

Summers, though, when cash is slow, you find yourself broke enough to venture out into the unspooling streets of Fayetteville, the pizzas ever cooler, about to call the Hut for directions, again, to be told, again, how to get there and then stand, again, with a tepid Large Everything, facing the face that says *No tip, buddy*, and hearing that eternal question: "Ain't it free if it ain't here in thirty minutes?"

"No," you grumble. "That's Domino's. Or was. They quit doing it because pizza drivers kept getting killed."

Is this true? Maybe.

Back in the car, back on the road, back into the Pizza Hut parking lot where Dave's Dodge pickup sits there chugging.

There's another thing about Dave. He has this youngish wife and this toddler daughter. You know this because they come to work with him, show up at eleven each day and sit there, in the truck, as Dave goes in for his first delivery. Then they ride with him as he delivers and ride back and sit waiting in the truck with the windows open as he pushes inside the flapping gray back door and emerges a few moments later with another box.

This is against the rules—ride-alongs—but nobody, Roger the manager or the twenty-one-year-old shift manager Rick, or you—

says anything. One of the perks of working at Pizza Hut is that you get a meal each shift. Whatever you want, within reason. At some point, a lull in deliveries, Dave will order three personal pan pizzas for him and his family. And breadsticks. They'll drink fountain sodas and sit there on the Ford's bench seat and eat facing forward, listening to the Cardinals. The girl reads sometimes, but the mother and wife, she just sits.

You pass them, not making eye contact, as you push back into the Hut, your padded delivery carrier still warm from the last pie. Dave's there watching the empty screen. Rick, the manager, long black ponytail, thin, is trying to get Dave to form boxes out of the stacks of cardboard on the shelves.

You cash in and come to the back and excuse yourself past Rick and begin making boxes. Rick gives you a grateful look, and Dave shoots you one that says, "You're a kiss-ass little college prick." Truth is, you like making boxes, the quick progress and product, faster the more expert you become. One thing you've always found to be true, when writing stories, is that when you're in the middle of figuring something out—a plot point, a character trait—any small, real-life accomplishment helps. A crossword puzzle, filling the recycling bin, making a pizza box, they all feel like a kind of progress; also, mindless handwork somehow frees your mind to find its own answers, fold its own boxes.

But not now. Now, as your fingers crimp and tuck, Dave and Rick engaged in a staring match, four addresses appear on the television.

"Watch it," Dave says as he steps past Rick, closer to the screen, and squints through his bifocals.

"102 Olive," he says, going to the ticker and tearing off two tickets, the first and third.

You say, "That's out of order."

He barely looks at you. "So?"

"What's the logic," you say, perhaps the wrong way to phrase it, "in you taking whatever address you want?"

"The logic," he says, looking over his glasses at you, "is that I'm faster than you."

"What he does," you tell Rick, "is take the addresses with the best tippers." You hate how your voice sounds, like a tattletale, and that the authority figure you're tattling to is a decade younger than you are and the peer you're tattling *on* is twenty years older and getting mad. And how can you blame him? With his family out in the truck, waiting, living on tips, and here you come, hot snot, grad student, challenging him with logic.

"Well?" you say to Rick.

"Dave," he says, "that's really not fair."

"Fair?" Dave says, looking from me to Rick and back.

Dave doesn't know now that he'll be fired in a year or so for a scam he'll perpetrate, a selection of coupons he'll apply to a customer's payment, pocketing the difference. You, you'll graduate and with your new MFA move on up to being a receptionist at the Best Western Inn & Suites just off the interstate. Second shift, weekends. You'll find you're not suited for that type of work either.

But now:

"Fair?" Dave says again.

You could play the wife and child card. How they're outside, right now, against the same Pizza Hut Policy Machine that demanded you shave your beard. But if you did that, went and opened the back door to where they sat, patient as a photograph, said, "Ride-alongs are against the rules," what would happen then? Where would they go? The truth is, you're not entirely sure if the truck's not their home.

So you pull off your Pizza Hut cap and shirt and stand there in your t-shirt. Somehow, it feels right and even a little heroic. You say it. "I quit."

And you walk past Rick, who folds his arms, betrayed. Shaking his head, Dave is already looking back at the screen as more addresses appear. He'll get them all now, will take all four out at once.

You walk outside into the cool mountain air and nod to Dave's wife and child confined in their truck as some Redbird hits a liner up the middle. That's how you feel. You just got a hit. Not a homer, or even a double, but that great sweet-spot bonk as the softball zings off your bat past the shortstop's glove and you're racing toward first.

You get in your Nissan and crank it up. Well, you suppose, shifting into reverse, shouldn't every writer walk off at least one job? Won't you grow via experience, deepen into a deeper man? Certainly these cold pizzas will wind up in a story somewhere, sometime.

When Nobody Listens

by Tim Gautreaux

I've worked as a crab scrubber in a seafood factory, a supermarket bag boy, a waiter in a Bourbon Street beer hall, a receiving clerk at Sears Roebuck, a rebuilder of player pianos, a university professor for 30 years, and in retirement I'm a part-time machinist and steam locomotive fireman on a museum railroad. However, the job I held which most connects to my trade of fiction writing had to be my short stint as an AM radio announcer on a little south Louisiana 500 watt station back in the mid-1960s.

I don't remember how I wound up in an interview with the station manager, a thin, pale man with wiry black hair and a severe, downturned mouth. He glanced at me once, asked a couple of general questions, maybe just to listen to my voice, then hired me for fill-in work and to hold down weekends from noon till sunset. One dollar and five cents an hour.

My training consisted of reading a pamphlet on FCC rules. I drove to a pigeon-haunted graystone building in New Orleans, and in one of its echoing rooms where steamboat pilots used to be examined for their licenses, I took my test for a 3rd-class radio permit. It was simple and had nothing to do with the job, nothing about how to start a record or turn on a microphone. One of the questions was about what to do if an airplane crashed into the broadcast tower.

I came to work the first day expecting elaborate training sessions. Instead, the station manager gave a five-minute explanation of the buttons, levers, cassette players, rotary knobs, switches, turntables, dials, and meters and an admonition to say nothing on the air, just to play the records and shove in the eight-track commercials according to the written schedule. The manager then stood outside the broadcast room and watched through the soundproof glass. When I made a mistake, I would hear the insulated door open with a furious suck of air, and he would yell at me like I was a field hand who'd just wrecked a tractor. For the third or fourth mistake that shift (I'd opened the mike and announced the artist on the upcoming record) he came in and grabbed my shoulder, getting down in my face and crying, "Don't speak. Just don't speak about a record."

"But what if somebody wants to know who's singing?"

He gave me an amazed look. "Why is that important?" He stood up and left.

After working a couple of shifts, I realized that music didn't even show up on the manager's radar, and in his opinion no one had to know what they were listening to since it was just sound waves stitching commercials together. Considering that most of our music was something like alto sax interpretations of Pat Boone's hits, or Herb Alpert's calmer renditions, I began to agree. For the first two days he did the hourly news himself, coming in with streamers of teletype paper and waving me away from the console. Third shift, he told me to tear my own news from the machine, Scotchtape five minutes of it together, and deliver it on the air. He sat on the other side of the glass with his chin in both hands, glaring at me. I did a fair job, but when I looked over, his hands covered his face. After I had a record on, the door whooshed open and he pointed to the news intro cartridge. "You know how the intro," he began, "goes dada-dadankdank, dada-dadankdank in an endless loop?"

I nodded.

"You let it run for six dadankdanks," he scolded.

"Well, how many dadankdanks does the news need?"

"Just two," he said, straightening his back and holding up two fingers. "Haven't you ever listened to this station's news?"

I didn't answer that one because I'd never dialed up our station. But at that moment I got curious. After all, who was listening to *me*?

I knew that none of my friends at the college listened, but one day I was having a flat tire fixed and noticed that a little greasy plastic radio in the filling station bay had its dial set on the edge of the station, the manager giving the news, sounding like he was humming tissue paper against a comb. Over the next month I heard our station in the five-stool coffee shop, inaudible under the clash of ironware and guffawing of local cops who hung out there telling dirty jokes in French. When I went in to pay a parking ticket, I heard our station warbling on a Formica counter, Perry Como singing "Hot Diggity" under the chattering of the city hall clerks. I went to visit a friend, and her ninety-one-year-old grandmother had the station playing loudly as I walked through her kitchen. I asked her why she had it on.

She turned off her gas range and poured us both a cup of coffee, though I don't think she knew who I was. "It's just noise that keeps the house from being empty," she said. "And there's the news." Her eyebrows went up in silver rainbows. "You never can tell when something important will happen." I sat down and sipped coffee, imagining that once a year the approach of a hurricane or a celebrity murder in Hollywood would cause people to listen to our broadcast. But what about in between?

When I went to the dentist's, his waiting room speaker played our FM. I didn't know why we broadcast FM since it didn't run commercials, or maybe one an hour, and the music was designed not to be heard, a kind of white noise as emphatic as a distant tricycle's bell, stuff like 1,001 Strings plays the alto sax arrangement of a Pat Boone hit. I'm sure some people thought FM was a whole office building full of ad salesmen, engineers, musicians, and announcers. Actually FM was a machine about the size of a file cabinet that played two spools of tape as big around as old Cadillac hubcaps. Totally automatic. Same reels year after year playing largo orchestral string versions of the planet's dullest pop songs from the '40s and '50s.

When I was on the air I wondered how many people paid any attention to my droopy tunes or halting news. The broadcast was like wind in a hackberry tree next door or a distant train whistle or a garbage truck six blocks away crushing rot, just off the edge of hearing and consciousness, something to fill an empty space in a room or a head.

It was a good thing the politicians didn't understand how people didn't listen, because during elections season, the station made enough money to carry it over the slow times. The manager was good at selling fifteen and thirty-second spots promoting the local representative and senatorial candidates (in Louisiana as many as a dozen would run for each seat in the first primary.) There were always run-offs after that, and sometimes separate Democratic and Republican primaries that complicated matters. Besides state congressmen there were national candidates, sometimes a gubernatorial slate, plus local mayors, sheriffs, clerks of court, coroners, police jurymen, plus a raft of minor offices. And there were both regular ads and attack ads. During election time my console desk looked like a brick wall of eight-track boxes of ads, so many that I could play only half a record at a time before jamming in a sound bite of praise or condemnation. It was like feeding a furnace, a frantic one minute of news, 150 seconds of The Four Freshmen, eight political ads in a row, five seconds of time and temperature, another nine ads. I wondered if anyone was listening to such a barrage of yak. One afternoon the manager handed me a particularly nasty attack ad against the local sheriff. After I'd played it three times, I felt the hair lift on the back of my neck while I was giving the news and figured it was the receptionist pulling open the door. I killed the mike and turned to see a huge deputy wearing two stag-gripped revolvers and cliché mirror sunglasses standing right behind my chair.

"That commercial about the sheriff," he grunted, "gimme it." He held out a thick hand.

I quickly fished the tape out of the pile and handed it over. He pointed the cassette at me like a gun. "I ain't gonna hear this one no more. Right?"

I was tempted to say that he'd have to talk to the manager about that, but I glanced at the blackjack on his gunbelt and told him, "Yes, sir. That commercial's a gone pecan."

He nodded and left, and that was the last I ever heard about that ad. The deputy was scary, and I'll admit my hands were shaking through the next commercial and half-song. But it was nice to have a visit.

On weekends I was the only one in the building. I'd take over from the morning man at twelve and go till sundown, when all 500 watt stations in America had to turn off to clear the airways for the 50,000 watt big boys and the real DJs with real listeners. If I was a minute late with the national anthem, the manager would call up and give me hell.

The morning man was a squirrely trickster who would change labels on the commercial cassettes and add fake items to the Community Bulletin Board, a single sheet of paper on a clipboard hung on a cup hook under the desk. In the middle of a bunch of announcements about a Knights of Columbus fish fry or a VFW dance he would plant something like, "Tonight at seven o'clock Professor Wasserman will hold a discussion in Town Park about why the Pilgrims passed over Bayou Lafourche and settled for Plymouth Rock." The bulletin board was in paragraph form and the fake events would sneak up on me. One was about an Ocarina concert sponsored by the Sweet Potato Foundation, requesting that listeners call the station for tickets. I was worried when I read that one, but no one called. After a few shifts it got so I would just read the jokes along with the charity bingo games and coin club meetings since it didn't seem to matter. Nobody ever called in with a question. Even the manager didn't listen to the Bulletin Board.

Saturdays and Sundays I had to pull records from the moldy stacks of albums, many by singing groups that must have stayed together only long enough to cut one release. I'd paw through mildewed jackets of Xavier Cugat, Ezio Pinza, Patti Page, and some soft-edge folk music like the New Christy Minstrels or the Sandpipers. Al Hirt plays classical music. I can't remember what else, and it's no wonder.

The job was eight hours of work jammed into six hours. A teletype machine clacked its guts out as long as it was plugged in, and from a pool of green paper on the floor I'd rip off news three times an hour, cut out five minutes worth with a pair of dime store scissors and tape it together. It was mostly national stuff of no interest to the locals. Not much Lafourche Parish news made it onto the AP wire. I also had to record meter readings off the broadcast machinery constantly, make sure the FM reels didn't stall or break, play and log commercials, watch the phone buttons for calls that never came, unless the manager was listening. Sometimes FM would go haywire and just wouldn't play, so I had to put the Crap Record on the AM turntable and pull off the giant reels, clean the pickup heads with alcohol, and try to coax the damn system back on the air. The Crap Record was an LP with one band on a side, a continuous drone of 10,001 Strings versions of 1,001 Strings versions of alto sax versions of Pat Boone's hits. It was played when an announcer was holed up in the john or had to fight the FM machine. Somewhere across town, the station engineer listened for it. I liked to imagine this wordless seventy-year-old seated in a flowered armchair smoking a pipe and reading Edna Ferber, hearing not his station's content, but just its existence, the way he might listen to rainfall or his Spaniel's asthmatic breathing. When the Crap Record was on for more than ten minutes, he'd shamble out to his Rambler station wagon and drive the four blocks to the radio station, where he'd find me sitting on the tile, red-faced and trying to thread tape, sometimes backwards, into the bogged-down machine. He would point to the sound room with his pipe stem, indicating that I should rescue AM, that he would have FM back up in ten or fifteen seconds and spilling Mantovani all through the skies.

Audience was really down on weekends. Really down. I guess listeners didn't want more of the stuff they tried not to listen to at work all week. One Sunday a thunderstorm rolled over the town like a boulder and the lightning knocked us off the air. I kept on reading the news and playing records, failing to notice that the output needles on the wall cabinet had stopped wiggling. No one called to tell me. After forty-five minutes the engineer appeared next to my console, pushed a broad green button, nudged a toggle switch, and we were back on the air. He winked at me and left, as though absolutely nothing of consequence had happened. I'd rather have been yelled at.

Eventually, I learned to watch the main cabinet during the rip-snorting electrical storms. A lightning strike would cut a commercial in half and I'd have to bolt over to the wall of bakelite knobs and meters embedded in gray wrinkled steel, not far in appearance from Dr. Frankenstein's lightning-capturing machine, and coax the balky gizmo back to life. Sometimes lightning would knock the station off the air every thirty seconds, and I'd have to start over on the same commercial six or eight times.

The main cabinet was old, full of vacuum tubes, and the station's signal would wander over the airwaves like an Alzheimer's patient made of electrons. Now and then I'd get a call from a station in Biloxi, Mississippi, its engineer complaining, "Hey buddy, you're stepping on our signal over here. Get the hell back on your frequency." I'd have to throw switches, dial what looked like a rotary pay phone dial, and press buttons until I pulled our Petula Clark off of their Merle Haggard's back. It was embarrassing, but at least someone had called other than the manager.

After a few months the manager quit and we got a new boss, a nice guy who never tried to gum up the broadcast end of the business. I began to get somewhat better at holding weekends together, but it was still odd, never taking a phone call, talking out into a world that never talked back, playing the national anthem and getting out of the way as all over the central time zone little dust bunny stations did the same, opening up the night sky to the big show of manic preaching or real music or mind-full talking.

Saturdays were slow, but Sundays were a dead stop. At noon for many years the station played the Waltz Time Record, an old mono LP in use since the '50s and sponsored by a local funeral home, I think. The Strauss waltzes were furry with wear, a rote performance to begin with on par with the Crap Record, and as it revolved, I ground down with it, starting my shift with a whimper as across town the funeral home owners sat proudly around their table and ate, what? What white bread nothingness would go with this music?

Never a phone call on Sundays, and the silence wore on me as I broadcast alone, doing news and promos in my best voice and never seeing a button light up on the phone. I got the feeling that the whole town could catch fire and the last place anyone would think of calling about it was the radio station. An airplane could crash into our antenna, wherever it was, spilling passengers out of the sky, and people would ask, "What was that tower for, anyway?"

To get attention I tried goofy stunts, pulling from the awful vault of records operatic arias to play next to Eddie Arnold's "Cattle Call." Vin Bruce, the Cajun baritone crooned in French next to Mary Hopkin singing "Those Were the Days." Nobody called in a comment or complaint. One of our steady advertisers, a big dance hall out in the woods, asked us to write their promos, and I started giving them in French, thinking some of the francophones still living in the region would call in. Nothing. I began to deliver fake weather forecasts. Then, fake forecasts in French. Nothing. After a year or so, even though we were not a request station and would probably not be able to honor such a thing, I announced that we would take requests. I got one call from an old woman back in the swamp around Attakapas Landing requesting a record we, of course, didn't have, though I rifled through the music vault, raising mildew for a half hour, looking.

One day, toward the end of my job at the station, I opened the mike and offered a free Beatles album to the first caller. The record had come to the station gratis, and since we didn't play rock and roll unless I sneaked one in between Los Indios Tabajaras and Jo Stafford, I figured I might make a last attempt to connect with the outside world on Sunday. No one called. I played a Chet Atkins cut and invited anyone out there to ring in with the title and claim a prize, a gift certificate to a local café which I'd bought for an ex-roommate. Not only were there no Chet Atkins experts out there in radioland, there were no eaters as well. I looked in my wallet and found two ones and a five. I opened the mike with trepidation and offered five dollars to the next caller, no strings attached. I stared at the phone until almost sundown and then dialed a girlfriend to make sure the phone was still working.

Eventually I got a fellowship to study creative writing in graduate school and left my notice in an envelope on the turntable Sunday night. Two weeks later I came in for the last day and found my pay envelope where I'd left my notice. Money only, no comment. I was to work only until three PM, when a new guy would show up to end the day. At 2:58 I cued up a slow instrumental, some kind of cowboy mosey I'd found in the record stacks, and started to give my farewell, thanking the station and my listeners. In the middle of this, the new guy came in and plucked the needle off the record and I turned to him and said, on the air, "Hey, I was speaking over that," instantly recognizing that it didn't matter, that nobody was listening except maybe the dozing engineer. I was talking into a black hole and felt foolish that it mattered to me at all. But, and I remember feeling this at the time, it did. It mattered that I was talking on the radio, and who knows, maybe somebody out there got a laugh, heard the news, and that much contact was why I ever opened a mike in the first place. It was important that even if nobody heard, I was talking.

Around a quarter century later I published my first book of fiction and understood that all the years of creative attempts before were like working at that radio station. I'd send out my stories and get nothing in return but a terse printed rejection slip after many weeks of waiting, or I'd send out novel manuscripts that would float around in some mysterious sky of judgment for six or eight months of my life and then come back with no comment at all. For years I wondered if I could ever produce narrative that was worthy of a real letter or phone call from an editor. I kept reading that the novel form was in trouble, that no one published short stories much less, God forbid, collections of short stories. But I was determined to be heard and kept launching tales into the darkness of a post office slot, some of which would never come back because little magazines were dying like frostbitten gardens all over America. Revising and revising, mailing a story dozens of times, figuring out the art of writing, making what I wanted to say into what people consented to hear, and failing again and again. But I was used to that. Being ignored was like announcing on small-town radio, and I never gave up, because I'd realized on a Sunday afternoon a long time ago that failure is not a problem. Not trying is.

Fumbling for the Keys to the Doors of Perception:
A memoir, mostly true but with some stretchers, as Mark Twain once said

by William Gay

We'll starve to death, she said.

I was married then and my wife was appalled because I had quit my job.

Something will turn up, I said. I'll get another job.

I sounded confident but I wasn't so sure. New jobs weren't so easy to come by and I was young and possessed no marketable skills. The only thing I had to offer the job market was a warm body. I had been working construction but when that job wound down I had taken a position in a shoe factory for minimum wage, operating a sort of press that cut shoe uppers from sheets of leather. Nobody had made production on this job since about 1947 and things did not appear to be picking up any speed. I could hardly keep up with the hands reaching out for my cut uppers to carry them to the folks who were gluing them to the soles.

This factory was a place of clamorous noise and the smell of hot glue and leather and I had come to see it as a sweat factory run by petty tyrants and their footlings and toadies who lorded it over the folks like me who were just trying to work out a grocery bill or car payment. Its only advantage was it ran all day every day.

Which was another thing.

You all work every day? Sheets asked me once.

Sheets was a new hand hired fresh out of the log woods and was not yet acclimated to the doings of factories.

All day every day, I said.

No matter what the weather is?

There's a roof, I pointed out.

The hell with this, Sheets said. I ain't working nowhere you can't get rained out just every now and then.

Now that job was gone in a moment of outrage and I could not call it back. Could I have rewound events and altered them perhaps I would have. But probably not, for I had been sent for.

I was married then only a few weeks and used to drive home for lunch. Occasionally one thing would lead to another and I did not always make it back to clock in on time. On this particular lunch hour, the time I was sent for, I had decided to take the rest of the day off and get a fresh start in the morning.

About one o'clock a car drove up the gravel drive to the house and into the yard and immediately the horn began to blow.

Who in the world could that be? she asked.

I went to look. I couldn't believe it. It was my foreman from the cutting room.

Car broke down? he asked.

No. Why are you here?

The floor boss sent me. Thought you might need a ride back to the plant. We sure do need you out in that cutting room.

I was outraged. Sent for. Sent for like some incompetent who had forgotten the way to town or could not find something the size of a shoe factory.

That cutting room can kiss my ass. I quit.

Why Lord, you can't quit. There ain't no work. You'll starve to death.

I can maybe get you on at the boat paddle plant, my brother-in-law Curtis said a few days later. Curtis was new at the job himself but was the sort of confident fellow who fell easily into the way of things and saw no reason why he could not hire and fire after a couple of weeks on the job.

Curtis had himself been recently fired. He had been a city

policeman who had used a little too much force blackjacking miscreants and had been summarily dismissed. Or penalized for unnecessary roughness, as he called it. He had been outraged too. Hellfire, he said to me. That's what the law is supposed to do. I just made em too good a hand. What's the point of being a police if you can't beat nobody up.

What makes you think you can get me on?

There's a lot of turnover, he said. Folks comin and goin. There is generally some kind of opening.

Let's try it, I said. I've got to do something till construction picks back up.

The boat paddle plant was a couple of towns over, almost fifty miles away. We drove there in Curtis's lovingly restored 59 Chevrolet. Anyone else would have had a 57 but Curtis fancied himself a bit of an eccentric and much preferred the fine aesthetics of the 59. He was the opposing viewpoint to every proposition. The perennial devil's advocate, his head always cocked slightly sidewise as if listening for the first faint beat of a different drummer.

The plant was a huge sheet-metal building full of machines and the folks who ran them. Saws, sanders, lathes. The place was full of noise like the shrieking from a slaughterhouse. But it smelled like freshly sawn wood, which was already an improvement over the cutting room.

I could put you on the dipper, the foreman said. Son of a bitch walks off the job last night. Never said a word. But you have to work nights and you'd have to be here every night.

I'll be here, I said.

It's warmer back by the dipper too. That's a little benefit we don't charge for.

It is a little cold in here, I said. Why is it so cold?

It's December, the foreman said. December has been a cold month all my life.

When do I start?

How about right now, the foreman said.

It was indeed a little warmer back by the dipper. The dipper consisted of a circular concrete vat perhaps sixteen feet in diameter and filled to some unknowable depth with lacquer or varnish, some kind of waterproofing sealant. There was a crane-like device you operated to lift baled bundles of forty-eight boat paddles and lower them into the hot lacquer. You left them there a time and then raised them out with the crane and stacked them to the side to dry. You always had bales soaking up lacquer, bales waiting for their turn in the vat, bales drying, new bales being forklifted over from the sanders. Enough oars for the entire population of the world to be sitting in flat-bottomed boats rowing upstream. An imponderable amount of boat paddles.

Hell, this is a job with all the work picked out, Curtis said. The machine does all the lifting. You're in the tall cotton on the dipper.

It did not take many nights on the job to discover there was another aspect of the dipper no one had bothered to mention. You got drunk. You got high on the miasmic fumes rolling from the heated vat. Drunker as the night progressed. Not just gently high but drunk as a lord, drunk as a bicycle, drunk as a fiddler's bitch, sleeping it off in the gutter drunk. By shift's end your head would be filled with helium, your boot soles touched the concrete floor only occasionally and a strong wind would have blown you into the next county. It took enormous snake-eyed concentration to raise the bundled oars and sit them down gently on the concrete without breaking the bales. You ran into things. Things did not look right. Perceived distances were fey and compasses unreliable.

The ride home seemed endless or it passed in a flash. Time was a fabric gone slack on the loom or stretched tautly past the breaking point. Every morning you woke with a headache you had been aware of while you slept. It was there before you opened your eyes. There was a taste in your mouth like you had been drinking formaldehyde. Every morning was like sobering up from a two-week drunk.

I need a mask, I told the foreman, after a couple of weeks.

A mask? Who the hell are you, the Lone Ranger?

Some kind of safety thing to breathe through, I said, a filter like. Something to filter out the fumes. I get drunk every night.

And perfectly legally too, the foreman said. You ain't been hassled by the law, have you? You'll notice on your pay stub you're not being charged for these drugs. As a matter of fact you're even being paid for getting high. Drug addicts would tramp each other to death trying to get to this job. We ain't got no masks. The budget don't allow for no safety equipment. Take it up with OSHA.

Perhaps there was an upside to this, I told myself, ever the optimist. This was the twilit waning of psychedelia, of Timothy Leary and LSD, but rumors of mind expansion had drifted down to my hometown through the people at Rolling Stone. Perhaps even now my mind was being expanded. Dylan had used LSD, the Beatles had tried it. Writing about mescaline Aldous Huxley had quoted Blake's line about opening the doors of perception. I had always written and was trying to be a writer. Perhaps these doors of perception would swing wide and I would be ceded a wider vision of things. The gift of the world bestowed upon me. The world writ large, infinite distance made comprehensible, the imponderable mysteries of this world printed out in simple block letters like a ransom note. My mind opened to the windy reaches of the universe.

None of this happened. My mind did not expand. My mind went into a darkened house and closed all the doors and windows. It went down to the basement and sat down in the tiniest closet in the house and pulled the door shut.

I had been there a little over a month and the shift was close to over when I dropped a bundle of oars. Lacquer in the vat seethed and frothed like some malignant potion. The foreman came back. Boat paddles had scattered all over hell and some of them would have to be refinished. What the hell happened? the foreman asked.

I don't know, I said. I got dizzy and let them down too fast or something. I think I need some fresh air.

Maybe you need some fresh air, he said, as if he hadn't heard. Go outside and take a break. Curtis' machine is down and I'll put him on the dipper.

It was very cold outside. A starless expanse of sky, purple in the floodlights. It seemed very close to the earth, the air was freezing, going opaque. A few flakes of snow listed and fell. I sat against the side of the building and smoked a cigarette and thought about things. The cold was beginning to clear my mind. Blow out the smoky fumes that smelled like nightside chemicals.

Perhaps I was damaging myself, I thought. Perhaps what brain I had was shriveling instead of expanding, drawing down to the size of a walnut. Perhaps things were turning black inside me, organs charring, becoming brittle at the edges, and flaking off. My blood slowing, clotting in my veins until all motion ceased. I might be getting cancer, sterility, impotence. Perhaps generations unborn, generations unconceived, would be tainted by the blight of the dipper.

It was snowing harder when the shifts changed and Curtis came out bobbing and weaving like a punch drunk fighter, just a few feet this side of the blind staggers.

Goddamn I'm drunk, Curtis said. I feel like I fell in a whiskey barrel and had to drink my way out. Let's get the hell out of here.

Curtis cranked the Chevrolet and waited a few moments for the engine to smooth out then he revved the engine and dropped it down into first and stamped the accelerator. He came out of the parking lot into the street too fast. There was one tree there, an enormous elm, and he drove directly into it. He seemed to have aimed the Chevrolet at it and hit it dead center. The hood buckled and I grabbed the dash to keep from being thrown into the windshield.

Where'd that come from? Curtis asked. He had bumped the steering wheel with his mouth and his lip was bleeding a little. He wiped it with a sleeve.

It's been there all the time, I said.

I could have sworn that son of a bitch was over yonder, he said.

I opened the door and got out into the cold. It was snowing harder and beginning to whiten the leaves in the edge of yards, the cold metal roof of the Chevrolet. Curtis got out to inspect the damage. He shook his head as if to clear it, as if when he looked back all would be restored. Headlights unshattered, pristine paint made right. I've ruined my car, he said.

A good body man can hammer most of that right out, I said.

I believe I busted my radiator.

Is it drivable?

Are we on the same page here? Drivable with a busted radiator?

I started up the street toward the highway.

Hey. Where you goin?

To the house, I said.

To the house? Hellfire, the house is fifty miles away.

We'll catch a ride, I said. Thumb a car. Somebody will stop for us, let's go.

I can't leave my car.

It'll be here, I said. It's not drivable.

Somebody will steal all my tapes. Take my tape player out. Hang around and we'll catch somebody when the shifts change.

I'm gone, I said. I started up the street.

How'll you get here tomorrow?

I won't be here tomorrow, I said. I won't be back.

You mean you quit? What'll you do?

Go to the house, I said. If I see a wrecker I'll send it your way.

By the time I got to the highway it was snowing harder. What will you do? Curtis had asked, and I wondered that myself. I would find some way to make a living and I would write at night. I had no words for the way the snow looked drifting down in the streetlights and I wanted those words. If they were anywhere I would find them.

I thought of things I could do. I was working on a novel that might come to something but more likely would not. I did not yet know how to write a story anyone would publish. I did not yet know how to frame houses or hang and finish drywall. Perhaps I could devise a territory no one else was working. I might become a sweat expert, I thought. Go out to Hollywood and advise people making movies. You ever notice in scenes where people are working, a chain gang in the hot sun for example, the sweat is never in the right place? They need someone for that, to show the makeup people where it goes, someone who has actually sweated, a perspiration technician. They could create an award for that. And

for best art direction, perspiration department, the Oscar goes to
————.

I went on. I had no way of knowing what might happen. The doors of perception had not opened and I could see down the road no farther than the darkness permitted but I was on that road anyway. It was long but it was straight and wide and clean and my house lay at the end of it.

I went on into the night. I would just take what might come. And hope nobody starved to death.

The Underwear Salesman

by John Grisham

Most lawyers are fine storytellers. It's not that they're trained to spin yarns or that they absorb some special talent after they pass the bar exam. It is more a combination of two important factors. The first is the material. Lawyers, most of them, deal with clients who wouldn't be calling if their lives weren't screwed up in ways that are often hard to imagine. I'm sure there are bond lawyers and patent lawyers who deal with gripping issues at the office, but I've never met one of these people. I have met a plethora of lawyers who mine the rich depths of divorce, personal injury, criminal justice, medical malpractice, insurance fraud, toxic torts, and the list goes on and on. These lawyers see misery and conflict on a grand scale.

The second factor, and one crucial to good storytelling, is the tendency to embellish. Lawyers are paid to take one side of a messy dispute and to believe in that side, to advocate and argue vociferously, and this often leads to overstating the facts. Embellishment might be too kind of a word for what is often done by lawyers in the heat of battle. Whatever it is called, it aids mightily when the lawyer is later narrating the story for the benefit of his audience.

I never would have written the first word had I not been a lawyer. Writing was not a childhood dream. I do not recall longing to write as a student. It came later in life, after an incident in a courtroom.

Of course, I had other jobs before I became a lawyer, though none have yet inspired me to write about them. Just the opposite—I've tried to forget them. My first was mowing grass. We lived in the suburbs and most of the boys on my block tried to pick up a few bucks each summer hustling around with the family mower. Next, I earned my first steady paycheck watering rose bushes at a nursery for a dollar an hour. It was incredibly monotonous, standing there with a water hose, trying to look productive as I filled up one potting bucket after another. The man who owned the nursery saw potential, and I was promoted to his fence crew. For $1.50 an hour, I labored like a fully grown adult as we laid mile after mile of chain-link fence. There was no future in this, and I shall never mention it again in writing. But to this day, I still stop and look down a line of fencing to see if it is straight.

The summer of my sixteenth year I found a job with a plumbing contractor. I had no desire to be a plumber, but my parents expected me to find a place on someone's payroll. I was called a 'helper,' the lowest of the low. As a helper, for example, I was expected to crawl under the house, into the cramped darkness, with a shovel, somehow find the buried pipes, dig until I found the problem, then crawl back out to freedom and report what I had found. The plumbers were always helpful. More than once I heard, "Watch that snake over there." "Where?" I cried, from deep under the house. "Coming your way." Soaked with sweat and covered with mud, I would hold my breath to the point of almost fainting. It was in the midst of one of those episodes when, struck rigid with fear, I vowed to get a desk job. No inspiration attached to that miserable work, and I shall never mention it again in writing.

My father dealt in heavy construction equipment, and through a friend of a friend I got a job the following summer on a highway asphalt crew. This was in Mississippi, where July is as hot as anywhere. Add another 100 degrees for the fresh asphalt, and you get the picture. Part of the project was clearing dirt ahead of the paver, and one day a bulldozer operator got fired on account of a hangover. The foreman took pity on me and showed me the finer points of handling a rather large Caterpillar. I was a natural, and for a few weeks contemplated a future in the cab, tons of growling machinery at my command, with the power to plow over anything. Then the operator was back, sober, repentant, and got himself rehired. I returned to the asphalt crew and got serious about college.

I learned a lot that summer when I was seventeen years old, and most of it cannot be repeated in polite company. Hanging around a construction crew, half with criminal records, I was continually shocked at their sexual exploits, which, at the time, seemed superhuman. Now I know that they were, but what compelling tales. Against my better judgment, I accompanied my new friends to a honky tonk one Friday night to celebrate the end of a hard week. We consumed beer after beer, something new for me, and were in the midst of a wonderfully rowdy evening when a fight broke out at the pool tables. To my surprise, this seemed to be the moment everyone had been waiting for. Tough men who had been drinking and laughing and having a grand time fraternizing together one moment were suddenly punching each other the next, and for no apparent reason. Pool cues were snatched from the racks and flung about. Beer bottles were thrown and broken. Heads were cracked, people screamed and cursed. For a split second I thought about hitting someone, but I wasn't sure who, and for what? Which side was I on? It didn't matter. Instead, I wisely hid behind a jukebox and watched the chaos. When I heard gunfire, I ran to the restroom, locked the door, and crawled out a window. I stayed in the woods for an hour as the police hauled away rednecks. As I hitchhiked home, I realized I was not cut out for construction.

My career sputtered along with little to add to the résumé. Retail caught my attention, primarily because it was indoors, clean, air-conditioned, much softer than, say, asphalt or plumbing, and I applied for a job at a Sears store in a mall. The only opening was in men's underwear, and since I was in college and needed the money, I reluctantly hired on. It was humiliating. On those rare occasions when a cute girl came close, I would find something to do in the stock room and ignore the cash register. I tried to quit, but they gave me a raise. Evidently, the position was difficult to fill.

JOHN GRISHAM

I asked to be transferred to toys, then to appliances, but they said no and gave me another raise. (These were not big pay hikes, mind you.) I became abrupt with the customers, and I am compelled to say here that Sears had the nicest customers in the world. But I didn't care. I was rude and surly and I was written up on occasion by the 'shoppers,' spies hired by Sears to buy things and fill out reports. One of these 'shoppers' asked if he could try on a pair of boxers. I said no, said it was obvious to me the boxers in question were much too small for his rather ample rear-end. I handed him a pair of XLs, said I was sure they would fit fine, and he didn't need to be trying on our brand new underwear. He took offense. I got written up, but they still wouldn't transfer me. I asked for lawn care. No. I finally quit when a customer with obvious hygienic deficiencies insisted on returning a three-pack of low-cut briefs. Other minimum wage paid jobs came and went, none as exciting as selling underwear.

Halfway through college, and still drifting, I hit upon the notion of studying accounting, with the goal of becoming a high-powered tax lawyer. I would go to law school, and then make a fortune representing wealthy people who wanted to avoid paying taxes. To this day, I have no idea where this came from. I knew nothing about tax and certainly knew no one with money. Undaunted, I got a degree in accounting and enrolled in law school. The plan was sailing right along until I took my first course in tax law. I was stunned at its complexity, and lunacy, and barely passed the course.

At about the same time, I was involved in mock trial classes and I realized I enjoyed the courtroom. A new plan was hatched. I would return to my hometown, hang out my shingle, start up a new firm, and become a hotshot trial lawyer. Tax law was discarded overnight. And since no one offered me a job, I really had no choice but to go home.

This was 1981, and at that time there was no public defender system in our county. For indigent criminals, the judge simply appointed whatever lawyer happened to be in the courtroom that day. The system worked well, with the unwritten rule that the young lawyers would take these low-paying cases because the

110

older lawyers had already handled their share. Since I had no other clients, I volunteered for all of the indigent work I could get. It was the quickest way to trial. I often felt sorry for my clients, many of them charged with serious crimes, because they were forced to rely upon me, a rookie. But I learned, and quickly.

With the law office struggling, I decided to launch another low-paying career. In 1983, I ran for a House seat in the Mississippi State Legislature, and got myself elected. The salary was $8,000 a year, which was more than I made my first year as a lawyer. From January through March of each year, I was at the state capitol in Jackson, wasting serious time, but also listening to great storytellers. My colleagues came from all over the state. Most were veteran politicians who had learned their craft in the tough world of rural politics. They were accustomed to public speaking, and they understood the art of embellishment. I took a lot of notes.

Like most small-town lawyers, I dreamed of the big case, the big trial, the big verdict, that great moment in the courtroom when a career is made. And it happened in 1984, but not in a way I expected. As usual, I was loitering around the courtroom, pretending to be busy with serious matters, when in reality I was watching a trial involving a young girl who had been beaten and raped. Her testimony was gut-wrenching, graphic, heartbreaking, and riveting. Every juror was crying. I got choked up myself, and I remember staring at the defendant and wishing I had a gun.

A story was born. Over the following weeks it grew, the plot was defined, the characters were fleshed out, and I thought of little else. Since I had not attempted fiction before, I was not sure how to begin. But since I was a lawyer, I carried around my faithful legal pad. One night I wrote "Chapter One" at the top of the first page, and the journey began. The first lesson I learned was the most valuable: If I didn't write at least one page per day, the book went nowhere. I fell into the routine of writing at the office, very early in the morning. My office was on the busiest street in town, and by 5:30 most mornings the lights were on and my car was parked outside. People were soon talking about how hard I worked. This was good for the law business. Little did they know I was trying to write a novel. *A Time to Kill* was finished three years later.

But the first book didn't sell, and my dream of writing full time was delayed. I continued to sue people, defend criminals, prepare wills and deeds and contracts, and do a hundred mundane little tasks that were so important to my clients and so boring to me. And I knew that if I disappeared, those same clients would simply walk next door and find the same services. My work didn't matter. Nothing I did was unique.

But with the fiction, things were different. After spending three years writing a book that sold 4,000 copies, I was determined to write one with a broader appeal, and write it much faster. It would not be about a small-town lawyer like myself, but instead a Harvard star seduced by the riches of a big law firm. When *The Firm* was published in 1991, I said goodbye to being a lawyer, and I did so with no hesitation. I practiced for only ten years, but that was enough. At the same time, I also quit politics and never looked back. A new career was calling, and I pursued it with a fury.

My initial plan, if a fledgling stumbling in the dark can actually have a plan, was to alternate books between Ford County, the fictional setting of *A Time to Kill*, and the world of legal suspense. However, the success of *The Firm* changed things. My publisher prevailed upon me to stick with the legal thrillers, and it was an easy sell. The last thing I wanted was to wake up broke and be forced to reopen a law office. *A Time to Kill* sold 4,000 copies. *The Firm* sold a few million. Hello.

And there was/is no shortage of material. I watch and study the law, certainly not as a scholar—those days are mercifully over—but rather as a keen observer. Trials, litigation, disputes, Supreme Court rulings, conflicts, disbarments, even crimes. We have an insatiable appetite for stories about lawyers and the law.

Someone has to write them.

John Grisham
April 5, 2010
Charlottesville, VA

Job Experience

by Winston Groom

I had a bunch of jobs before I discovered you could make money writing books and not actually have to work for a living. I think I learned something from all of them.

My first job was a newspaper boy at age twelve. From this I learned I did not like to get up early in the morning.

*   *   *

My next job was as a summer construction worker at age sixteen. First day I walked into the office and this guy said, "Are you scared of heights?"

I didn't know, because I'd never been really high up, so I said no.

"Good," he said. "He is," and pointed to a black guy sitting in the corner. "Both of you come with me."

He drove us to a building in downtown Mobile and told the black guy to wait outside in a parking lot. He took a great big coil of rope out of the back of his truck and slung it over his shoulder. Then we got inside an elevator and went to the top of the building—eight stories. We climbed some stairs to the roof and he went over on the side to where there was some scaffolding and said, "This belongs to us. We got to take it down."

I didn't know what he was talking about, but he stepped out on the scaffolding and undid a piece of scaffold pipe, tied it on the rope, and began to lower it to the ground, eight stories below. Down there was the black guy, who was supposed to fetch it, untie it from the rope and put it on the truck. He was so far down he looked like he was barely an inch tall.

"He's got the worst job," the guy says. "One of these pieces is apt to fall on him."

Well, I climbed out on the scaffolding, which was very shaky, and was hanging on for dear life. The wind was blowing and we were so high up I could see ships way out in the harbor.

"Turn loose of that scaffolding and take off that pipe," he said, "and tie it on this rope."

It was like dismantling a big erector set with yourself inside it. Or making up a bed while you're still lying in it.

Anyway, we took apart scaffolding most of the day until the pickup truck was full. The guy said he don't do any more than one pickup load a day because it is "kind of hard on the nerves." So we knocked off and drove to a site where we pickaxed hard clay to put in curb footings.

We made about a half-story a day taking down the scaffolding; it took two weeks.

From this job I learned that if anybody asks if I'm scared of heights, say yes.

*   *   *

My next summer job was encyclopedia salesman. I had just graduated from high school, and there was an ad in the paper that said, "Make loads of money, easy work, good hours, no labor involved, meet interesting people"—or something to that effect.

I went to the motel room where the ad said go, and there was this thin guy with slicked-back hair in a cheap suit and a pencil mustache, who told me to go on inside. There were about thirty people in the room. Before we even got started, one guy asked, "Say, is this about selling encyclopedias?"

And the slicked-back guy in the cheap suit answered, "No, we don't sell anything here. We *place* them in homes." The guy that asked the question just got up and walked out.

I should have followed him.

First, I found out we had to put up a $100 deposit, and then he showed us how to "place" encyclopedias in people's homes: "You go into neighborhoods and look for yards with children's toys. You never work on weekends, because that is when the men are home. You do NOT want to talk to the men."

This slicked-back guy could sell damn near anything. We'd been at it about a week and I had no sales, so he says, "You come with me today, I'll show you how it's done." He drove a yellow Buick convertible.

We went to this really poor-looking house that needed paint and the only toy was an old tire hanging on a rope from a limb. A woman came to the door and you could hear kids crying in the back. Before I knew it, old slick had talked his way in, and we were sitting on the couch. He started his spiel. When he laid out the encyclopedia pitch she said, "Wait a minute—is this about encyclopedias?"

Slick said, "Yes—the finest encyclopedia in the world!"

And she said, "Well, look over there" and pointed to a bookcase filled with encyclopedias. "That was last year," she said. "They talked me into buying the entire *Encyclopedia Britannica*. I'm still paying for it—and don't nobody ever even use it."

"Well," Slick said, "that's your problem. That encyclopedia is no good for kids—it's too smart for 'em. It's for college kids. What you got to have is our encyclopedia," and he went on about how great it was for kids.

I looked out the window at her kids playing in the yard, and from what I could see, those kids needed *clothes*, not some damn encyclopedia. But after an hour or two of Slick browbeating her, the woman agreed to buy our encyclopedia for about $1,000 that she could not afford, I was sure.

When we got into the car, Slick said, "I bet that gal knows how to have a good time. I'm gonna phone her back this afternoon and find out."

I did not go back to the encyclopedia place again. My daddy gave me back the money I lost in the deposit. From this job I learned I did not want to be an asshole. Or sell encyclopedias.

* * *

Next job I had was actually fun. I was editor of the student humor magazine at the University of Alabama, which was called *Mahout*, and they actually paid me a salary. Our job was to lampoon things and be really ironic and make people laugh and say, "See—hah, we told you so!"

At the time there was much to lampoon in the state of Alabama. For one thing, there was the governor, who was George C. Wallace, who had just gotten his ass handed to him by federal marshals on the steps of the University of Alabama Admissions Building so he would step aside and let black students in.

So for one of my first magazine covers I pasted a picture of the governor being flushed down a toilet, with his hand up kind of like he was waving bye-bye.

When this appeared, both the Dean of Men *and* the Dean of Women went apeshit. I was hauled onto the carpet and informed in no uncertain terms that besides being governor, Governor Wallace was also "*de facto* chairman" of the University's Board of Trustees, and, as such, he could, if he wanted, close the University down—permanently!

I made a lot of apologies and bowed and scraped and promised not to insult the governor anymore and they were satisfied it was all smoothed over—until they saw my next month's cover. I had pasted pictures of the Dean of Men *and* the Dean of Women being flushed down the toilet.

Once more they were furious. How could I demean their important positions by having them flushed down a toilet on the cover of the student humor magazine, and what was I thinking, and so forth? So next issue I just put a picture of myself on the cover getting flushed down the toilet. Five minutes after the magazine hit the streets my phone rang and there was all this hollerin' and yellin', and I was in the doghouse again.

"Groom," they said, "You have got to lose that toilet!"

From my job at the humor magazine I learned you can push people just so far.

* * *

Following the end of my magazine career at the University, I had another job. Sure, it paid me a little money, but I don't think I would have taken it if I had known where it would lead.

Back then, for the first two years at the University, if you weren't in ROTC you had to take PE, and I didn't want to take PE. Also, in those days there was the military draft, and if you didn't go through ROTC and become an officer, you were liable to wind up in the army as a private. I didn't want to be a private either.

ROTC wasn't so bad at first. We got to parade in dress uniforms on Tuesdays and Thursdays on the Quad, and I didn't have to worry what I was going to wear to classes twice a week. The courses were easy. And it wasn't like there was a war on or anything.

But unfortunately, by the time I graduated it was 1965, and there was a war on for sure. Anybody who thought he was going to spend his tour of duty as a shiny brand new second lieutenant over in Germany or someplace had another think coming.

For one year I got additional training. They trained me like I had never trained before, shooting cannons, rifles, humping through the woods, camping out, jumping out of planes. Always somebody was hollering at me. Finally the yelling stopped and they sent me to Fort Bragg in North Carolina to the Special Warfare School.

"Fort Bragg: Home of the 82nd Airborne," "Home of the Special Forces." Bullshit! It wasn't anybody's "home." Fort Bragg was a damn halfway house running people in and out of there on their way to Vietnam.

In the psychological warfare course I learned how to trick the gooks into surrendering, or telling us things we wished to know, or how to just plain scare the hell out of them. And when I was sufficiently schooled, they shipped my ass out to Vietnam—literally, on a USN troop ship, the USS *Gaffney*, out of San Francisco and across the Pacific Ocean.

From the deck of the USS *Gaffney* five weeks and one typhoon later, Vietnam looked lush and luxuriant, with mountains and rice paddies, palm and banana trees and what looked like pretty flowers. That picture was deceptive. The place was a dump.

First off, the air smelled bad because nobody had proper toilets like those I had put on the cover of the magazine. Villagers just mostly "went" where they pleased, even in the rice paddies—hell, *especially* in the rice paddies. And then they ate the rice!

The Vietnamese threw their garbage where they pleased, too, which was mostly in the roads and streets. It rained most of the time and when it wasn't raining it was hot as hell, kicking up a stink.

I was assigned to the First Brigade of the Fourth Infantry Division to be the "Brigade Psychological Warfare Officer," which turned out to be a joke. I was a flunky for every damn major who wandered in or out of the TOC, the Tactical Operations Center tent.

Do this! Do that! Go out in the woods and stand in for Lieutenant So-and-so who was sick, relieved, wounded, on R&R, killed, or under arrest.

Every once in a while I got to do my psychological warfare thing, which was not as fancy or fun as it sounded. Basically, the job was this: Whenever one of our operating units stepped into deep doo-doo, I would hustle up a team—loudspeaker operator, Vietnamese interpreter/translator, power battery carriers, couple of riflemen—and we went out on a helicopter to the scene of the action.

There we would try to convince the bad guys to give up. The interpreter would interpret what I told him into the mike and it would bellow from the loudspeaker and we'd wait to see what would happen. Usually they would shoot at us. I guess on account of our loudspeaker was so loud it disturbed their fighting. Or maybe they didn't approve of our message.

In any case, very little good was accomplished from our broadcasts, but from time to time it was exciting. (About halfway through my tour we were told not to use any more Vietnamese translators, but instead to spread our message using pre-inspected tape recordings played from the loudspeaker. We discovered that some of the translators were actually VC, and were not telling the enemy to surrender, but to fight harder).

What I learned from this job was:
1. Do not volunteer for anything. Ever.
2. Do not join the army if you consider yourself a sanitary person.
3. Vietnam: If You Can Make it There, You Can Make it Anywhere.

*   *   *

When I got out of that mess I went to New York City, certain that because I had been the editor of the humor magazine at the University one of the big magazines like *The New Yorker*, or *Esquire*, or *Time*, or *Newsweek* would be glad to put me on their staff to write columns, make suggestions for cover art, or whatever.

It did not work out that way.

They were polite enough, but all said the same thing: "Boy, you got to get some experience before you can come up here asking us for a job."

I asked them where I might get that experience, but nobody knew.

So I went on back home to Mobile and started trying to get some journalism experience. My hometown paper wouldn't hire me because they said there wasn't any room for another reporter, which was basically everybody's answer down to and including a little two-bit paper over by the Okeefenokee Swamp in Georgia. It was a hell of a thing. I was running out of money and wound up taking a job for a dollar an hour putting up shelves at a plant that made canvas tarpaulins.

What I learned from that job was that if you are tall, like I am, you will always be told to put up the highest shelf. Top shelf or not, it was a hell of a comedown from being an officer in the United States Army commanding men in combat in Vietnam.

* * *

Just when I was feeling so low I had to look up to see down, some luck came my way.

There was a big wedding of the sister of a good friend of mine and I was asked to the after-rehearsal dinner party. At one point I stepped outside to get some cool autumn air, and there was an older guy there who I figured was probably a newspaperman because he had on a tuxedo and brown shoes.

We got to talking and he asked me what I did.

When I told him I was "retired," he asked what from, and when I told him, he asked what I wanted to do.

I said I wanted to write, but nobody would hire me, to which he replied, "Well, you want to write, why don't you write me a letter saying why, 'cause I am the managing editor of the *Washington Star*." He was also the uncle of the bride.

You could have knocked me over with a feather.

A couple of weeks later I was headed to Washington, D.C., to be a reporter on a big city newspaper in the nation's capitol. On my way out of the drive my mother called and said the editor of the local paper was on the phone. Turned out somebody quit or got fired and they now had an opening. I told him to go...well, let's just say I said I wasn't interested.

I had never been in a newspaper office like the *Washington Star*. The newsroom was the size of a football field and a hive of activity, with desks as far as you could see and reporters coming and going and everybody typing and hollering "copy," and teletype machines clattering away and bells ringing and people shouting stuff I didn't understand, but it all looked pretty impressive.

They put me in the "Editorial Training Program," which meant I got to sit at a desk taking dictation from reporters on Capitol Hill, or places like Paris and Rhodesia. And you daren't make a mistake or typo, or it was your ass. Nobody gave a flip-shit about whether I'd been in Vietnam, or what I did there, which was okay by me. They didn't look like the sort of people who would have appreciated it anyhow.

I worked all night about half the time, and my only writing was doing little public service notices and obituaries and stuff, and the most exciting thing was when they asked me to go way out somewhere and cover a county commission meeting.

But I got the hang of it, and wrote some feature stories of my own, and sure enough, before you know it, they made me a reporter.

As luck would have it, this was not really a good time to be a new reporter on general assignment. It was April, 1968, and Martin Luther King had just been murdered in Memphis. The reaction in Washington was immediate and furious.

I got into the office the morning after King's death and there was smoke rising over parts of Washington. The city editor was a guy named Sid, who was worse than the worst major I ever encountered in Vietnam. They didn't call him the Smiling Cobra for nothing, and you didn't want to cross him. There weren't any cell phones in those days, and during my training program Sid made me take a test proving I'd memorized the location of every single pay telephone in Washington, D.C., so I'd know where to phone in stories from.

Anyway, Sid told me and this other guy, Rusty, that there were reports of "something going on" way up on 14th Street, and for us to get up there and see what it was.

I will tell you what the something was. It was a goddamn riot, was what it was!

I had never been to a riot, but let me tell you, it was weird—and scary to be the only two white guys among about two hundred thousand rioters enraged because somebody had gunned down their head man.

We could hear the riot before we could see it. We had parked on Massachusetts Avenue about three blocks away, but when we turned the corner of 14th Street it was pandemonium. First thing happened, glass was breaking all around us, cascading down the brick wall of an apartment building we were pressed against. We looked up and people on fire escapes were throwing beer and soda bottles at us.

Out in the street in front of us we saw cop cars and cops crouching down with weapons drawn. We looked at each other and made a dash for the patrol cars in an avalanche of bottles that shattered at our feet, just lucky our heads were spared. When we were clear, what we saw took our breath away.

Every burglar alarm up and down the street was clanging and sirening. People were busting plate-glass windows with bricks and stealing stuff from storefronts. Bright orange flames and billows of black smoke were pouring out of some buildings. The liquor store across the street had been broken into and everybody we saw running seemed to have a bottle of something. I kind of wished I had one myself.

The noise and sight of so many people, the mob that seemed to be everywhere, that was petrifying. You could see for miles up and down 14th Street and it was jam-packed with people hollering and yelling, singing and shaking their fists, or running, looting. Rioters had broken into the supermarket and had run helter-skelter with grocery carts piled with loot. Some people were shooting firearms out of the windows of the apartments above the storefronts. And it was only 9 AM. It sort of reminded me of Vietnam, except I didn't have my weapon.

The cops looked at us like we were crazy. "Get the hell out of here," they said. We had our press cards around our necks. We told them we were there to cover the riot.

"You damn fools, can't you see what's happening here?" one sergeant said. "We're trapped. They're setting fire to the patrol cars down the street!"

Oddly enough, some of the rioters did not seem to me overcome by grief, or even angry. Some in fact almost seemed to be enjoying themselves. There was a filling station about half a block away where I saw a phone booth. My partner and I worked our way down there, getting not only glares of surprise or hostility, but also a few nods of "good morning," if we smiled and pretended to be casual.

The filling station was on fire inside and my partner jumped in the phone booth to call the paper. I looked across the street, where it appeared people were beating someone with boards. It turned out some kids had hauled one of the mannequins out of a broken storefront and were acting out with it.

But when I turned back, to my shock, people had surrounded the phone booth with my partner in it, and had shoved it over. I could see him inside, horrified, obviously worried how long it would be before the fire got to the station's gasoline tanks. Luckily I got him out of there.

We had a story to cover, and we sort of hung around, hoping to look inconspicuous enough to get out alive. We took out our notepads and tried to be very workmanlike and if we saw anyone with an approachable face, we asked questions, such as, "Why are you rioting?" "What do you want to accomplish?" "What is your reaction to the death of MLK?"—stupid and inane things like that. Which is what reporters do. "Name, address, where do you work?" Jesus—it almost made me want to join the riot myself.

The riot continued most of the day and the mood turned uglier. By late afternoon there was pretty much nothing left to steal, nothing to distract from our presence. A few people made threatening comments to us as they passed. Our problem became, "How the hell do we get out of here?"

Oddly, somehow, there in the mob it seemed safer. If we got on side streets, no telling what we'd run into. The cops were still there, stuck like everybody else, weapons still drawn. They had been pelted with food, glass, and other things from the upper story windows.

About then came a big roaring racket from up the street, and a US Army armored personnel carrier appeared with a big .50 caliber machine gun at its turret. Manned and loaded. Loudspeakers told people to move off the street. A string of these vehicles had been ordered down from Fort Meade, Maryland. Martial law had been declared by the President.

Soldiers cleared the streets of people, and the cops got back in their cars and sped away. Unfortunately, while the column of APCs cleared the people off 14th Street, they were merely shoved back into the side streets, and when the convoy had passed they came back out and were hopping mad, cursing and throwing things, and the riot broke out all over again.

My pal and I were sure we had overstayed our welcome and made for a side street, followed by a hail of bottles and other debris. By this time all our newspaper deadlines for that day had passed, so we stopped at the first bar we saw and had a drink. Actually we had more than one drink before we went back to the office to file our accounts of the riot.

I stayed at the *Star* for nine years and got to cover some interesting things and meet some interesting people. In fact, I met four presidents and any number of senators, congressmen, supreme court justices, ambassadors, and assorted hoity-toity, as well as my share of hoi polloi. I was there for Watergate—in fact I was the imbecile who cost the *Star* the story. I knew Carl Bernstein and Bob Woodward fairly well, and thought they were making most of that stuff up. It seemed too good to be true.

I was the legal reporter at the paper, and whenever they'd come out with a story of some monumental wrongdoing by the Nixon Administration, I would call up the United States Attorney's office and ask if it was true. Routinely I was told it was untrue, and would duly report this to my superiors. Having been raised with a lawyer for a father, I simply could not, or would not, believe that a United States Attorney would deliberately lie to me.

So I missed the big story. But in any case, by then they had started paying me pretty well, and it became clear to me that if I wasn't careful I'd wind up in journalism the rest of my life. If I ever wanted out, I'd best find a new line of work.

So one day I resigned. Not only that, but I sort of cut my umbilical cord, too. Deliberately. I told them I was leaving to write a book—a novel about the Vietnam War.

I knew that in many of those desks in the back of the newsroom where I sat, old reporters kept, above all else, three things: a pack of cigarettes, a pint of Seagram's in a brown paper bag, and the half-finished manuscript of a novel. I didn't want to wind up like that, so I quit, knowing that after telling everybody why I was leaving, I could never come back.

What I learned from my job as a newspaper reporter was a valuable lesson from Sid, the city editor: When you are standing in a phone booth on deadline, and about to dictate the story of a triple ax murder, there had better be no such thing as "writer's block."

And I have never had writer's block.

So there you have it, the Odyssey of what I learned from all the jobs I've had, in a nutshell, a little something from each of them, job experience wrapped in the sum of a life's experience. And if you expect to be a writer, you'd best be able to draw on what you know from what you've done pretty heavily. Good luck.

Why I Worked at the P.O.

by Silas House

For seven years I worked as a rural mail carrier for the United States Postal Service. It was pure hell, but it was also the best thing I ever did for my writing.

Forget that image of a mail carrier as someone in a smart, crisp uniform with an eagle patch on the sleeve and a clean little postal-service-supplied Jeep like you see on the city routes. Rural carriers drive whatever they can get—the more junky the better, since a vehicle tends to get pretty banged up on the mail route (bad roads, mailbox lids that fall open and scrape down the door)—and wear whatever they want. In summer my uniform was a pair of shorts, a tee shirt, Chuck Taylors, and a cigarette hanging out of my mouth. In winter: a union suit under the heaviest flannel shirt and jeans I could find, hiking boots, and a cigarette hanging out of my mouth.

My mail car was a rusting 1984 Thunderbird that sent out funnels of black smoke and made a sound like a train approaching, or sometimes like a plane in the process of crashing. I bought the car cheap because it had been wrecked; the entire passenger-side fender was caved in so that sometimes I had to pull over and readjust the flapping metal so it didn't grind against the tire. The console was the size of a small home and since I had to drive from the passenger side (the steering wheel was on the driver's side, as it usually is), this meant that my leg had to go across the console to reach the gas and brake. Only a person with long legs would have been able to reach the pedals easily or comfortably over that gigantic console, but I managed to do it. At the end of the day I often felt as if I had spent hours doing leg stretching exercises and I believe I grew at least a couple of inches in the process.

Strangely enough, I felt that I drove better from the wrong side of the car. I was more alert and somehow had more control. Children loved to inquire about this. Many times I was detained by kids who stopped riding their bicycles to lean against my door and ask me if it was hard to drive from the passenger side. "Just about impossible," I told them. "And don't you ever try it."

The word *rural* in *rural carrier* is important: sometimes I had to ford creeks to deliver the mail and I climbed muddy roads that required me gunning it up the mountain, slip-sliding every whichaway. Often I would drive for an hour without seeing anything but trees and cornfields and mailboxes, as the houses were way off the road down some winding gravel drive. Some days I didn't see a single person, but I was perfectly happy to see nothing but poplars and pines, river banks and railroad tracks. I liked them better than people anyway, for the most part.

I can't think of a better job for a writer. I got to listen to music and smoke cigarettes and drive. I was in my early twenties, and listening to music, smoking, and driving were three of my favorite things anyway.

The best part of working for the P.O., however, was I could think about my first novel all day long. Sometimes I composed entire scenes between runs of mailboxes. One of my mail routes was about 80 miles long and one day I finished it with absolutely no recollection of delivering my mail because I was so caught up in thinking about an intense chapter of *Clay's Quilt*, my first novel. But, as far as I know, none of the mail was delivered incorrectly that day.

But best for my writing, I discovered things as a mailman.

The main things I discovered are that people are wonderful, people are terrible, and that we don't really know nature until we're forced to be out in it.

At the first of the month, people often stood by their boxes waiting for their checks or their bills, mostly older people because they were retired and at home during the day. The older most people get, the better they get because they start to figure out that the main thing we need to be doing is loving one another. Not all people figure this out, but most of the older people I knew on my route had come to this epiphany. They were good to me, kind and courteous, even though I brought them a lot more bills than checks. My customers gave me Ziploc bags full of pennies and nickels to buy books of stamps. In the summer, they gave me tomatoes (still warm from the sun), messes of green beans (which would sweat in their plastic grocery bags before I could get them home), or—once—a whole gallon of blackberries, from a man whose fingers still bore the stain of picking them.

One lady on my route always watched for me to come up her road and brought me out a big glass of blue Kool-Aid. I never did like blue Kool-Aid as I thought it looked exactly like windshield washer fluid, but I was awfully grateful for it on those days when the air was so hot it was like driving through a furnace. The Thunderbird's humungous V-8 motor made the 100-degree summer days seem twice as hot as it burned and churned near my legs. I have never, ever forgotten her kindness, and the blue veins in the tops of her hands.

In the wintertime, people helped to push me out of ditches I had slipped into or they asked me to come in and get warmed up. It was a blessing to go in and rub my hands together by their fireplaces. After all, nothing will make you long for warmth in the cold of winter more than driving past hundreds of houses that are pumping out coal smoke. But I had a job to do, and some days I had to drive past.

I knew all of my customers by name.

There was America Morgan, who bought postal money orders from me to pay her bills because all the banks were owned by Communists. She kept her cash safety-pinned to her brassiere strap. In summer we sat on her front porch while I made out her bills. She always sat on the cool concrete floor of the porch and swung her legs like a little girl. I still think of her. Often. And I miss her.

There was Shade Owens, who always put a tiny Milky Way in the box when he had outgoing letters as my payment for picking up his mail.

There was my Aunt Dot, who was very proud that her nephew carried her mail. If I drove up and she happened to be out in her yard she would stroll over to my car and lean in the window and kiss me on the forehead the same way she had done when I was a small child.

There was the day two little boys hid behind a tree and waited patiently for me to pop open a mailbox, only to find the black snake they had propped up inside. I slammed the box shut so hard that it tore loose from its wooden post and I screamed a certain curse loudly enough for their grandmother to hear it inside her house and come rushing out to see what was wrong. The boys nearly died of laughter. Over the years these two also put in the mailbox: a dead squirrel, wads of garbage, a rotting watermelon rind swarming with ants, a flaccid condom that was undoubtedly used and discarded on the side of the road. Their favorite item to put in the box was a dog turd, which happened at least once every couple of months. I truly hope there is such a thing as karma and would love to watch it arrive at their mailbox, so to speak.

Twice I had a gun pulled on me. Once because the man was out of his mind and thought I had stolen his disability check. He had his children line up across the road to block me from passing while he propped the shotgun on my window sill and proceeded to interrogate me. The children wouldn't move and I thought he was going to shoot me, so my body took over and left my mind to watch as my arm popped the gear into neutral, my foot slammed on the gas, the engine roared its best plane-crashing snarl. The children dived for the side of the road, thinking I was going to run over them. My arm—without my mind's consent—snatched the gear down into drive and I sped away, leaving the man and his shotgun in the middle of the road and his children pulling themselves out of the brush. Yes, I reported it.

Another time a man trotted toward my mail car with a pistol in hand and I sped away from there, too, no questions asked. Several days later his neighbor, C.W. Spurlock, sauntered out to get his mail. I had come to know him a little bit over the years, so I asked him why the man would have brandished his pistol. C.W. spat a stream of tobacco juice between his feet while he looked through his Kroger circulars and bills. "He's kindly skittish," C.W. said. "Got the biggest crop in these parts." I didn't have to ask what kind of crop needs protecting with a Smith & Wesson.

Once a man came out onto his porch to sign for his food stamps clad only in his tighty-whiteys and ostrich-skin cowboy boots. Another time I caught sight of a naked woman. She had opened her front door and was divided from the world only by her glass storm door. Living way out in the country, she was used to having her privacy, and people often forget that the mail carrier visits every day, and now and again might need to come up on the porch to leave a parcel. So there she was, leaned over and dusting her coffee table in her full glory while she sang "Don't Rain On My Parade" along with Barbara Streisand, who was turned up loud on her stereo. The woman must have caught some movement out of the corner of her eye because she looked up just as I stepped onto the porch. Her eyes went wide, her mouth fell open, and one arm went high and one went low as she instinctively covered the two most private areas of herself. I just nodded and scampered away. I didn't know what to say, and wouldn't have been able to speak anyway.

A mail carrier knows more about you than you might realize. I could tell which people were in debt up to their eyeballs (collection agencies don't make a secret out of what they're doing on their envelopes), which people were hypocrites (there was the Baptist preacher who took a subscription to every dirty magazine known to man...perhaps he was just doing research?), and which people were missing someone (they got long, handwritten letters with beautiful penmanship on the envelope). I knew who was bored (they received every catalog possible), who was unhappy (they were delivered a package from QVC or the Home Shopping Network every day), who was a music lover (back then people still became members of cassette and CD clubs), who was a dog lover (updates from the animal shelter), who was sick (prescriptions are delivered in white plastic bags), whose henhouse lost chickens to foxes or snakes (chickens can be ordered through the mail and cluck and titter and cheep and crow and have bowel movements all along the entire mail route).

The people on my route gave me stories—sometimes by not even saying a word, but just going about the business of living in plain view. I saw people working in their gardens, playing with their children in their yards, changing the oil in their cars. Sometimes, they told me things. A woman who was ecstatic to finally receive her divorce papers by certified letter spilled all about her abusive husband. A man who lived at the mouth of Hawk Creek stood by his box every single day for a month waiting for me and hoped that I was delivering news that his black lung disability had finally been approved. Each day he seemed more out of breath from walking the short distance between his house and his box. He knew all about the mines and told me about his work, in words lyrical and strong. He once said to me that when he entered the mines, it always smelled like a spring evening, "just after a good rain, with the smell of something baking in the air." He died only days after I brought him the letter he'd been waiting for.

Everyone knows the old post office brag about rain, hail, sleet, and snow. They say a writer should write about what he knows. Believe me, I'm on personal terms with the weather, having been a rural carrier. We all know what rain smells like, the way it feels. We all know the way a storm sounds. But you don't know anything about rain, or storms, or snow, or hail when you're watching it from your living room or running through it to get from one place to another. You truly know about the weather when you don't have any other choice but to be out in it. I tried to fight the weather for a time, but after a while I just gave myself over to it. I got so I would walk my normal pace in the pelting rain from my car to the front porch to deliver food stamps or parcels. I stopped rolling the window up between mailboxes when the snow was falling in wet clumps. When the sun was at its noontime highest and it seemed the whole world was baking like a slow cake, I let it be and folded myself into the heat and accepted it.

In summertime, when I first got out on the route, morning mist still lay above the pastures. By the time I was done in mid-afternoon, the heat bugs were screaming. When winter came, I worked for hours in the snow and ice while teachers stayed home with their own children because school was called off. Roads in Eastern Kentucky are treacherous enough without snow. And since we don't get snow on a regular basis, no one knows how to drive on it. A half-inch of snow leads to the entire region shutting down. Except for the mail. Sometimes on those frozen roads I got so aggravated from sliding into every mailbox that I would just stop for a little while. I sat there with the window rolled down, and looked around, listened. Snow has a sound. It sounds like *huuuuuuusssssssssshhhhhhhh*. Snow sounds like the whole world has stopped moving and everyone is holding their breath. They can't teach me that in a writing class.

Carrying the mail was a great job in retrospect, now that I'm a writer full time, but those mornings when I'd saddle up that old Ford, it was just plain misery. Typically rural carriers work at least five years as part-time employees, or substitute carriers, before getting their own routes and full-time status. So I carried a different route almost every day, which meant that I had to often put the mail in order for routes I didn't know well, a four-hour Easter egg hunt and no fun whatsoever. But, if you hold your mouth right, as the old timers say, there's something worthwhile in every unpleasant thing we do.

Early on in my writing education, I was told by the great writer James Still that the best thing a writer could do was to "discover something new every day." The mail route was the perfect place for that. When I try to explain this to people, they always laugh and say that my mail must have always been a mess since I drove my route dreaming up stories. People assume that my letters ended up anywhere but where they were supposed to be. And that was sometimes true. But not often. As a writer, I learned to have my mind going two ways at once. As I sold books of stamps and money orders, I could listen to the stories people told me. While I was putting letters in order, I could steal a minute to look at the way the land flows down to the river or draw a slow breath and take note of the way the morning smells.

I suppose you could say I worked two full-time jobs at once.

Eight months after my first novel came out, I was lucky enough that I could quit my job as a mail carrier. Ever since, I've been doing what I love, writing for a living. On winter mornings I watch the snow fall, get a little closer to the fire, and say a little prayer for all the mail carriers out there.

I don't miss carrying the mail one bit on those snowy mornings or on those blistering days when the noontime heat is sizzling on the horizon. But I miss the people. Nobody leaves Kool-Aid out for me on a hot day anymore, blue or red or any color. Sometimes I miss sitting with America Morgan on her cool concrete porch and listening to her laugh, which sounded like a little song. I miss driving for hours listening to my radio (I quit smoking, though— one of the great accomplishments of my life.)

And sometimes I miss that little distance between mailboxes when I'd pull my car over to the side of the road and prop my chin up on the window and take in the fierce world in all its beauty and ugliness.

Hiding out with Holden Caulfield

by Suzanne Hudson

Some lawyers are fond of saying that they keep secrets for a living. I am not a lawyer, but I do a whole lot of observing, listening, and keeping my mouth shut—except when I am required to open it. So I'm part spy, part Catholic priest, and sometime tattletale. The workaday world I navigate involves being thoroughly entertained, hearing all stripes of stories, and, for all the toil of it, has a big red cherry on top: staying in touch, on a daily basis, with my inner Holden Caulfield. Neither Holden nor I ever did *really* want to grow up. Lucky him, with his red hunting hat, to be frozen in fiction as THE adolescent of the twentieth century, commenting on the quality of farts at prep school assemblies and such. Lucky me, to have this job, where farts abide and never fail to amuse or humiliate. I am a grateful and wounded resident of middle school world, having come to the land of public education in a roundabout way.

It went down like this: The not-so-sad fact is that, like Dobie Gillis's buddy Maynard G. Krebs, I was never much of a fan of work and, at college in the 1970s, felt my true calling was to be a professional student and world-famous author—fairly effortlessly, of course. Screw a life of real work and the burgeoning societal desire for the acquisition of all that stuff the Mad Men of the '50s had foisted upon a generation. I was above all that, all the "phonies" Holden and I hold in disdain. I was an *artiste* with no bra and the armpit hair to by God prove it; I would live the good bohemian life, thank you very much. However, my parents, the funders of my educational adventure, did not concur, even though I'd actually had some success getting a couple of stories published and winning a writing contest or two. The minor Armageddon that ensued led to that time-honored, age-old question: What the hell do you actually *do* with an English degree? Answer: get certified to teach, a prospect that kind of turned my stomach, having denigrated education degrees as not very, shall we say, "challenging." Ultimately, though, the humbling of my academic snootiness turned out to be my salvation and made any other job I've held seem like a Dickensian tale of woe and cold gruel.

Having done tours of duty as a cuff clipper on a textile assembly line, a waitress in a college beer joint, a brief graduate assistantship in an English department followed by a year of teaching high school seniors (I wasn't paid nearly enough to give up my personal life for the honor of grading really bad term papers), I finally landed in a place where I truly, *truly* belonged—a place riddled with stories and peccadilloes and royal fuck-ups to be observed and filed away in my one-day-to-be-a-writer-again brain. Middle school was a land of double-dealing and plotting and subterfuge and intrigue, crawling with denizens eager to engage in all manner of posturing and preening on one end—and slinking away and fading into the background on the other. These beings were unpredictable, impulsive, and irrational, which led to all manner of grand entertainment for me. They also harbored a deep fascination with bodily functions. Old people were gross and anything that was annoying was gay. I was surrounded by crude, tasteless, base immaturity. I was home. And, over the years, as the job evolved into a career (with four books published, I never quit this, my day job), I gained all sorts of insights—into these hormonally challenged little beings, and into myself. The latter ultimately made it possible for me to write again.

Most sane adult folk see the (sub)human creatures in grades seven and eight as unbearable at best and torturous at worst. And they are correct. Drop an untrained adult into a middle school and its citizens catch the scent of fear very quickly, subsequently gauging where the weak spots are, picking, grinning, circling, and feasting like vultures upon the kill. I've seen many a cocky substitute teacher from civilian world reduced to a tearful, quivering mass of Inner Child by twelve-year-olds who cut their teeth on subs. This pack mentality—even including the onlookers who are too sweet or too shy to join in—is an ugly thing to witness but certainly goes with the territory.

No amount of university schooling can prepare one for the land of the adolescent. Perhaps it is because so many of us have blocked out those traumatic memories of the days when we were tormented by bullies, by the onset of our menstrual periods or our impromptu erections, by our imagined imperfections, or by just the god-awful uncertainty of it all. (When I try to coax memories of my junior high days they become a blur of Clearasil, Kotex and the attendant elastic belts, awkward penny walks and bottles spinning, slam books, crushes on teachers, the Beatles, both yearning for and fearing success at getting a boyfriend—because, hey, *then* what?— Midnight Sun hair coloring, tent dresses, whispered judgments, snapped bras, and Yardley cosmetics.)

Once certificated and supposedly ready to be a Giver of Knowledge, I attempted to get my students to be amazed by the wonderful, intricate, scintillatingly complex world of . . . grammar. I was the English Teacher. (I would become the secret-keeping guidance counselor later, like ten years.) Painfully, I learned that no middle school teacher should ever use an outdated film that refers to "grammatical boners"—not ever. "Don't forget your period," an English teacher might sing out as a reminder to punctuate. Not in middle school. And no way in hell could we conjugate the verb "to come." When it came to literature, the "climax" of a plot was territory fraught with snickers, as were any mentions of a "nut" or a "ball." And God forbid that an author of a classic poem or story might have used the words "queer," "gay," or "breast" in some sort of confusing context. Even a seemingly safe vocabulary word like "flagellation" would bring gasps and giggles. In middle school there is not much that is not about sex.

Or about self. And how best to hide that real self.

I accepted that grammar, when held alongside sex, is pretty boring. I began to wish that I had minored in theater since it was becoming clearer all the time that I was going to have to be a goddamned actor/entertainer if I wanted them to take an interest in appositives or infinitives or the subjunctive mood. So I mugged and strutted. I did dialects. I did the hambone, for Christ sake. And I maintain that the fact that I succeeded to take their minds, fairly often, away from the teeny-bopper drama du jour qualifies me for an Academy Award.

But it was not the parsing of the language that brought me the most joy to impart; it was the smithing of the words that was heady and rewarding. And royally amusing. For middle schoolers do not possess the filters of their older brethren; middle schoolers will write or say anything. Any parental unit who thinks his/her child will be either tasteful or discreet is in a mighty state of denial. For example, ask for an expository or a narrative essay and one might get informed about how Aunt Marcy's toxic farts are known to be akin in stench level to those passed by Spence, the family dog; or told the story of how grandmaw got loose last Saturday and went running the streets nekkid, stopping only to hump light poles and parking meters; or how Cousin Eddie got arrested the other day when he showed his pecker to the little kids on the First Baptist Church playground.

In spite of the great stories, after about a decade spent observing a deteriorating state of parenting, a growing tolerance for disrespectful students, an element of pettiness and small-mindedness among teachers, and an overall system of inflationary grading along with the elevation of mediocre standards, I was burning out. The peripheral shit had sucked the spit and energy from my classroom persona. Holden's exterior world was becoming stale with superficiality while his terrified inner one was beckoning like the Grim Reaper.

And so it was that into the 1990s I marched with a Master's degree in school counseling. I set up shop, determined to listen, nod, question, nod, listen, reflect, nod, empathize, etc. No longer was I in the role of taskmaster, Nazi rule-maker, enforcer of learning and discipline. All of a sudden I was that which only the most egregious of teachers dare attempt to be: the "good guy." Now I got a more up-close look at farting aunts, nekkid grandmaws, and pervertoids like Cousin Eddie—not to mention abusive stepdads, cancer-ridden uncles, evil best friends, bipolar moms, meth-head dads, tormenting older sisters, a cast of thousands. Kids used for Internet porn, rape victims, cutters, children who served as weapons for their warring parents or who had been abandoned or were doing drugs because Mom shared with them. Those stories took on a wash of darkness that had not shown itself so boldly in the classroom and it was beyond disturbing. And of course it was only the tip of the iceberg, too, since the messy, silly, nanny-nanny-boo-boo trivialities played out most of the time—locker room bullies, girlie-girl dramas, and my-teacher-hates-me delusions. Still, all their stories, whether dark and disturbing or shallow, silly, and trivial, trickled down to the storyteller at my core. I began to miss the writing, and more than just the exercises I once did along with my students in class. I began to feel a need to reach out to that part of me that was twin to my middle schoolers. Writing was the only way I knew.

And then, out of nowhere, the stories took a turn, inside out. An eighth-grade girl defied statistics, put a gun to her head, and pulled the trigger. One of my children committed suicide. Not a girl who was neglected by her parents, or afraid of academic failure, or criticized by her teachers. This was a bright, beautiful young person, a leader among her peers, with a loving family and a constant smile for everyone. The utter tragic dissonance of it all snatched me into the real reason for Mr. Caulfield's tale and how much the surface is such the mirage, especially at an age when you're a chameleon, with the undeveloped brain of a lizard that eats its own tail. It's the flip side of Holden's funny, sarcastic musings. He is, after all, trying to hold together in the face of the most traumatic event of his life: his brother Allie's death. He also has the specter of a former classmate's likely suicide breathing down his neck. He occupies that place where self-destruction and self-awareness cleave, running scared from the truth of his own flawed reality. And that is what we have to always wonder about Holden. Does he make it? Or does he fold in on himself, like my dead student, collapsing under the weight of that youthfully false perception of hopelessness?

Adolescents hide. That is a given, of course, but I mean they really, *really* hide. They change personas sometimes in the space of a day. They only show a few of their cards to that one or those few who are trusted—or to no one. They hide from every shred of humanity for which they can maintain denial. Sure, some of it pops out—in some children quite frequently. But stripping emotionally naked is not something an eighth grader is likely to do, even behind the closed door of the guidance office.

I had lost other students to tragic accidents, but none self-inflicted, none so accusatory, defiant, and guilt-wrenching as that. It was a death that demanded answers, for the sake of those who might visit and revisit such a choice. Thus began the second-guessing, the what-iffing, the retracing of steps to try to find the moment when such an unthinkable act could have been prevented. But there was no comprehending. The full-bore, scorching sadness dug into me in a way I had never expected—*could* never have expected—yet, surprisingly but slowly—trudgingly slow—it began to dig me out of the hole that, I was discovering, had been my residence for too long.

I'm sure it's no coincidence that this was around the time I was also in the midst of a fallen-over-the-cliff, smashed-up, twenty-something-year relationship. I had scores to settle, even though I've never looked kindly on the settling of scores. There was a flux of mish-mashed karma riding the ether—a confluence of events coaxing me from that camouflaged perch occupied by the school marm/guidance counselor personas. It began to dawn on me that, like these kids to whom I was drawn, I had been hiding from my own expression, that I had spent a couple of decades as an adolescent. Literally.

But now I set about re-emerging as an author after the long hiatus from word-working. I took a deep breath and "came out," spending two class periods a day, back to back, with one group of students for both English and literature. We called ourselves "The Writers' Block." We read. We wrote. We scorned grammar drills in which students picked out prepositions for an hour and then picked out more for homework. We sneered at templates for formulaic paragraphs that cookie-cuttered the mainstream into an imitation of style. Instead, we masterfully dissected one sentence per day—obliterated it—went grammatically medieval on its ass—then got down to the really important business of books and words. Those were the most delightful years in my teaching career—when I re-birthed myself and was surrounded by some amazing students who were much braver than their peers in what they shared on the page. A few in the bunch even put me in mind of Holden C., and I put a copy of *Catcher in the Rye* in their hands, even though it was probably on some "banned" list or another in this conservative county where I toil against the tide. Of course, no student to whom I ever gave that book did not love it.

I don't do The Writers' Block anymore. I'm winding down, hopefully into full-time writing mode. A year or so away from retirement, it feels lucky and right and symmetrical that these adolescents, who would rather die than reveal themselves for who they really are, have actually taught me that it's fairly safe to show myself, through the writing. Interesting little critters, these acne-fearing, angst-ridden troubadours, who have told their stories to me and trusted me to really listen. Sure, some of them have been a pain in the ass—some downright disturbing in their skewed sense of reality—and one in particular has become the ghost-voice in my head that begs me to give them all the benefit of the doubt, because the overwhelming abundance of them truly do want to become human, to become themselves.

It has been a dozen years since that ghost-voice was born of a gunshot, and as I write this it is only days since another young lady, a local high school student, died under similar circumstances, but in a murkier atmosphere. In a freakish clustering of events, she was preceded in death this academic year by the suicides of two teachers at her school within the span of a few months, teachers who laid out the blueprint for her and possibly for others. And now comes the collateral damage, the ruined families, the emotional fallout further scattering across the entire community, trickling down to my middle school charges, picking at my own squelched-down guilt and inciting the kind of rage that senseless death taunts out of us. Hearing about such a thing makes the heart of any parent go numb with the sudden severing of possibilities and a story incomplete, unwritten, cut off in a second's worth of irrational role-playing that has no do-over.

We have to think deep and dark, even as we enjoy our inward snickers at the shallow goings-on in 'tween and teen world, grown ever meaner with the folding in of texting, sexting, online communities, and the viral exposure of images and self-expressions that once were deeply private and respected as such. As for Mr. Caulfield: not so lucky after all, to be character-frozen at that point of cleavage between innocence and despair, between humanity and isolation, between protector of children and conspicuously consuming adult. That crazy red hunting hat, with its Elmer Fudd earflaps. That whole '50s vibe of dry martinis and materialistic myopia. Juxtaposed with the electronic age, Holden Caulfield is *so* very post-World War II, *so* twentieth century. But his outward bravado and inner uncertainty transcend the subsequent decades since his creation, to expose the sometimes brittle fragility of adolescents everywhere, who, like yours truly, fight to defy the hiding.

Tote Monkey

by Joshilyn Jackson

When I saw the classified ad for a receptionist job, the first thing I thought of was Jennifer on WKRP in Cincinnati, laughingly refusing to do everything her boss asks. When he finally demands to know what her actual duties include, she smiles her wide, white smile and says, "I'm a receptionist . . . I receive." That sounded about right. I was tired of bartending, giving out good drinks and sympathetic smiles and bad advice. I was ready to receive.

According to the ad, a small, family-owned car parts business wanted a lady—the ad was specific about that—to sit at the front, greet people, and route the phones. She didn't need to know computers, which was great, because I was still hacking away on a word-processing abomination that resembled what might happen if a real computer and an IBM Selectric had a defective baby. This thing faithfully stored my early attempts at fiction on oddly sized floppy discs no other machine on the earth could read.

I could bang out 100 words a minute on it using my right middle finger and thumb, supplemented by my left index finger to hit the keys that lived west of the G. My gaze never moved to the screen to see all the typos because I had failed my touch typing class the same way I had failed every other class at UGA. That's why I was living in a crime-addled, depressing piece of Atlanta, renting a room with kitchen privileges week to week, avoiding my concerned parents' phone calls and trying to learn to write.

According to the ad, the sought receptionist did not have to type, either, although a little light filing might be required. My current skill set was exactly the same as every other college-aged, chemically-altered, would-be bohemian art fart. My main strength was my Irish peasant's liver; I could drink grown men under the table. My forte was writing huge chunks of prose that I never revised. I thought Smirnoff was good vodka and was still young enough to believe a poem didn't need images, as long as it accurately explained how alienated I felt and didn't rhyme. There were not a lot of classified ads seeking employees with these attributes, even in Creative Loafing.

But this receptionist job paid a buck-fifty an hour more than minimum wage and looked possible. I knew how to answer the phone. I knew the alphabet. And I had a wardrobe of barely worn, prepped-up, khaki-heavy outfits that my hopeful mother had gotten me at Gap to wear at college. They were almost new, as I had pretty much left them packed. I'd bought myself a slew of slouchy thrift store men's jackets and ripped up jeans and disappeared inside them. But I could see myself putting on my Gap 5 pockets like a costume and heading off to play a receptionist; I'd planned to study playwriting at UGA, after all.

I got an interview, but I didn't get the job. It went to a skinny-nosed duck-bodied object named Donna. I thought it was strange that they called me up to tell me this, but then the owner went on to explain he had another opportunity for me. He needed an office assistant, and it paid the same wage. I wasn't sure what an office assistant did, but I had made it clear in the interview I didn't touch type and had never seen Excel. I said, "Sure. I will be an office assistant. Why not?"

I know the answer to that now. The job should have been called Paper Tote Monkey. Because that's what I did. I toted paper. All day long, a row of dot matrix printers ground out orders. When a stack about as thick as a couple of phone books had accumulated under one, I would take it back to my cubicle and peel the rind off the edges. Then I would separate the copies: white to the files, blue to processing, pink to receiving, and the last, the goldenrod copy, went a mysterious place called Back Up. Whenever I got ahead of the cranking printers, I gave Donna a break on the phones or made fresh coffee or went to my boss's outbox and picked up things that needed to be faxed. But a good seven hours a day were spent peeling dot matrix printer paper edges and sorting sheets by color.

I learned quickly that since I had flunked out of school, gotten in a fight with God, moved away from all my friends, and was so ashamed that I was desperate to avoid my family, boredom was the worst thing for me. Being the Tote Monkey gave me too much time to think, and I spent it dwelling on all the ways I'd failed.

I think that's why I got so invested in the lives of the women who worked around me. In my Gap costumes with my hair in a neat tail, I looked like one of them, but listening to the conversation that went on all day through the cubicle walls made it clear we had nothing in common. I was in them but not of them, and eavesdropping made me feel I was playing a silent and a surreal game of Sesame Street's Which One Of These Things Is Not Like the Other.

They were all mothers, while my closest relationship was with a sweaty stray cat with a scab disorder. Their churches were full of ladies organizing fundraising lunches for foreign missions. I sporadically attended a small, gay church that had no funds and no ladies. They read cheerful things, like *People Magazine*. I was so low I was obsessively rereading Jerzy Kozinski. They had mortgages and backyard gardens. I had a rented room with a sleeper sofa and a cardboard dresser. They had husbands, while I had an alcoholic landlady who liked to prowl through my dresser, hoping to find drugs.

Listening to these women chatter got me out of my own head, and to my surprise, I started liking them. They seemed to be living in color, while my life felt sepia at best. I developed crushes on their basic happiness, especially Polly's. She was a short, wide lady with a clear mole on her lip and a husband she fondly called "That One." Polly had lost half a lung to cancer, and she tracked my course with sorrowful hound dog eyes every time I went outside to smoke. She'd say, "I'm not telling you how to live, but quit if you can," in a tone that was kind enough to sound motherly but not motherly enough for me to rebel against it. I wanted to crawl up in her lap.

I liked the others, too: Addie, who had a good figure and a bad husband. Sheryl, a perky blonde who loved Bunko and dogs and celebrity gossip. Cara, whose teenagers were driving her batshit. The only one I didn't like was Donna, who had taken my rightful receptionist job and stuck me with Tote Monkey. She had a nasally voice, and she hot-rolled her hair into puffy sausages. She liked to slyly remind me we had been up for the same job, and she had gotten it. She acted as if that gave her the right to tell me what to do instead of asking.

As I peeled my endless reams of papers and trit-trotted silently back and forth to the file cabinets, I began to want a place in their endless conversation. I was bored and lonely as hell. I wanted them to treat me as if I were the girl my mother had bought all those clothes for. They would like that girl, I thought.

So I started talking, trying to be her for them. At first, my conversational gambits were like sloppy dams that the stream of conversation had to work around. My cultural references were wrong. I'd never heard of Coach purses, and I hadn't seen *When Harry Met Sally*. I was almost constantly hung over. So I'd insert a remark, and there would be a slight pause. No one would respond directly, and then the conversation would politely navigate around me and resume its course.

The day I finally broke in, they were discussing a new romantic comedy, and kind Polly, who was always trying to help me along, said, "What about you, Joshilyn?" I had no intention of seeing it, but this was an opening, and I wanted to slip into it. My mouth opened and words came out. "You know, it's not my kind of thing, but my boyfriend Dan wants to see it. He's taking me this weekend."

My Boyfriend Dan was a magical phrase. Boyfriends were apparently of interest in a way that existential angst was not. All at once, these women were asking me questions about My Boyfriend Dan, who was so freshly invented he was as amorphous as a blastula. I quickly gave him a job in insurance, and black hair, and a Maserati. I knew nothing about cars but I thought it sounded fancy. Maybe too fancy, based on their reactions, so I back-tracked and said he got it used and fixed it up. My Boyfriend Dan was apparently mechanically inclined.

On Monday, My Boyfriend Dan resurfaced again when they asked me how we had liked the movie. I'd spent the bulk of my weekend hunched over my word processor, slinging out 100 unhappy words a minute and drinking room temp beer. I told them that even though the movie was Dan's idea, he hadn't enjoyed it. In fact, he'd blamed me for "dragging him to a chick flick." My righteous indignation covered my ignorance of the movie's plot, and it was catching. I had stumbled on a major theme in their ongoing conversation: What the hell is wrong with men? They spent the next hour gabbling about it, and I joined in, happily ragging on Dan and all men by extension, just as if I were a real and solid member of the office lady posse.

Not only did My Boyfriend Dan give me a wedge into the conversation, but I learned I could give him my actual opinions on politics and movies and culture. My new friends would rail against him instead of me. And Dan made the long hours of paper rind peeling go faster as I bent to the writerly task of developing his history and character and keeping his personal timeline straight. He had lost his mother at a young age. One of his brothers had died of leukemia. He was deep and wounded. Dan could be very funny and yet also very cruel. He was quite a few years older than I was. He had beautiful hands and a racing bike and an embarrassing tattoo from his wild college days. I started taking notes on My Boyfriend Dan at home, spending as much time building him as I used to spend pouring out unrevised chunks of fiction.

I'd only had him a couple of weeks when his non-existence became a real issue in our relationship. At lunch one day, I was telling them how Dan had showed up at my house the night before with a bag of groceries and made me the worst meatloaf marinara I had ever tasted. He was so proud of it that I had forced myself to choke down every bite. Donna narrowed her eyes at me and said,

"It sounds like you two are getting serious. How come he doesn't call you?"

"He calls me," I said.

She looked down her long nose and said, "I'd know if he did—I am the receptionist."

My heart stuttered, but then I realized she was not implying that Dan did not exist. That had not occurred to her. Her subtext was that her job was superior to Tote Monkey. It was gratifying to have Polly and Addie rush to my defense, pointing out that My Boyfriend Dan and I had only been seeing each other a few weeks, and anyway, we weren't supposed to get a lot of personal calls. Even so, I realized how tricky maintaining My Boyfriend Dan was going to be.

The smart money would have been on breaking up with Dan right then. But I loved My Boyfriend Dan; I couldn't imagine going back to all the silent thinking about failure I'd been doing before he came into my life. I decided I simply had to find ways to work around his limitations. Over the next few weeks, I carefully seeded my conversations with explanations for things that had not yet become questions.

When Polly showed me a picture of herself holding new her grandbaby, I lamented the fact that I carried no pictures of me with my (purely fictional) nieces, and by extension, no pictures of Dan. "It's because I hate having my photo taken," I confided.

I handled the phone issue by going to Sheryl, the most reliable office gossip, and telling her in strictest confidence that I had asked Dan not to call me at work; he had one time, I said, and I was pretty darn sure that Donna had listened in on the conversation. The next time Donna brought up Dan's lack of calls, I watched Sheryl exchange significant glances with Polly and Addie, and then Addie nudged Cara, who changed the subject in an arch tone.

As the weeks went on, my constant need to pre-argue for Dan's existence made him develop so many personal ticks and foibles that I began to wonder if the poor guy had OCD. The ladies stopped liking him. They began to speak of My Boyfriend Dan in the same way they spoke of Addie's awful husband—as if I deserved better.

I liked how they all rallied around me and took my side. I began to slant the Dan stories. He cancelled on me a lot at the last minute. He bought me a gym membership for my birthday because he said I was "pushing maximum density"—a line I stole directly from *The Breakfast Club*. He promised to join me at the office Christmas party, but he never showed. I paged him several times, to no avail, then crept theatrically away to pretend to cry in the bathroom. I thought I would sit in a stall for a little and then use Dan as an excuse to leave early, but Polly came after me, coaxing and insistent, until I had to emerge. I opened the door, swinging my long hair down to hide my dry eyes. She hugged me and said I could do better, I was worth more. As she snuggled me up under her arm and patted at me, I was surprised to feel a couple of real tears rising. It was as if her belief in my pretend was making it truer. True enough to cry over.

A few weeks later, my car broke down, and I had to take the bus to work. Before this could raise suspicions, I revealed that Dan had not driven me because he never spent the night. He had horrible insomnia and could really only sleep in his own bed. As I added this most recent detail, I noticed Polly and Sheryl were exchanging significant glances. They began asking me more and more questions about him, and I lied and tap danced. His quirks and history became so convoluted I was lucky I had the whole thing documented, or I surely would have made some fatal error. I was terrified that they had figured out that he was imaginary and were trying to trip me up. They hadn't, though. They had put their heads together and decided he was married.

Their questions—had I ever seen his house? Did I have his home phone number? Did he ever take me out, you know, in public—and the pregnant pauses after my answers let me figure it out. I decided that was brilliant. Dan was married, obviously. It explained so much about him, and I decided my character should be completely oblivious to it.

I began shaping my answers to enhance this idea: No, I hadn't been to Dan's place. It was all the way out in the suburbs, and anyway, he said it was a typical bachelor pad. He liked my place.

No, I didn't call him at home. He never checked his messages there. He liked me to call his pager, and then he'd ring me back. No, he didn't like eating in restaurants, preferring to get take-out and go back to my place.

I also decided that if he was the kind of guy who cheated on his wife, he should be even meaner to me. Dan became verbally abusive. When I asked him for his home number, he accused me of being clingy. I became downtrodden, and my audience responded with more sympathy. By creating Dan, I had made something that had more of an effect on the world around me than peeling the rinds off car parts orders ever could. When I unfolded the couch in my rented room each night, the middle bar grinding into my spine, making up Dan stories to tell the next day were the only lullaby that could conquer my insomnia and soothe me off to sleep.

As Dan and I celebrated our sixth month anniversary with a cheap bracelet I bought myself and a fight because he wouldn't take me out to this new tapas place in Midtown, the ladies in the office decided to stage a Dan-tervention. One day, when we had planned to go out for lunch, the office ladies one by one dropped out, giving each other significant glances. By obvious design, I ended up alone with Polly at a nearby Subway.

I thought she was going to tell me Dan was married. I was already staging the confrontation in my head so I could report back to all of them. I couldn't decide if he would confess or try to cover, if I would believe him or dump him or go on seeing him, explaining that his wife was an ogre who truly did not understand him and he was only with her for the kids.

But Polly didn't tell me that Dan was married. She didn't talk about Dan at all. She began speaking to me about her own excellent husband, That One. She was more personal with me than she had ever been, giving me a window into her rather lovely life.

She told me the story of how her husband proposed. It wasn't that great. He took her to the beach, sunrise, kind of a cliché. But her heavily fringed eyes got round and moist, and she was breathless in the memory. She told me how he made her breakfast in bed last Mother's Day. He made the best eggs. Just how she liked them. She talked about how he'd stood by her through the chemo. She said he was kind of a tough guy, not a big talker, but he cried after her surgery and told her she was strictly forbidden to stop fighting.

The more she talked, the more it hit me that every word she was saying was the truth. She was telling me something real, that meant something personal to her. She wasn't playing. She was doing this to help me, because she had come to feel a genuine affection for the girl I'd pretended to be. She wanted better for this girl in her Gap pants, a girl I had invented as much as I had invented Dan.

I started crying into my seafood salad, and Polly took my hand and said, "You know why I am telling you this, right? I want you to know what a relationship should be like. Honest and faithful and fun."

She was talking about her husband, about my Dan, but I applied it to her and me. I was the cheater, telling stories and keeping my timeline straight, and what she was offering me now was genuine.

There was no way out. Even if Dan and I broke up, I still wasn't the girl I had made her care for. I wasn't a duped, sad object who was eating the crumbs of affection from a married man's table. I was a lying rat who was stealing warmth and kindness, stealing her real stories. And the worst part was, even as I wept over it, a part of me knew I would one day incorporate her story into one of mine, knew that I would take this moment and use it.

I got up and went to the restroom and threw up my seafood salad. When I came out of the bathroom, I was shut down and silent. Our lunch hour was up. We made our way back to the office. I went directly to my cubicle and began peeling paper, letting the conversation wash around me, not even listening to the words. I peeled paper rind and filed, blank-minded, until 4:59. Then, as everyone else left, I stopped by my boss's office and quit. No notice. Just said I was done working there. Effective immediately.

I went back to the house where I rented a room. My landlady was passed out on the sofa in a cloud of rum-smell so dense it was almost visible, with the scabby cat kneading her stomach. I filched her copy of the paper and started circling the waitress jobs.

A couple of weeks later, I had to go back to the old office to pick up my final paycheck. I went in early, hoping only my former boss would be there. I got in and got the check, but as I left the building, my luck ran out. Polly and Addie had both pulled into the parking lot. We had a fast, awkward conversation, purely superficial. Polly blinked at me sadly with her heavily fringed eyes, and I found I couldn't meet their gaze. I got in my rattletrap car and watched them walk inside. I had this urge to run after her, to tell her thank you, to tell her I had ditched My Boyfriend Dan and I was living a much better life now. I wanted to give the girl she was invested in a happy ending, or at least a hopeful one.

It also occurred to me to tell her that Dan had been a construct. I could see it. I would go in and drop my head in her lap and weep and confess all, and then promise to be truthful henceforth and evermore. I would assure her I would find myself a nice boy and go back to school and stop slinging out endless reams of made-up words, both on paper and to the people around me. I would promise to stop being such a screw-up. I would promise to become a good person, a more honest, kinder, and happier person, and assure her that it would be because of her.

But none of those things were true. They were as invented as My Boyfriend Dan. In the end, I started up my car and drove away.

Note: In the interest of full disclosure, you should know the names of the people in this essay have all been changed. Except Donna's.

For the Good Lies

by Barb Johnson

I'm standing on a temporary layer of plywood that I've laid along the joists of a second-floor side gallery. I am 35—this is quite awhile back, but even so, I've been a carpenter a long time at this point— and my assistant, a man about my age, is on an extension ladder, bracing a new corner post while I bolt it in place.

"You helping your husband?" a guy on the sidewalk asks.

"Nope," I say.

"Well, your boyfriend, then?" the man persists, jutting his chin at my assistant. My assistant smiles. It's the third time someone has stopped and asked me this question. It's the same question I'm asked everywhere I work.

I ratchet the bolts, and my assistant gives the post a shake to test for sturdiness. The post is a Victorian reproduction I've made. "I'm a carpenter," I tell the guy.

Sidewalk guy cocks his head in disbelief. "A lady carpenter?" he asks, as though I am a species with a beak that has somehow learned to peck a tune on a little piano, or perhaps an animal that can add long strings of numbers and tap out the sums with its hooves.

I was a carpenter for almost thirty years. In all that time, I don't remember ever walking on a jobsite and not getting that same kind of double-take. On a jobsite, though, who you are or what you're about isn't as important as your skill and what you bring to the party. The trades party was an ever-changing family of sorts, the Guy family. There was Early-Riser Guy, who opened up the jobsite, making it possible for the rest of us to sleep in. Fisherman Guy brought his catch in for fish-fry Fridays. Impressive-Sweating Guy changed his shirt several times a day and was very enthusiastic about his sandwiches; he also liked to quiz Recovering Alcoholic Guy about drinking: "But you could have like a beer, right? Not whiskey or anything, but just like one beer?" Amazing Drywall Guy could run a perfectly smooth skim coat of mud that required almost no finish sanding. He could whip a twelve-inch knife around the base of a ceiling fan in a single swipe, all while wearing plasterer's stilts. It was pure poetry. Once you've proven your skill on a jobsite, people mostly forget about all the other. And so I was Carpenter Chick Guy, the one who could fix broken tools. A handy Guy.

I was the kind of kid who felt compelled to take things apart to see what made them run. I had three brothers, and they were all the same way. My mother was a single mother raising four kids on minimum wage. Out of necessity, she had to fix things when they broke, so I grew up expecting to do all my own repairs. If the car wouldn't start, you raised the hood and fiddled with stuff until it did. I learned that you didn't necessarily need to know the names of the parts to fix the whole. This predisposed me to enter a fixing occupation, I think. A making occupation. A dislike of uncomfortable clothes sealed the deal.

When people ask how I became a carpenter, I find they're really wanting to hear a romantic story that goes with the romantic notions everyone has about things they don't do for a living. Carpentry, in particular, for some reason. I want to tell them that I met an old man from Italy, a real craftsman, who never had a son and who really, really wanted to pass along his wisdom before he died. I want to say that I was so inspired by the beauty of his work that I apprenticed with this old man—let's call him Antonio—and he taught me everything. Old school. Hand tools. Precision joinery done without a jig of any kind. And on the last day of my apprenticeship, I want to tell people, he gave me the two-foot level his father had crafted from rosewood and passed to Antonio upon the completion of his own apprenticeship.

If there was any indication early on that I would eventually be a writer, it is contained in this impulse to tell the better story, the one people want to hear. The better truth is usually a lie.

There was no Antonio, alas. How I actually became a carpenter is that I heard I could make more money working inside than I was making outside in the blistering heat, standing on a ladder two stories in the air, scraping lead paint off the side of a house. This is one of many jobs I worked at to put myself through college, and the one which, having earned a degree in English, I kept for the better part of the next thirty years. I walked in that house and the Guy asked me if I had carpentry experience. I gave him the story he was longing to hear. I said, "Look at this saw," and held up my battered circular saw, which was not battered from frequent use but because I'd bought it second-hand from a Guy on another job. It was missing its blade guard. I didn't tell him an outright lie, but I let his assumptions take the story where I wanted it to go, a critical storytelling technique.

That saw in my hand was the best kind of lie. It got me hired, and it got me the respect of the men on the job. Because of the ever-present possibility of bloodshed provided by that missing blade guard, the Guys forewent the hazing they felt they had to do. Once, when I was just starting out, I was working as a laborer. We were putting shingles on a second story roof. A bundle of shingles weighs seventy, maybe eighty pounds. I weighed a buck and a quarter. One of the Guys had me haul bundles up a ladder at the rear of the house, a huge house with a steep, cross-hipped roof, and no one holding that ladder steady at the bottom. Nothing OSHA would've approved had they been anywhere near. After about three trips, the Guy on the ground sent me to get his toolbox from the front of the house, where I found a giant truck parked out in the street, a conveyor belt running bundles of shingles up to the roof. Hazing. Ah-ha-ha. You got me. Being good-natured about hazing was the quickest road to becoming a Guy.

Waiting to see me get what was coming from that guard-less saw was better than any hazing those Guys could think of. And less work on their part. The Guy I'd bought it from got rid of it because that same lack of blade guard had resulted in a forty-stitch gash in his thigh. He confessed to smoking a joint just before the accident, and I figured as long as I steered clear of the weed, I'd be fine. What could possibly happen? Twenty-four carbide-tipped teeth spinning at 5500 rpm a half an inch from my bare knuckle. I mean if I was careful, right? In fact, nothing bad happened, and the vigilance required to use that saw became my habit when using any tool.

I'm not going to idealize carpentry or make romantic connections between being a woodwright and a writer. Or maybe I am. Using the word "woodwright" evokes the romantic. It's a way to make people think of that guy on PBS, the one who only uses hand tools and dresses like it's 1890. I don't have much interest in tools that don't have cords or batteries that make them go. Why work harder if you don't have to? But I am constantly thrilled by the way that careful word choice can completely color an otherwise neutral statement. Because I chose it on purpose and because it sounds romantic, using "woodwright" makes the first line of this paragraph a lie.

As with all lies, intent is everything. A good lie is interesting. People want good lies almost as much as they want the truth. When I was a carpenter, my customers didn't just want a table or a renovation. They wanted a good story about that table. They wanted to hear secret things about their houses. They did not want to hear about the giant splinter I got while making the table. A splinter so large and so deep it had to be removed in the emergency room, the cost of which more than cancelled out the payment for the table. They wanted to hear that I made that table from a sinker, which is a log that sank in the river on the way to the mill a hundred years ago, and which was fished up only recently and dried in a sand pit for a whole year. They were interested to know that the wood from the log was used to repair the floor in a house in the French Quarter. (Insert ghost story here.) They wanted to hear that I was working on that jobsite and hence had access to the scraps left over from the giant, ancient log from which I made a one-of-a-kind table. Their table. Everyone longs for these sorts of lies.

So, except for the sawdust and heavy lifting, carpentry and writing are practically the same thing. In addition to a good lie, there's a lot of engineering and architecture in both. And a consideration for beauty. Here's the space. Here's what we want to do with it. What will it take to support all that? What style should we use? What are the right materials? The mistakes made at both generally hang around to embarrass the makers for far too long.

Embarrassment is one thing; losing a finger is something altogether different. Though I never had an accident with that guard-less saw, twenty years later, I lost the end of one my fingers to a dado blade. A fluting bit. There's no revision in woodworking, so that single moment of inattention cost me the ability to play guitar. It was months before I turned that machine back on, and months after that before its menacing hum quit affecting my heart rate. Losing the end of my finger didn't put me off carpentry, but it certainly made me look more closely at its price.

There used to be this thing we did on the job, those of us who were older. We didn't own our own homes, and we didn't expect to. We'd never had health insurance and assumed we never would. We were not stupid, but there wasn't much use for our intelligence, it seemed. We'd sit in the bed of one or the other of our ancient trucks and make big talk about how, yes, those bastards with the desk jobs and air-conditioning, they had it all. Or they thought they did. But they didn't have the kind of freedom we had. They couldn't make their own hours. And they had to spend a fortune on bullshit like free-range this-and-that and fricking bottled water. They'd never know the pleasure of eating in the bed of a truck, the guts of a broken recip saw laid out in front of them, fixed before the meal was over. When those guys with office jobs needed something fixed, they had to call one of us.

All that big talk floated on top of a hot river of panic, of course. We were too old to be doing what we were doing, and we knew it. By the time you got to be our age, you were supposed to have a bunch of people working for you. You can't make money by the sweat of your own brow. Everyone knows that. You can buy groceries with it and keep a roof over your head. But not necessarily all at the same time. That big talk? That's another example of how people really want lies. Really need them. You can tell any story about yourself that you want to, and that will be your truth until you change the story.

By the time I was forty-five, I was pretty chewed up. I was in pain just sitting there eating my dinner. Clearly, I needed to turn my attention to something new. Maybe go back to college. I'd heard that there were graduate degrees in writing, and that didn't sound as though it would get me any kind of job, but it did sound like a whole lot of fun. *Really? We're just going to make crap up and that's the schooling?* As I understood it, the university would pay me to study and give me a little sit-down kind of job. Sallie Mae would kick in a few bucks, too. If I'd had the ability to imagine it, I would've said I was going back to school to study writing so I could become a writer. It never crossed my mind that such a thing was possible, though, so wanting to be a writer was nowhere near the story I was telling myself at the time.

Ten programs turned me down that first year. I looked like crap on paper, apparently. I came to understand that when a website said that they were interested in diversity, they didn't mean broken down bottom feeders from the Deep South who spent their days covered in dirt. I'll be forever grateful to those who turned me down, though, because that wholesale rejection ticked me off so much, I was able to focus all my energy, all my desire, on proving that I'd been underestimated.

When I applied to schools the next year, the University of New Orleans took me in, one of only a few schools to show a little imagination. What I thought was going to happen was that I would learn about writing, get a little rest, do a little carpentry to pay Caesar. When it was all over, I planned to sell my business to pay whatever debts were left from my academic vacation and go to work for someone else. I was completely dedicated to succeeding in graduate school, although I had no idea what that might entail. As it turned out, forty-seven was a perfect age to start something new because I was old enough to know what interested me, and I had the ability to give it my full attention. Writing stole my heart in a way that my carpentry business never had. I was waylaid by the love of it.

Then Hurricane Katrina ate my carpentry shop and everything in it, and I got a new story, that's for sure. That new story was almost about how I threw myself into rebuilding my business, working ceaselessly to regain the ground I'd lost. It eventually became clear that would be impossible. There were simply too many obstacles and not enough money. So it didn't happen in an instant. Not like you see in movies, where ta-da! someone has an instantaneous transformation. It was a long, slow, wave goodbye. Letting go of the idea of something is much more difficult than letting go of the thing itself. But once I had cleared out the notion that I was always going to be a carpenter, the new story was perfectly obvious to me.

I threw myself into writing. I was manic with misery after Katrina. Every day I put as much of my physical world right as I could, and then I sat down to work on a whole different world, one that didn't have a thing to do with hurricanes and heinous presidential acts. By the time I calmed down, I was graduating from UNO, fifty-one years old with a book deal in my hand. It was a fairy princess story, except for how, as I mentioned, I'm not a fan of uncomfortable clothes. And also, princesses don't seem to work very hard. If I had a magic wand, I probably wouldn't work hard, either.

Now I'm in a whole new world, a world of writers, where I'm still not familiar with the customs. When other writers hear that I was a carpenter for most of my life, they get a certain look. "Oh," they invariably say, "you have a skill. I wish I had a skill." As though writing isn't a skill. As though they're not building things every day of the week. That feeling of being useless is part of the deal for writers, I guess. Playing pretend all day. Running characters around the page and having them do exactly what you want them to do. It doesn't seem very connected to the real world or even to an adult life. But it takes real skill to bust through the hard candy shell of things and talk about what's underneath, and it involves a lengthier apprenticeship, I suspect.

I could say that writing has its own dangers. The psychic pain of the story that won't do right. The pressure. The loneliness. But that would be bullshit because that's not how I feel. Writing has its downsides, to be sure, but for me they aren't any of them the tortured-artist kind. When people start talking about suffering for their art, I always want to say, Shut up and write, you lucky bastard, and quit telling yourself that story. You want to eat factory chicken your whole life? Get all your water out of the tap? Because that's what carpentry taught me. You are the story you're telling about yourself, and your story will take you exactly where you expect.

I don't miss being a carpenter, and that is no lie. I enjoyed it the whole time I did it, but I don't miss sweating and sucking down sawdust. Lifting heavy things all day. I don't miss coming home and slapping a pack of frozen peas on each knee. It was most definitely not a romantic occupation. But occasionally I miss spending my days at a task for which all the tools lie on the outside of me. All the material right there in front of me. And a sure knowledge about how the parts fit together.

There are days when it's sunny outside—usually in the fall—that I wouldn't mind dropping the tailgate on my truck and having lunch there. I'd like to think I haven't lost the knack for eating while covered in sawdust, moving slowly so as not to startle the hovering wasps that are attracted to the smell of wood resin. I like to imagine my whole truck bed filled with the Guy family, and maybe there'd be a recip saw to fix. That's something I really miss, I guess. The clear, sweet truth, the simple yes or no, of a machine working. And some Guy telling me the story of it all, a good lie to lay on top of the uncertainty.

My Life as a Spy

by Cassandra King

I don't want to open up the old debate of wanting-to-be-a-writer versus wanting-to-write except to say this: I've loved writing more than being a writer. For me, writing will always be a treasure hunt, a thrilling adventure down the rabbit hole. Being a writer, on the other hand, is more like a trip to the underworld. A writer's life is made up of contracts and agents, editors and publicists, signings and tours, reviews and Amazon rankings. Sales become survival. No wonder we have to work other jobs.

In order to write, and thus become a writer, I've worked as a waitress, barmaid, cook, tutor, teacher, editor, journalist, and spy. I was best suited for the latter, and for good reason. I spent almost as much time preparing to be a spy as I had becoming a writer. Spies are born, but we are also made. I always knew I'd be a writer, but wasn't so sure I'd make it as a spy. Spying is tough business. One slipup and you're toast. The powers that be will deny your existence, and you have no one to turn to. Who would believe you, anyway? You might be doubting me now, and I wouldn't blame you a bit. Spying is the one job I can never put on a résumé.

I can tell you something about how I got into this line of work, the training involved, and my first assignment. But I'll have to be careful in doing so, so bear with me. Spies are secretive, elusive, and close-mouthed by nature, otherwise you wouldn't last a day. Not everyone is cut out to be a spy. Aptitude and desire count a lot, but there are less tangible factors. Some of us don't make it through no fault of our own. You have to be physically nondescript, not too fat, thin, tall, short, freckled, pale, good-looking, or ugly. Personality traits must be tempered as well. Those of us who make it are neither flamboyant nor meek, loud or overly soft-spoken, fiery or passive. It's a fine line, the right degree of invisibility. Too much of it, and your contacts will look right past you. Too little, and you'll scare them off. As a spy, you learn early to dress down. Calling attention to oneself is not only undesirable, it can ruin everything.

I started my training as a child, when it felt more like a game. It was a game then, and I ordered the tools of my future trade from the ads in comic books. My mother didn't approve of my allowance being wasted on such foolishness, and I couldn't tell her what I was up to. It became my first lesson in subterfuge. I had the orders sent to our rural route, but used a classmate's name instead of mine. Then I told my mother it had been delivered it to the wrong address, and I'd take it to my classmate the next day.

To inspect my loot, I climbed a tree. The importance of hiding places was something I learned early. The main thing, your chosen spot couldn't look like what it was. If you're found out, there should be a reason for your being there. High up the magnolia, which was taller than our house, was the place I'd always gone to read. The leaves were a perfect shelter from the prying eyes of my little sisters and ever-vigilant mother. And the book I held concealed the stuff I'd ordered. In the magnolia, I learned when and how to use invisible ink. I mastered the periscope that was designed so you could peer around difficult angles without being seen. Best of all, I had an adjustable, fake-onyx ring, which came with a secret compartment (though I never figured out what you were supposed to put in it).

It would be four decades before I got the chance to practice my trade. That's common in the business of spying because an unquestionable identity must first be established. A low profile is not necessarily the goal of a spy, but a certain degree of ordinariness is. Here are some of the guidelines: Achievements should not be under or over. If you make the papers, let it be for community service. Head up the Relay for Life or the United Way, maybe, or trick-or-treat for UNICEF. Political activism is discouraged. Religion is fine, if mainstream. My family has always been staunchly Methodist so I was okay, even after I became an Episcopalian. Religious zealots may be found among Baptists, Catholics, or Orthodox Jews, but never Methodists or Episcopalians. Speaking in tongues was a deal-breaker, though I'd argue the point if it were up to me. What better way of delivering a coded message?

In establishing an identity, a spy's day job is critical. Mine— teaching composition to college freshmen—was perfect. Few occupations offer such anonymity. The main problem with teaching is the low pay; most teachers have to supplement their income. And that's where you have to be careful. As an English teacher, your marketable skills are limited. Journalism is a likely field of employment, but it's prohibited. Trust me; any journalist accused of spying has been framed. There's only one acceptable way of writing for a newspaper, and I was lucky enough to find it. I wrote human-interest features for a local paper. Writing about the yard of the month in Small Town, Alabama, was not likely to compromise my secret life as a spy.

Another iffy field for spies is publishing. On one hand, it's a good cover because a writer doesn't have the time or desire for a secret life—or so people think. On the other, writers sometimes find themselves in the limelight. That's when it becomes a balancing act. Modest success as a writer is desirable, since "dabbling" in writing is too obvious a cover. Calling yourself an unpublished poet, for example, raises more red flags than the student section at an Alabama game. (Oh, come now—what do you *really* do?) Publish all you want, but if you achieve fame doing so, be prepared to forgo your secret life. You won't be allowed both.

When my time came, I was set up as well as I'd ever be. I was an instructor at a community college, a journalist of the harmless variety, and a writer of minuscule success. I was ready, but even so, the assignment came out of the blue. After years of waiting and preparing, I opened my mailbox and there it was. Had I not known it'd come that way, I would've overlooked it, or dismissed it as a scam. A plain envelope, no return address, and my name, almost illegible, either handwritten or made to look that way.

I called the number provided, gave a few basic facts, then waited for the packet as I'd done all those years ago, a young girl on a rural Alabama farm. I was now a middle-aged woman living alone, so no reason to have the material sent to another address. Like the initial contact, it arrived in a plain manila envelope. This one, however, held only one piece of paper with an oath of confidentiality, availability, and willingness to perform the assignment. Once I'd returned that, another waiting period followed. I knew my long-awaited assignment had finally arrived as soon I saw it in the mailbox: Like the contact and agreement, it came in an unassuming envelope, with no return address.

There were several pages of instructions, restrictions, and warnings. One word about my secret mission, and I'd be immediately terminated. (Take that however you wanted.) Likewise if I got caught, messed up, or failed to follow the intricate directions exactly as worded. No excuses, no second chances. Once the mission was completed, there was a number to call where I'd leave only my last name and assigned code, then wait by my phone for the return call.

Following the enclosed orders, I disguised my assignment as a shopping list. Good thing, since there was a lot to remember. A specific time was set to execute the mission, and under no circumstances could I deviate from that time frame, even by a few minutes. When the day in question came, I had mentally rehearsed the procedure several times, and was more than ready. Even so, my hands were shaking when I approached the destination. Which wouldn't do, so I took a couple of deep breaths to steady myself. I've been waiting for this for a long time, I told myself firmly as I got out of my car.

What I'm about to tell you is general enough that it can be safely revealed. On that particular day (yes, there were others to follow), my rendezvous took place in a distant town at a large discount department store. I can't reveal the name, but you'd know it if I did. These stores may have a few disparaging nicknames attached to them, but they're the place to go for bargains. It wasn't bargains I was looking for that day; I was following instructions which were written out to look like a shopping list. Matter of fact, shopping for myself was a part of the assignment, essential for the appearance of normalcy. And a bonus: I'd be reimbursed for all items purchased—up to a certain point, of course.

Moving purposefully from one department to another, I checked off the items: toothpaste, bandaids, a three-ounce bar of oatmeal soap for sensitive skin. If the latter was unavailable, I was to go to the pharmacy counter and inquire, but only of the pharmacist or assistant. I was to make note (though not in their presence) as to whether or not an offer was made to order the unavailable item. In the next department, I got two mechanical pencils, computer paper, a greeting card. The card was to be returned on a follow-up visit. There were several checkpoints where note-taking wasn't allowed. Since I'd be questioned later, everything had to be committed to memory.

The assignment was completed in less than an hour, as planned. Back home, I called the secret number, gave the information, then waited for the return call. When it came, I was speaking to a real person, not a recording, and she identified herself only as my case manager. I was questioned extensively—drilled, I guess you could say—then told to wait by the phone for another call. When it came, another voice gave me verbal instructions for the follow-up visit. No written instructions would be issued, so I was careful with my note-taking as I listened and wrote. The follow-up assignment was similar to the original one, except for one difference. At the end of my call, I got the affirmation I'd hoped for. My unnamed case manager, she of the brisk, business-like voice, concluded our conversation by saying, "Good job, King. A new assignment will arrive in due time."

I wish I could tell you that I'm happily retired from spying now. Or, that I occasionally take on an assignment if it's interesting enough to lure me from my writing desk. But revealing one's status is not allowed under any circumstances. Even on your deathbed, or to your nearest and dearest on his or hers. Reading this, you might question such a policy. You might even wonder if any of this is true. At one time, I would've done the same. But spies don't ask questions. We take our assignments, or we don't. If so, we carry them out exactly as directed. We never know the outcome, or whether or not the mission was successful. Maybe what we did changed someone's life, or maybe not. Despite that, we do it because it's what we love doing. I guess spying is a lot like writing in that way.

The Things we do for Love

by Janis Owens

Writing about a day job presents me with a small conundrum, as I haven't been gainfully employed since roughly 1986, the year my second daughter was born. Even before that, I never had an actual full-time, regular-paycheck, permanent job, but represent the last of a dying breed; what the old census takers used to call a Housewife and Mother—or I was, before my children grew up on me and flew the coop. Now I am a full-time, semi-paid writer who supports her literary aspirations with occasional editing work, frequent speaker gigs, and a lifelong calling as a kept woman.

It's a tough job, but someone has to do it.

I am kept by one Wendel R. Owens of Truman, Arkansas, who is also my husband of thirty years, and takes a lot of pride in the fact that his wife is educated and free to pursue a life of arty leisure. The pride stems (like all pride) from pathology, as we come from poor stock, and have grandmothers who cleaned houses for rich white folk for a living. Mine even took in ironing (and if you ever wonder what job is rock bottom on the Southern labor chain, well, take my word for it: Ironing is right down there with mining phosphate or working the spool room at a textile mill.)

The pinch of having a servant grandmother hasn't quite lost its sting for Mr. Wendel, though I don't lose much sleep about it, myself. I've never been what you might call a worker bee, though the economic realities of my early life meant that

I was thrust into the work force at a tender age, as a cashier at a tiny Winn-Dixie on the poor side of the tracks in Ocala, Florida. Back then, it was still called Quik-Chek, and the male/female division of labor was rigorously maintained. Boys were put to work as bag boys, then stock men. Girls were cashiers or nothing, though if you put in enough years, you could become Head Cashier, and sit in the front office, high above the fray, and count money and chat with the Bosses. I never made it to that point of Valhalla but I did get to handle money and wear a cool electric blue polyester uniform.

I'm thinking I got paid $2.65 an hour, but I might be overstating. My industrious oldest brother was third-man (that is: third in line to manager) and he's the one who snagged me the job, the day I turned seventeen, which was as young as it got for cashiers. Winn-Dixie had just begun opening on Sundays (Publix still observed the Sabbath) and I remember that it required a little soul searching on my part before I'd take a job with a company that had so blatantly spit in the face of the Most High. But hey—I needed the money and they didn't open till noon, after preaching was officially over, and closed before evening service began. I could hit both services if I was truly devout, which, as it turns out, I wasn't. Our church was on the way home and as I merrily sailed past every Sunday night, just as the first hymn was cranking, I'd think: ah, the life of the capitalist.

I was a senior in high school at the time, and not the most academically gifted Cracker the Florida public school system ever produced. A keen-eyed high school counselor, rightly perceiving my college career wouldn't be without effort, recommended I learn the single skill that became my magic carpet out of poverty: typing. I had failed at piano as a child and for the first month of my typing class feared I'd fail at that, too. But I persisted, and in a crazy paradox of hand-brain wiring, proved to be unnaturally fast— thirty, then sixty, then a hundred words a minute, which in those days of huge, boulder-like typewriters was very fast, indeed. I couldn't spell worth a crap (still can't) but I could churn out the words, and upon graduation from high school, I proceeded down the cow trail of social betterment, circa 1978, rural North Florida: I enrolled in a community college and got a job in an office.

My family of origin had supplied so much first-hand knowledge of mental eccentricity that I had decided to cash in on all that anecdotal evidence and major in psychiatry or psychology. I didn't know which because I didn't know the difference. I could seldom remember how to pronounce the former, so I usually told people I wanted to become the latter. I was going to school on Pell Grants and college-funded work grants, and another wily counselor set me up in a work-study job as a clerk typist at a community mental health clinic. My whole purpose was to type in-take notes for a crew of post-Woodstock generation hippie therapists. I was possibly the only native Floridian in the place and was quiet as a mouse, tucked away in my corner with my typewriter, but on the frequent employee lunches reverted to church girl mode and brought in homemade apple pies and homemade brownies, and Mississippi Mud Cake. It was the one part of communal life I knew, and if I am remembered for nothing else at the North Central Florida Human Resources Center, I am sure I am remembered fondly for my Fresh Apple Cake.

I was eventually adopted by a smart and efficient supervisor named Delores—a local black woman who knew a thing or two about native Florida life. She took one look at my apple pie, my words-per-minute, and my fresh-faced, church-girl desire to please and knew that she was sitting on a gold mine. She moved my desk to a corner of her office and soon had me doing everything from typing to doing in-takes on our unhappy patients, who suffered from every emotional malady known to man. The clinic was free or nearly free, and my job was to ferret out all the sensitive information of their personal lives: medical histories, financial history, exact number of abortions, failed marriages, and live births. Such were the requirements of government-sponsored clinics, and it was at the tender age of eighteen that I realized that as a species, human being were, above all, duplicitous, with interior lives that seldom mirrored the outward product. I never blinked an eye at anything they told me or worried too much if they were lying. I knew I'd be the one typing their session notes later in the afternoon. They could run but they couldn't hide; sooner or later, their secrets would be safe with me.

It was interesting work, with the twin benefits of making money and accruing college credit, but after two years of it, I began to have grave doubts about working with the mentally ill; I was too empathetic. If I talked too long with a schizophrenic, I absorbed it; I got a little paranoid myself. Typing up notes on depressives made me melancholy and documenting the actions of wife-beaters made me want to punch someone. I was a walking sponge, and though that quality would later prove invaluable in my real calling, at the time, it was just annoying.

I began casting about for a different major, with many heartfelt suggestions from my mother. In her day, there were four jobs a respectable girl could land and be happy: working for the phone company, the bank, or, if they were real go-getters, as a nurse or a teacher. She tactfully indicated that I didn't have the smarts for medicine (I didn't), and at some point decided I should be a teacher. I wasn't averse to the idea, but nurtured a well-known desire to be a writer, one noted in my high school yearbook ambition ("to write a book that will shock the world"). It sounded good on paper, but few people supported such a pipe dream. Writing was the pastime of the gentry and the well-connected; the lolling F. Scotts and the bohemian Zeldas.

Everyone urged me to stay at the clinic, but I was deaf to all entreaties, afraid the next suicidal client might talk me into joining him. I was desperate to break away and searching the horizons for a sign when it appeared at church one morning in the form of one Wendel Ray Owens, a native of the far-off state of Arkansas, who'd moved to Florida to get his Masters at UF. He was twenty-three at the time and had been raised in The Assemblies of God, but was at that moment in his life technically a backslider, which suited me. I was always one for paradox, and since I naturally and sincerely believed, I had confidence in my ability to sway the most hardened sinner.

There was a certain Tommy Lee Jones thing about his punk expression that lit him all around with the allure of the bad boy—

bad, but not *that* bad, attending church that morning because his best friend's mother had nagged him into coming. I was wearing a lavender linen wrap-around skirt and a peasant blouse, bought at Sears or Penney's, but a little thin for church. We were introduced over a pew, and when we shook hands, it was a magical moment. I looked at him, he looked at my chest, and it was a done deal. It was Cracker kismet. Within the week, I had confessed my desire to leave the typing pool and strike out in a more artsy direction, and he was vociferous in his support of my ambition, partly because of the thinness of my blouse, partly because he really did have faith in my vision; God knows why.

He'd been raised the oldest son in a household that teetered perpetually on the brink of destruction, and was used to going into rescue mode. The night he asked me to marry him he promised to put me through UF and square it with my father—two things I would not marry without. I didn't care about diamonds or freedom or the stigma of being a teenage bride. I did care about being stuck in Ocala, and as far as college went, UF was my only choice, for reasons of poverty (they were cheap) and convenience (thirty miles away.) They had an open-door policy on community college transfers and slipping up to Gainesville was as easy as popping out a pan of cornbread, as long I was legally married—which I was, in short order.

In May, we moved to Gainesville with precious few possessions but, thanks to the economic challenges of our youth, well set in job skills. Wendel had been supporting himself since he could hoe cotton (and yes: in case you wondered, his grandfather was a sharecropper) while my experience with the mentally afflicted had given me a jump on clerical work. I pulled my weight with a variety of typing gigs, though my real career was being a wife, and, shortly thereafter, a mother, which surprised no one. Unexpected pregnancies are the great fruit of the premature Cracker marriage— like it's written in the stars. And we weren't all that hot on birth control, now that I think of it.

In any case, my first daughter came along in my junior year, and it was sometime during the pregnancy, when I was big as a manatee, wearing a homemade maternity dress a friend of my mother's had made me (in pity), that I first had the courage to take a run at trying to get into the Creative Writing classes at UF. Smith Kirkpatrick was the head of the program, but Harry Crews was the fearsome face of it; fearsome by reason of his tattoos, his reputation, his drinking, and his habit of getting into bar shuffles around Gainesville. I was still a shy church girl—a knocked-up shy church girl—and feared him as a Missionary feared a cannibal. I made my sister-in-law (eighteen at the time, who would herself be pregnant by summer) come with me to our first meeting, for courage, and when I found his office empty, left a note stuck to his door.

I later learned that he had notes pinned there all the time and would routinely snatch them off and wad them up while he unlocked it. But I was a hopeful little manatee and once I got the ball rolling, was intent on getting into one of Harry's classes, which wasn't easy. He was a local legend and famous for his generous grading curve. He didn't give many A's but he seldom gave less than a B unless you insulted him to his face or turned him in to the department for public drunkenness. His classes always filled the day the section opened, but the summer after I delivered my little pink baby girl, I finally made the cut and got in for a summer session.

I was on the official list of CWR 101, which met in a tiny room two floors down from the English department, designed to comfortably seat maybe twelve people. At least fifty showed up the first night of class, hoping to talk Harry into letting them in—so many that they lined the hallway and sat around the walls. Harry had lately been in hot water with the department over being late, and arrived precisely on time, an enrollment list in hand. He seemed perplexed by the mob, and just made his way in the door and looked at the classroom number, the list, then back at the sea of shining, expectant faces, his first words a weary: "Why is my life so fucked up?"

I think all my Crews memories could be encapsulated in that first, despairing line. After chastising the wannabes and trying to shoo them away, he finally sat down and started the class, and by the end of it he said what-the-hell and let everyone in. This was beginning, basic fiction, and you had to make the cut with an A in order to be formally invited to the official realm of Creative Writing. Getting an A from Harry Crews wasn't an easy proposition, and much of your success was based on a short story he assigned that first night that had to have at least one scene set at Crystal Hamburgers, across 13th Street.

Well, I was an obedient Cracker and did as I was told, though some of my fellow pupils thought the caveat about setting a scene at Crystal was insulting to their First Amendment right to set a story wherever they pleased. They actually complained to the department and poor old Harry was back in hot water. As a result, of that entire herd of eager writers, I was the only one who made the cut to the official Creative Writing Program, where the professionals on staff taught me many valuable lessons in writing that I carry with me to this day. Things like: Beware of plot devices; don't mimic other writers; don't get caught in the mill of academia if you can help it; and pace your whiskey consumption so that your liver and your lifespan go out at the same approximate time.

They taught me other things, too, but those are the most profound, and once I had my degree under my belt, I set myself to the task of writing the Great American Novel. Just like that. I had, after all, the two requirements for writing fiction, as put forth by Virginia Woolf: money and a room of my own. Actually, I shared the room with a husband and two babies by then, and would shortly have another—all girls and all my real life's work— but I didn't mind. I adored my girls and the money part of the proposition was provided by old Mr. Wendel, who proved to be that most rare of all Crackers: a workaholic (and let the church say: *Amen*).

On money borrowed from my brother, we'd bought a house in the little hamlet of Newberry, fourteen miles west of Gainesville, and an eon away, culturally speaking, which suited me to the ground. Newberry was still Cracker Florida, and my neighbors were farm wives who'd turned over the farms to their sons and built houses in town for the company. They found my intact, old-fashioned family life par for the course, and only friends who'd known me since college knew that beyond the small-town respectability of our custom-built picket fence and matching Easter dresses, a small obsession was wildly and freely pursued by the lady of the Owens' house: writing.

From '83 till '96, I wrote at least four hours a day, and sometimes round the clock, if the plot was cooking and the girls otherwise occupied. My college typewriter had died a natural death and I had no money to replace it, and for the first few years wrote in long hand, on yellow legal pads, from the first page to the cardboard, then flipped it and wrote on the back. I wrote in bed, at a desk, nursing an infant; at night, at dawn, at mid-morning when the girls were at school, and in the afternoon when the preschoolers were napping. In short, I wrote whenever I could, and in due time produced two novels that never have (and never will) see the light of day.

I was bracing for a third when my great aunt died on the West End of Marianna, unexpectedly, of a neglected medical condition. She was the last of Grannie's generation, and I was heartbroken at losing her, and a little crazed from post-partum depression. When I came home from her funeral, I ditched my previous books and began feverishly scribbling out a novel that was purely displaced biography; not mine, but my mother's. In real life, they were the Rice family, of the West End. In fiction, they became the Catts, and oh, how I loved them. They provided the perfect outlet for my grief, this shadow family, whose history and struggles drew from both my current life there in downtown Newberry, and my mother's hardscrabble childhood on the West End of Marianna on a grid of row houses called Magnolia Hill.

It consumed me creatively, and for five years, while I went about raising my own daughters in the never-ending treadmill of cheerleading, softball, and VBS, I spent my mornings and nights perfecting my mirror universe. It wasn't exactly my job, this writing thing, but more of a personal obsession: cheap therapy for a working-class mother with refractory depression and a bad case of insomnia. I never thought I'd make a penny in it, as I was (and am) thin-skinned when it comes to rejection. After my first novel was turned down in '84 (when I was all of twenty-four years old) I came to the (premature) conclusion that I was a hobby-writer and would never publish anything I wrote. I decided Southern letters were dead; our stories told; our history mined. And I was too cut off from the pack to try and crack NY publishing and too thin-skinned to try. I had no writers on my Rolodex except Smith Kirkpatrick, who had retired shortly after my graduation but still called me every Christmas Eve and encouraged me to keep at it. He told me I was one of the best writers in America.

I thought him a charming liar, but I kept at it. I wrote and wrote and wrote, between waxing floors, teaching Sunday School, nursing daughters through childhood measles, chickenpox, the F-Cat, and the Clinton Administration. I eventually grew ashamed of my private obsession and quit talking about it, except to Wendel, who accepted it as a quirky part of a quirky nature. I never sent anything out till sometime in the autumn of '96, when I happened upon a book at a local library on neo-Cracker architecture, called *Classic Cracker*. The two words seemed to fairly sum up my life, and on a whim, I sent the publisher—a regional press in Sarasota—my latest version of an old manuscript that had been moldering in a chest in my sunroom for three years.

I had no particular hopes it would be accepted, but later in the spring, I got the call every writer remembers: the breakthrough call from an editor who wants to publish their book. I was getting ready to go to the grocery store when the call came in; was so stunned that I immediately called my great friend, Joy, to tell her I'd done the miraculous! I'd sold a book! She was happy, but confused. I'd never, in all the years I'd known her, so much as mentioned I was a writer. She hadn't a clue what I meant when I said I'd sold a book.

"You mean, like, at a garage sale?"

"No! I sold *my* book. I wrote a book. I just sold it."

There was a silence on the line, then she asked, in disbelief, "When did you have time to write a book?" as three of her four children were best friends with my girls, and we'd just come off a heavy Pop-Warner cheerleading schedule that had eaten up our entire lives.

It was a valid question, one I was asked more than once that first heady year, and I'm not sure anyone really believed I'd actually written and sold a novel till it came out the following spring: *My Brother Michael*. It was only when they read the curious story of my alter ego, Gabriel Catts, that they began to get an idea of the latent schizophrenia of the writer mind, and its peculiar ability to weave the essence of many lives into a single, seamless cloth with the tenacity of an industrious silk worm.

There was much speculation, en famille, over which family member had inspired which character, but my oldest brother, Jay, who claims *My Brother Michael* is the first novel he ever read, nailed it best. "All of us are all of them," he said, and a finer bit of literary criticism I've never heard.

I wrote in secrecy for so long that I actually came to prefer it. Even now, twelve years and four books later, my life tends to split into two parts: my Writing Life and my Real Life. My Writing Life is the stuff of dreams and dragons, and spent in solitude, hashing out plots, or on the road far from home, standing at podiums and dissecting those plots to people who have never heard of Newberry, Florida. My Real Life is spent much as it always was, thrift shopping in High Springs, going to Mama's for Sunday dinner; gardening and eating barbecue and cooking supper every night for Mr. Wendel, who still puts in a formidable work week, and prefers home cooking in his lunch pail. The two lives draw from each other, but seldom do they meet, which suits me. Those poor schizophrenics taught me a thing or two, back in my youth in the clinic, about insanity and emotional splitting, and obsession. When you're a writer, it all goes into the mix.

Message in a Bottle

by Michelle Richmond

You might have known me as Charity Strong. That's the name I adopted in Knoxville, Tenneessee, in 1992, while selling *Popular Mechanics* subscriptions over the phone for a company called Dial America. The call center consisted of a single large room with a dozen or so rows of cubicles. Each cubicle held a computer and earphones. Upon arriving at work each night, I would pick up the script beside the computer, log on, and wait for some stranger's phone to ring, somewhere in America.

The object of the telemarketer is to keep the person on the other end of the line from hanging up. The longer you keep him on the line, the more likely you are to make the sale. But there would come a time, somewhere around the middle of my shift each night, when the sale itself would become irrelevant, and I would find myself engaged in a game of beating my own clock, trying to keep the customer on the line for two minutes, three minutes, four. I would engage them in conversations about their families, their jobs, their lives. The people on the other end of the line—like most people if you give them a chance—were endlessly fascinating. Everyone had a story. For a semester in high school I'd volunteered for a suicide prevention line, and telemarketing felt alarmingly similar: all that loneliness pulsing through the air, all those people just dying to talk. One night, my boss called me into his office and pointed out that I'd been on the phone with one potential customer for twenty-three minutes. I'd made a sale, but that was beside the point. When I reeled off the names of the customer's children and related a story he'd told me about being stuck upside down in a ditch by the freeway for twenty-nine hours following an accident in a rainstorm, my boss seemed unimpressed.

"I was building rapport," I said.

"It's fine to ask about the weather," he replied, "but you're not auditioning for a part in their wedding."

After that, I had to find new ways to entertain myself without running up the clock quite so obviously. The boss could tune in any minute to a call. The window of his office looked out into the call center. At least once each night I'd glance up to see him watching me, earphones on, and I would know that he was listening. Everything about the job became a game, a way of passing the four-hour shift. I found that, by using a breathy voice and making double entendres that stopped just short of being risqué enough to get me fired in the event that the call was "being recorded for quality assurance purposes," I could frequently up-sell someone to the three-year subscription. It's not difficult to make double entendre out of car talk. You know, all those radiators and gear shifts, all that body work, all those purring engines. It helped that my call list consisted entirely of current or previous subscribers, almost exclusively male, frequently willing to talk about the cars they had or the cars they wanted, how they'd found their cars or how they planned to acquire them. Once, a potential customer complained to me that his wife didn't understand why he needed to spend so much time with his '67 Mustang—"but *you* understand," he said. "You, I can talk to." Telemarketing is like dating that way: Use the right tone of voice, say mm-hmm in all the right places, and you're halfway there.

Later, at the same company, I moved on to selling *Sesame Street Magazine*, but I quickly discovered my telemarketing skill set was limited. Whereas *Popular Mechanics* had been a cash cow, *Sesame Street* was a dead end. Nobody wanted to hear what Charity Strong had to say about Big Bird, and young mothers, no matter how lonely, are generally too busy to spill their hearts out to some stranger on the phone. Every bad job you sign on for has its breaking point, a moment when you look up at the clock and realize that you simply cannot do it for another minute longer, the point at which another hour in the proverbial saddle seems like a death sentence. For me, *Sesame Street* was the breaking point.

The night I punched my last time card for Dial America, one of my colleagues took me out for drinks. She was a tall, thin, dark-haired woman who taught freshman composition at the community college and who kept saying, "Can you believe I'm forty? I don't look forty, do I? The secret is to drink lots of water." I thought she did look forty, but didn't have the heart to tell her. At the time, it seemed silly to me that she would care so much whether or not she looked her age, but now that I'm thirty-nine, I understand exactly where she was coming from.

Next stop: a restaurant and bar in Knoxville's Old Town, a hip little place that featured live music on the weekends. We had a surly chef with a thick black beard who chain-smoked beside the salad station and who was utterly committed to producing cuisine that fell just short of mediocrity. The menu was Cajun-inspired in general spirit, but without the attending flavor. We sold red beans and rice, jambalaya, soggy fried frog legs dipped in honey-mustard sauce. While none of it was exceptional, all of it was cheap, so the place was often packed. After a couple of months as a hostess, I was promoted to wait staff, although for the most part I only got weekend lunch service—which mainly consisted of refilling iced tea and bread baskets for the after-church crowd, bringing ladies extra lemon for their water, explaining why I could not substitute the cheese fries for the coleslaw at no extra charge, and pretending not to notice when a guy in a cheap suit made a thinly veiled comment about my ass. (The Sunday lunch crowd in the Deep South has surely done more to tarnish the reputation of fundamentalist Christians than Ted Haggard and Jim Bakker combined.)

Depending on the clientele, waiting tables can feel way dirtier than telemarketing, with the added disadvantage of physical contact—but show me a writer who's never been broke enough to wait tables, and I'll show you a writer whose fiction is probably stuck on the golf course. Forgive the sweeping generalization, but a person who has never truly struggled to pay the electricity bill is at a deficit when it comes to attempting to understand the struggles of others. Being poor per se may not make a person a better writer, but there's a good chance that financial hardship, and a childhood and young adulthood spent on the wrong end of the class struggle, makes a person a more careful observer of humanity.

I was eventually promoted to cocktail waitressing during live music shows. At first, I was thrilled. No salads to make, no entrees to time correctly, no complicated side orders, and when it came to tips, drink service was the holy grail. The later the hour and the louder the band, the bigger the tips. Not to mention, it was fun. Anyone who's worked at a restaurant can recall the general camaraderie inspired by the night shift, the sense of looseness and fellow feeling that ensues once the last customer has left, the stations have been broken down, the salt shakers topped off, the night's receipts counted, the credit card tips distributed. After the kitchen closes, the party starts, and the hierarchies of restaurant life seem to magically melt away.

One night after hours, the owner of the restaurant turned to the bartender and ordered "one of your special Lemon Drops—for her." To my surprise, he was pointing at me. I hardly knew the owner, but it had been a long night and I welcomed the drink, not to mention the implicit approval of the boss. The next thing I knew the floor was spinning, and he was offering to take me home. Then I blacked out. At some point, I woke up in a house I'd never seen before, flat on my back in a strange bed. My boss was having sex with me. I told him to stop, but he didn't, and I passed out again. The next morning, it took a minute to orient myself, to understand where I was, and that I was naked from the waist down. My boss was snoring beside me. When I got up to go to the bathroom, I realized there was a used condom inside me—a fact which would, in coming weeks, send me into a panic and provoke me to go to a public clinic to be tested for HIV. At the time, I'd only had a couple of sexual partners, one of whom had been a serious four-year relationship, the man I'd planned to marry, the one for whom I'd "saved myself," the way Southern Baptist girls are taught to do. What I mean to say is: Even if the sex with the boss had been consensual, it would have been significant within the limited context of my life up to that point. The fact that it happened off my watch, the fact that it was done *to* me rather than *by* me, was devastating.

Years later, it's the condom I remember most, along with one other odd detail. The bed was tall and elaborately dressed, fitted out with all sorts of pillows, as if my boss's mother, or maybe his sister, had chosen the comforter and pillow shams. I remember a fussy combination of maroon and forest green. I remember gold piping, a square pillow with ropey gold fringe.

Of course, in this day and age we all know about Rohypnol, and there's a name for what happened that night. If I'd been smarter and less broke and less ashamed, I might have pressed charges. But I was twenty-two years old and desperately afraid of losing my job and my apartment. Beyond that I was mortified, and I had no desire to have my entire personal life trotted out for public display. So I just avoided the boss from there on out. When he reprimanded me later that week for some mistake I'd made on the floor, pressing his hand into the small of my back and muttering, "I've got your number," I had no response. It's the silence that I think of now—the fact that, back then, I couldn't find the words, so I said nothing. When one of the veteran waitresses said, "Oh, I hear he got you, too," and pointed out the marks on the office wall where he and his co-owner kept track of the waitresses they'd bedded, I tucked my shame in tight and acted like none of it mattered, biding my time until I could find another job.

Fortunately, it didn't take long. I happened to have a friend at the restaurant, a woman my age, whose day job was in graphic design. Before the event in question, I'd been blindly wandering through my post-college year, writing stories and occasionally sending out résumés, in no big hurry to find a proper job. When I told my friend what had happened, she took me on as her personal project. She introduced me to a friend in the advertising world, which led to a freelance job, which led to an interview at an ad agency, where I was soon hired as a copywriter. While the salary was small, the job felt like a gift. Much to my astonishment, I was given a corner office with a view—the first and last such office of my fairly short-lived nine-to-five life. My boss, Hal Ernest, was a former military man who had cut his advertising teeth in the '60s. He took me under his wing with a kind of paternal concern that I'm grateful for to this day, and he proceeded to teach me the ins and outs of client relationships, product positioning, and how to shoot a commercial in front of a green screen. He also was one of the most caffeinated individuals I've ever known, and his unique method for making a particularly intense pot of coffee has seen me through many a deadline. Call it luck, or call it cause and effect, but something very rotten led to something very good. I never worked in a restaurant again, and I've never in my life had a better boss than Hal.

When I left the restaurant, I told the boss I was going to be a writer. I'm not sure why it mattered. I think I wanted him to know I was more than what he saw: the girl who carried the drink trays during the live music shows, the unresponsive body that he had arranged to his satisfaction on the bed, so meaningless to him that he did not even bother to remove the condom after he was done.

As I write this I'm wondering how I got here—how I set out to write an essay about telemarketing and ended up revisiting that long-ago moment when I was passed out in the boss's bed. I haven't thought of it in many years. Though it sickened and humiliated me at the time, it left no lasting scars. Now that I'm thirty-nine, married and a mother, coming across that ugly old memory hardly even stings. It does make me mad, in a hazy, distant way—but the anger isn't personal. It's more a general anger for the sorry old state of things, the kind of anger that makes me want to take my teenaged nieces by the shoulders and tell them to be careful.

* * *

Writing, like any other job, almost always ends up taking you somewhere you didn't mean to go. After writing this, I did what so many of us do these days when a name from the past pops into our head. I looked my old boss up on Facebook. There was someone with his name in Knoxville, so I sent a message: "Did you by any chance own a restaurant in the early nineties in Knoxville named —?" He wrote back within the hour. "I did." Along with his message was a friend request, which isn't surprising, considering the careless way in which "friendships" are formed on Facebook. I didn't get the feeling he recognized my name. Why would he? Dozens of young women must have waited tables at his restaurant before it finally went under sometime in the mid-'90s. By the time it closed, I had left Knoxville, cycled through a few more jobs, and gone off to graduate school.

Through the mercurial mechanics of Facebook, this person who had been an ugly blip on the screen of my life became, quite suddenly, an open book. Under relationship it said, "engaged." Under religion it said, "Christian." In his profile photo he looks much the same as he did eighteen years ago. He's gained a little weight and lost a little hair, but aside from that, I recognize the face, the cocky smile, everything. If I'm honest with myself, I just wanted to take a peek, to have a voyeur's sense of satisfaction in looking into his life without telling him who I am. If I were to remind him of that night, I doubt he would take it seriously. Surely I'm not the only waitress who accepted a drink from him and woke up half-naked in his bed. In his mind, I'm sure it hardly even registered. And besides, one of the great cosmic gifts of growing older is that the people who once held power over you and wielded it badly eventually become nothing to you—just part of the periphery detritus, something vaguely unpleasant but ultimately unimportant floating on the edge of consciousness.

I don't "work" anymore, in the real sense of the word: by which I mean I don't have an office or a classroom where I must show up at a certain time on a certain day, I don't have a boss to answer to. In the last few years, something happened that I could never have predicted, something so out of line with my expectations that

I sometimes have to pinch myself to believe it: These days, I write novels for a living. I don't know how long the good luck will last, but I do know that literary fortune has a tendency to ebb and flow. I'm certain a time will come when I have to go out into the world again to earn my living. But that doesn't bother me much, because there's one thing I always believed during my fifteen-plus years of working whatever job paid the bills—not just telemarketing and waiting tables, but credit card sales, copywriting, a receptionist stint at a tanning salon, and too many adjunct teaching gigs to count: I always believed that a writer, no matter how she makes her living, is a very lucky person. Because a writer can take any unpleasantness, any drudgery, any sadness, any comic madness, gather words around that thing, and spin it out into the world like a Frisbee.

I don't much believe in writing as revenge. But I do believe in writing as information, as memory. As record and reminder. For years, I rationalized the long hours and paltry paychecks—and worse—by telling myself that, one day, I'd put it all in a story. What writer hasn't considered just such a possibility, the moment when some past silence is turned on end? What writer hasn't imagined the moment of recognition, when the impersonal sentences on the page begin to clarify, to coalesce, and the reader looks inside the story and sees himself? What writer hasn't imagined slipping her true story into the mailbox, with no return address, no note, just a scrap of paper to mark the page? Like a ghost of Christmas past. Like a message in a bottle.

A Summer at the Phone Farm

by Clay Risen

Generations of Risens, stretched in a belt across the wide hips of the Appalachians between North Carolina and Kentucky, toiled in coal mines, textile mills, and horse farms. Even when they came into some money and went to college, they worked summers picking vegetables or digging ditches, grinding calluses into their palms and furrows into their brows.

I got lucky. I worked in a call center.

This was back when I aspired to join the business world. It was more an adolescent aspiration than a fully formed plan. I struggle with math. Socially speaking, I was a die-hard Type B personality. And, fortunately, given my eventual profession, I'm relatively indifferent to making money.

The dream had more to do with that old boyhood malady of trying to follow in my father's footsteps. Dad was an executive for a fiber-optics manufacturer. He spent my late childhood jetting around Eastern Europe and what they used to call the newly independent former Soviet states, signing deals with Poles and Estonians and Kazakhs, coming back with vodka from Warsaw and real fake Rolexes from Moscow. My classmates' moms would flirtingly ask him if he was a spy. This was Nashville in the early 1990s, and I guess for those ladies, anything involving Eastern Europe and technology still carried that scent of Cold War intrigue.

It was also the dawn of the dotcom boom. First came the post-recession era of grunge rock, *Reality Bites*, and Douglas Coupland novels, when news magazines ran covers about how kids with English degrees were night managing at Taco Bell.

By the time I graduated, though, those same kids were leaving their fast-food gigs for the bright dawn light shining from Silicon Valley, where venture capitalists were pouring millions into technologies and services no one understood, including their creators. I read *Wired* and *Popular Science* and saw a lifestyle of fun and success, filled with visions of open-plan offices with pool tables and in-house coffee bars. I was about to graduate; why couldn't I be a part of the magic?

Do I need to report that, in 1995, the dotcom wave had yet to break on the shores of Nashville? That my hours spent navigating the local message boards on AOL's "webcrawler"—"browser" was not yet the settled nom d'Internet—put me at the cutting edge of the city's digital elite? If not, then I don't need to explain why I leaped at the first vaguely tech-oriented job that I could find.

For reasons that will become readily clear, I'm going to call the company Expertech. But suffice it to say that its real name was one of those new-economy neologisms, akin to but not at all the same as Expertech, names that companies pay consultants tens of thousands of dollars to devise, names that scream "cutting edge" without actually meaning anything.

It didn't bother me that I had no idea what Expertech did. This was the mid-'90s, after all. In the '60s people joined political movements without knowing what they stood for. In the '70s people had sex with complete strangers. In the '90s, we let ourselves be seduced by anything vaguely high tech. How else will historians explain digiscents.com, a company that raised millions promising to transmit smells over the Internet?

Not only did I not know what Expertech did, I didn't even know what I'd be doing there. Since I got the interview through a friend of my mom, a woman whose husband was an Expertech vice president, I figured it would be something in the executive assistant range—learning at the knee of a wise old CEO, or CFO, or COO; anything C would have been fine with me. Sitting in on meetings? Sure. Taking minutes? Why not, a bright young man like myself? Of course, there'd be the occasional mundane task. Filing. Making copies. I'd even answer phones.

Things started to go awry when, rather than meet in an executive's corner office, a few minutes after arriving I found myself in a cubicle, hammering away at a typing test. Then I filled out a long form asking about prior arrests and drug abuse. I'd have to take a urine test, the form told me, so I should tell the truth. The truth was, I had led a pretty sheltered childhood, and a few sips of rum at camp was the closest I'd come to illicit substances. I took a gamble and left it off.

Then I waited in what passed for a visitors' lounge. A few hard sofas, a coffee table stacked with trade magazines. Through the picture window I watched cars drift by along Maryland Way, the main drag in a mega-complex of office parks (an office park park?) in Nashville's southern suburbs. It was built on the site of an old horse farm, and the side roads had names like Winners Circle and Thoroughbred Lane. Maryland Way had the only sidewalk within twenty miles of my house, though I never saw anyone use it. The quarter mile on either side of the road was zoned exclusively for offices, all under five stories, each surrounded, like belles at a free-enterprise ball, by flowing asphalt skirts, empty save for five eight-hour periods a week.

Finally a woman in sensible shoes, a pink cotton pantsuit, and hair befitting a Whitesnake groupie called me into her office. She was the company's lead HR associate—they were all, she told me, called "associates," not "employees." Her accent put her from somewhere in the Rust Belt, born of a working class very different from the local Tennessean variety. I handed her my résumé. She said thanks and set it aside.

Ms. Whitesnake explained the job. Expertech provided credit cards for trucking companies, a sort of AmEx for the CB world. Using a single card, drivers could buy gas, food, personal items—usually copious amounts of pornography, I later learned—with each purchase under a different category with a different limit.

Expertech monitored their purchases and reported them back to their clients.

My job was to be a customer relations associate. From one until 9:30 PM I would sit at a desk in Expertech's "phone farm" and answer calls from drivers. If a card didn't work, or the driver had lost it, or he'd maxed out, I'd be there to provide calm, professional assistance. I would get an ID card, and from the moment I came in the back door to the minute I left the office I'd need to swipe it to get into doors, to check into the call center, to leave for lunch, trailing a precisely calibrated, chronological record of my daily movements behind me. Expertech, Ms. Whitesnake made clear, didn't put much stock in individual responsibility.

Why did I say yes when, a few minutes later, she offered me the job? Wasn't it suspicious that I was apparently the only candidate for the job? Didn't I wonder if maybe Expertech had such high turnover that I wasn't up for a job at all, but just a slot in a procession of short-lived stints in a modern-day sweat shop (albeit an air-conditioned, manually undemanding one)?

I have a hard time saying no to anything, and I don't think too quickly on my feet, which is probably why none of this occurred to me at the time. Waxing more thoughtfully, all these years later, I think I took the job out of some sense of dues-paying, that I was starting on the first rung of a corporate ladder. But I also wonder if, in some quasi-genetic way, as a Risen I'm given to accepting drone labor. Even now, few things are more satisfying to me than shoveling ditches or filling out forms. I look forward to the Census, and I'm a sucker for online surveys.

A few days later I returned to Expertech as its newest employee, a post I held for approximately forty-two hours, until the next newest employee arrived. And I never saw Ms. Whitesnake again; my badge didn't give me access to the building's upper floors. Instead, I found Stephen, my supervisor.

Not to belabor what should by now be an obvious metaphor, but Expertech worked like the setting for a dystopian novel. Stephen—not Steve, he told me as we shook hands—was an alpha. He had a business degree and a smile designed for upper management. His

ID gave him access to the upper floors, and no one questioned that within the year, he'd be up there full time.

Stephen-Not-Steve loved to devise new and overly intricate metrics for associate performance, but he took special pride in the Gridiron. On my first day, the only time I sat in his office, he pulled out a black binder and explained how it worked. Our monthly progress was measured as yards gained down a football field. Mistakes—a few minutes late, dropped calls, losing your cool with a driver—constituted penalty yards. If you scored a touchdown by the end of the month, you got a prize, like $15 off at Applebee's. This system made him very popular.

Most of us, though, myself included, were betas. We were a motley sort: moms dipping their toes back in the workforce; overqualified middle-aged men who bore an unexplained mark of professional Cain—maybe an embezzlement conviction or alcoholism, or a demonstrated inability to play well with others. There were a few kids like myself working for the summer, but most of the young people had passed on college completely. Some were well aware that the job was a dead-ender, but others seemed to see themselves following Stephen-Not-Steve. It wasn't going to happen, but they either didn't know or had deluded themselves into believing otherwise. They wore skirts and slacks instead of jeans. They took copious notes when talking to a supervisor. And most of them were gone before the end of the summer, out of frustration or incompetence, replaced by a new crop of C-grade strivers.

Whatever sociological insights I could gather were limited by the call center's ingeniously soul-sucking design. The room was shaped like a Greek cross, with four wide apses sticking out from a central podium. Each apse was about 10,000 square feet in size. Three were filled with rows of low-walled cubicles; the fourth held offices and the break room. The center of the cross had a higher ceiling to accommodate a raised platform where the shift managers sat, peering over their computer banks at the rows of associates.

Each cubicle had a computer, a phone, and a pen and paper. Associates weren't allowed to bring food or magazines or books to their desks, or even bags or purses, to keep us from being distracted for even a fraction of a second that could be better spent serving Expertech's clients. We were randomly assigned a different desk each day to make sure we didn't leave a secret stash of cookies or books behind. I developed a habit of rifling the drawers of my desk-for-a-day as soon as I sat down, in case some kind soul had left a scrap of entertainment behind. Occasionally they did—I once found an Amway catalogue in the top drawer of that day's desk, and I relished its perfume and ladies' undergarment ads for a few fleeting hours.

I relished them carefully, though, because we were under constant supervision by the shift managers, not to mention video cameras poking out of the acoustic ceiling tiles all around the room. Everything, it turned out, was monitored, measured, analyzed, broken down and reconstituted into numerical bits of hard data that someone much higher up used to decide whether we were doing our job.

At the start of a shift, I'd swipe my badge beside a computer at the entrance to the call center. I could be no more than five minutes late (or early, for some reason). The computer would spit back a seat assignment. Then I'd sign in again once I sat down. That simple procedure gave Expertech three vital data points: that I was there, when I arrived, and the span of time between when I signed in at the entrance and when I registered at my desk.

The last bit of data was incredibly important, because it told Expertech whether I was a dawdler. If there was a significant lag between when I came in the door and when I sat down, it was probably because I was chatting with my neighbor, or pausing to look out the window. At the end of each month, we'd each sit down with Stephen-Not-Steve in a small office off the call center floor and give a sort of confession—he'd ask why our lag time spiked on the 23rd, or why we signed in early for three days in a row. Forgive us Stephen-Not-Steve, for we have dawdled.

The job itself was numbingly easy. A driver hauling diapers across South Dakota would call from a Flying J outside Spearfish, unable to fill his tank because his Expertech card was maxed out.

Open the account file, see if he's approved for a credit increase, click a box and tell him he's set. Hang up, pick up, repeat.

Occasionally we couldn't increase his credit, and we'd try to calmly explain why, for reasons unknown to us, he was now stuck outside Spearfish, South Dakota, with a truck full of diapers. He would then explain, somewhat less calmly, why and how we could go fuck ourselves. Then he'd amend himself and say no, he was going to come find us and do the job for us. We were not allowed to show the flaw in his plan—that, while we knew he was in Spearfish, he had no idea where we were. All we could do was tell him to call his dispatcher. He would then explain why and how his dispatcher could also go fuck himself—although, if his dispatcher was a woman, he might have a specialized, anatomically specific vocabulary of options set aside for her.

By break time I'd be brain-stunned. I'd sign out and go sit in the break room. Because our breaks were staggered and randomized, we couldn't easily bond with fellow associates. Not that many of us were in the appropriate mental state to carry a conversation—we just sat staring at the TV, slowly chewing our food, like patients in an Alzheimer's ward.

Other times I'd sit on the patio, where a few picnic benches poked into the parking lot, and cast my gaze over the acres of asphalt behind Expertech, abruptly ending at a line of pine trees, behind which ran a row of brown-brick ranch houses. A basketball goal on a rusty pole stood off to the side of the lot, though I never saw anyone use it. Expertech had mastered the art of projecting camaraderie while doing everything it could to prevent it.

I left the company a few weeks before school started. I'd like to say I learned a lot from the job, that I grew to be a better person, that it pushed me toward becoming a writer. But all I learned was that, contrary to all the years of Protestant, preppie work-ethic indoctrination I'd had growing up, work is not always fun, or enlightening, or an opportunity for personal growth. I learned that even in the vaunted new economy, most people are going to spend their lives doing drone labor for someone else. Sometimes—most of the time—work sucks. I learned that the mills, coal mines, and fields of the old New South have been replaced by less physically taxing but no less soul-destroying call centers and data-processing farms. I wouldn't trade my work at Expertech with my great-great-grandfather's coal mining, but I doubt he'd have traded with me, either.

Refuse

by George Singleton

I'm pretty sure that my blind headfirst leap into writing fiction occurred for the same reasons it occurred with my brethren: I had discovered some new types of music, I'd been scorned one too many times by a woman, and my summer job involved driving a garbage truck. I'm no expert in astronomy or anthropology, but it seems plausible and likely that the alignment of Tom Waits and the Sex Pistols, of "Get lost, I hate you," and of "You gone have to drive the garbage truck that don't have power steering," said by a man named Lonnie, will only result in a kid spending late-night hours with pen to paper, trying to be as existential as possible. I'm not so sure that I've ever thanked any type of Supreme Being for the Summer of 1978. Maybe I shouldn't.

It doesn't matter about how I went from listening to the Grateful Dead to either punk or cry-in-your-beer narratives bellowed out by a gravelly-voiced seer. And I certainly understand now why a college girl would think to herself, Man, what was I thinking when I started dating this guy? No, what had the most impact was the summer job, which started off as my needing only to drive a special flatbed truck with a giant forklift on back instead of the bed. This was for the city of Greenwood, South Carolina, my hometown.

In the previous summers, since the age of fifteen, I had driven dump trucks and water trucks, working for the "beautification committee." I had cleaned up flowerbeds around town, watered the plants, spread pine straw, and that sort of thing. I hoed around the town fountain, dipping the hoe into water when I saw quarters. I spread mulch, and dug ditches, and pretended that I knew what I was doing. I'd spend hours trickling water from a fire hydrant into the water truck's reservoir so I could take a nap in the shade. I'd driven the dump truck (which you could get going about forty miles an hour, turn off the ignition, then turn it back on in order to make the truck backfire) with my coworkers—college kids— out to Lake Greenwood to gather up pine straw from one of the summer-job coworkers' parents' lake house. We'd buy beer at this little store along the way, load up the truck in about five minutes, go swimming and fishing, drink beer, then drive back just before lunch. After lunch we'd unload the pine straw and make a second pilgrimage to the lake house, et cetera.

I don't want to tattle on everyone involved, but Charlie, Phillip, Eddie, and Scurry—what a name, *Scurry!*—all ended up being productive, non-criminal citizens, from what I understand. For some reason none of them chose to write, or quit early on like rational beings should. They listened to regular music and had steady girlfriends who liked to dance, I imagine.

Anyway, for some reason the bosses deemed me responsible enough, finally, in the summer before my junior year in college, to promote me to the Sanitation Department. Originally, I was in charge of washing out Dempsey Dumpsters with a steam hose of sorts, then painting the insides with a brown de-ruster. I painted the outsides green with a roller and, more often than not, signed my name somewhere on the inside. It was my job to drive to the dumpsters with the flatbed truck with the forklift on back, pick up the bin, and bring it back to the shop area. Sometime in the middle of the night these dumpsters had been emptied by the third-shift driver, a man named Fletcher. What a sweet job he had, with no one named Lonnie to yell at him.

I should mention this: There are people who work at department stores and pharmacies and such who steal from their employers. I know that it's hard to believe. But on occasion

I would drive my fancy forklift-in-the-bed truck to a Dempsey Dumpster, lift the lid, and learn that the bin wasn't empty. Did Fletcher forget part of his route last night? I would wonder immediately. Then I would notice how there didn't seem to be actual trash in the dumpster. No, somebody had placed perfectly good, say, albums, clothes, hair dryers, cigarettes, boxes of Russell Stover candy (which melt in a dumpster, by the way), candlesticks, candles (they melt, too), pipe tobacco, pipes, belts, sandals, and a Velcro-type dart game into the dumpster. Could it be that an employee of Eckerd's Drugs, or Belk, planned to come back after work and take what he or she had placed in my Dempsey Dumpster? Could it be that I should take said items, in order to make the employee understand that life isn't fair, just like it's not fair in the world of American fiction, of which I wanted to be a part?

So there was that wonderful part of the job. This "stealing from the thieves" part of my job, I feel sure now, had some kind of effect on my writerly beginnings. But it wasn't enough.

Again, I'm no anthropologist, but surely some scholar has delved into the world of typical work weeks and noticed how many sanitation department workers don't show up on Mondays. So was the case in the summer of 1978. Hangovers and knifings and jail time seemed to be the prevalent reasons. One early morning Lonnie came to me and said, "We ain't got no drivers this morning, two in jail, fellow stabbed Leon, ain't enough with licenses, you drive one the trucks?"

Lonnie had a head like God's bowling ball. His eyes bugged out and his mouth never closed. Lonnie kept his head shaved way before it was fashionable. He yelled at everyone constantly, except a barrel-chested, long-haired white garbage truck driver named Henry who came back to the shop after his route and practiced shooting his high-tech bow and arrow at a target placed right beside where I steam-cleaned dumpsters.

I had already declared my philosophy major in college, so I didn't know enough not to say, "'Ain't got no drivers' is a double negative. Do you mean? . . ."

I think he actually pulled me by the ear, up the slight hill to where the trucks were parked.

My coworkers on these Mondays, and then usually Tuesdays and Wednesdays, were named Honeypie and Esby. Because one of the newer trucks was always in for repair, I had to drive a garbage truck manufactured circa 1965 that didn't have power steering. Listen, when it was heavy with what my townspeople discarded daily, I had to get the thing going about thirty miles an hour before I could turn the wheel.

Again, this particular truck was used only when no other was available. I got in, and Honeypie and Esby jumped in the front seat with me for the ride to our route's first can. Honeypie said, "Something stink."

It was a fucking garbage truck, I thought. Cause and effect! Philosophy 101.

Honeypie reached beneath my seat, between my legs. He pulled out a grease-stained brown paper bag and extracted a tin foil-covered meatloaf sandwich that had been there since the last time this truck saw use. Let's say it had been two weeks. I don't know what the gestation period is for the types of flies that hang out at sanitation department yards, but that rancid meatloaf sandwich had enough maggots squirming between bread and beef for an entire hospital wing of patients with necrotic tissue in need of clean-up.

"Summody wasted a good sandwich," Esby said. "Who don't eat they lunch, who don't eat they lunch?"

It was Monday. Maybe I, too, had a hangover. I opened the door, sick to my stomach.

*　　*　　*

Oddly, this is the first time—thirty-one years later—that I've written about driving a garbage truck. All in all it may have been my best job ever. I got paid a couple bucks more than minimum wage. If we finished routes at one or two o'clock, we were done for the day and paid eight hours' worth of work. If I had understood America's obsession with junk and antiques that occurred years later, I would be a millionaire, for Honeypie and Esby probably threw Tiffany lamps and Chippendale chairs and antique Royal typewriters into the back of the truck. I worked my shift, I returned to my parents' house, and I wrote fiction that concerned characters living in New York and Paris—places I had never visited at the time—who worked as doctors and lawyers—things I would never do, or really care to know about.

When there were enough drivers for the trucks, I returned to picking up dumpsters and cleaning them up. Filled with the anticipation of finding a dishonorable and disgruntled employee's stolen goods, I drove to my sites—the same feeling I get nowadays when writing a story. When there were zero nearly-stolen products hidden away, I felt deflated—the same feeling today when I get a rejection in the mail. The highs and lows of sanitation work, baby, are the same highs and lows of writing daily.

Only later did I understand that perhaps Honeypie and Esby didn't understand their occupations as the best jobs ever created. Honeypie said more than once, "Sheet, I'mo kill Lonnie and get me a guh goddamn job." More than once Esby said, "Bitch don't realize I working my ass off while she down on Waller Skreet drinking beer." Waller Street—aptly named—was a short alley off Main that held three or four juke joints. Back in previous summers I'd driven my dump truck down there too fast, turned off the ignition, and watched the windows shake to my backfire.

They never looked me in the face when they spoke. One time Esby was in the truck's trough in back, riding to the next stop, when I heard him yelling, then in my side mirror saw him running in the road. A rat had crawled onto his lap, and he jumped. When there were narrow driveways or alleys with cans far away, they asked me to back my way right up to the cans, which took much longer than their walking to the garbage and bringing it back. I think it was their way of saying, "This isn't supposed to be an easy life, boy." I think it might've been their way of saying, "Remember these days when we're still here and you out of college, with a good job, like roofing, or painting houses, still a decade away from ever having a story published."

And then there's this: One day with Honeypie and Esby, we idled in line at the county dump. They sat up front with me. Esby kept yelling, "Hurry up, man, I gots to get me home." In a non-power steering garbage truck, one needs to wait back in line, then drive as fast as possible toward the man with the bulldozer once the previous truck exits the area. At the last second one turns the wheel hard to the right, in order to eventually back up toward where the garbage truck's contents should be discharged.

Honeypie hummed. He said, "I ain't looking," but I didn't know why.

Esby said, "It ain't right. Gone happen to us one day."

"That man ain't got no soul, do what he do."

I thought they were, perhaps, hallucinating, or had been reading Faulkner and were in stream-of-consciousness mode.

This man named Dalton, who worked as the dogcatcher and whom I called Dalton the Dogcatcher, had been in his pickup truck right before me in line. He'd shoved off what appeared to be a refrigerator box. He drove away and looked at me—college boy—with his beady little eyes. I looked in the rearview mirror as the county dump's bulldozer man shoved the box further up a heap. The box split open, and I saw probably ten stiff dogs emerge, legs out, eyes like sad peeled muscadines. I don't think, at the time, I thought about how those poor strays would be buried in what trash I was about to dump out. I didn't think about how Esby and Honeypie might've felt that their lives were on about the same course as a stray dog's, but I do now.

Faulkner's Place

by Matthew Teague

My recognition of William Faulkner's brilliance came shortly after a sick cat flipped around and sank its teeth into the meat of my thumb. His genius only grew every time I scraped handfuls of dog feces from a cage into a weakening cone of newspaper, or, depending on the dog's health, sopped it up with a wad of the same. So for a long time the sight of the *Vicksburg Post* created in me a tension between the beauty of words and the metallic tang of canine parvovirus.

I was sixteen, and worked off the books for a veterinarian in town. I made two-thirds the minimum wage, which was just enough to cover fuel. I enjoyed the animals, but the veterinarian seemed to hate them and me with equal force; once he had picked the biggest dog in the outdoor cages and kicked it with his snake-proof boots until it snarled. Then he grinned, handed me a pill the size of a man's fist and said, "You're going to want to get that into the throat good so he'll swallow it."

About that time I came across a paperback copy of *The Sound and the Fury*. I'd like to say I huddled with it between the cages, poring over its tattered pages, illuminated by Faulkner's grace and power. But after the first paragraph I suspected he was insane, or had hoodwinked the world. I had spent my whole life reading, drifting with Huck Finn and Robinson Crusoe, but I had never seen literature as broken as this. I showed it to an older friend, who said, "He drank a lot."

William Faulkner came from just the other side of the Delta. He performed terribly in school. And yet—the brilliance—he had persuaded all these people, including the people who gave him a Nobel Prize and a million dollars, that he had something to say. That he belonged with, or above, Mark Twain and Daniel Defoe.

I came from the Delta. I was a terrible student. And most importantly I had the advantage of sitting three times a week in a Southern Baptist church where our preacher placed drinking somewhere between prostituting and stabbing. One day a bar opened up a couple of blocks away on Cherry Street, and our congregation prayed that God would close its doors. When it burned to the ground a short time later, the owner complained to the authorities that the Baptists had hit him with a miracle, and he planned to see us in court. So I had sobriety on my side.

If William Faulkner could write, I figured, then so could I.

*   *   *

I wasn't sure how to get started, so for about a year I wrote poems in the white spaces on the backs of book jackets and napkins and failed math tests.

Everything changed, for better or worse, in my last year of school, when my friend Shea Hammond hit on the idea of a trip to New Orleans. Louisiana beckoned us and terrified us at the same time. When the preacher in Vicksburg needed to make a point about debauchery and bacchanalia, he would simply point west, across the Mississippi River, where even the children staggered around drunk. Parents in Vicksburg allowed their teenagers to roam free in the evenings, because unlike the cloven-footed people of Louisiana, our state required its citizens to reach the age of twenty-one before they could drink alcohol.

The sons and daughters of Vicksburg knew, though, that just across the river bridge there sat a tin shack with one window, where an old woman sold lidded cups of hard liquor to cars full of teens. I had only ever visited there once, by accident, in a car with braver friends. "Can I help y'all?" the old woman asked. To safeguard against drunk driving she distributed the cups with their straws still wrapped, and warned us to keep the lids unpunctured until we got home. The river bridge, luckily, had rails; later when I read *Inferno* I pictured Dante crossing the river Styx to find a drive-through daiquiri joint on the opposite bank. So making a trip down the river to New Orleans—the heart of sin itself—seemed like an almost impossible notion.

We were five: my friends Shea, Jerry, Greg, me, and a fellow named Jack. We left town on Friday, and as we made the short trip south to New Orleans it seemed strange to me that Shea, Jerry, Greg and I had lived our entire lives so close to a city so large, yet to my knowledge none of us had ever seen it. I didn't know Jack, and about the time we crossed the state line he said, "I've got to get back in the morning. If I miss work again I'm going to get fired."

I asked where he worked.

"At the newspaper," he said.

Like a spitting, sparking electrical wire his answer touched my brain and left me paralyzed for the duration of our ride. I had never conceived of the newspaper as a thing with physical origins. In my mind it had always simply existed, as distant and abstract as elephants or England. Not a place where locals worked.

We made our way to the French Quarter, searching for Bourbon Street. We gawked at the flesh swirling there, eddying in bars and nightclubs and cascading down from the balconies. The sound of trumpets and snares rippled from open doors. We had learned in school that the whole city lay below sea level, but now we could feel its wonderful lowdown nature, a sunken place where people pooled and collected like confetti in a gutter, all sparkle and stench, a hundred-proof mash flowing toward a drain we couldn't yet see. In the doorways men with unfamiliar accents shouted names of drinks as though they were accusations—Slippery Nipples! Hand Grenades!—but in the car Greg had explained the legendary properties of the only true New Orleans drink, called a Hurricane. It could so thoroughly obliterate a man that he might not remember drinking it at all, which we all agreed sounded like a fine time.

I secretly prayed that Hurricanes were a myth, but we found them immediately, and everywhere. As the group started to drink I slipped away, too scared to partake and too embarrassed to refuse. I wandered off Bourbon and was shocked to discover rows of homes with doors and flowerpots and trash cans just like real houses back in Mississippi; it had not occurred to me that anyone actually lived in the French Quarter. Near the cathedral square I saw a street called Pirate's Alley, and followed it. Midway down I passed a tall, yellow, and lovely row home bookstore. I stopped to peer in the window with an older couple. They were dressed up, and seemed merry. After a while the man said, "This was William Faulkner's house, you know."

"The writer?"

"That's why it's called Faulkner House."

Another revelation. I had imagined Faulkner as a sort of word farmer, digging up manuscripts from a plot of north Mississippi loam. But he lived here, too, in this beautiful home with wrought iron and hard wood and a garden across the street. He had come from just the other side of the Delta, yes. But he had left for a while. I looked up at his old home and imagined myself as its owner, sitting in a small third-floor library, overlooking a courtyard from a high-backed chair, setting aside a leather-bound volume to take up my pen. My imagination stopped there because whatever lay beyond the taking up of the pen remained a mystery. But if he could do it, so could I.

"The good artist believes that nobody is good enough to give him advice," Faulkner told *The Paris Review* in 1956. "He has supreme vanity. No matter how much he admires the old writer, he wants to beat him."

And now, standing on the slate pavers outside the great author's house, I felt an urgency, a compulsion, that I could not articulate.

* * *

In the early morning I found my friends in varying states of inebriation, scattered around the Quarter. The Hurricanes were starting to blow through and, surveying the aftermath, we discovered only a horror of chaos and destruction.

I remember anger flaring, a sort of self-righteous perturbation, as I helped them walk to the car, flop into it, and pick our way through the rubble toward home. As we climbed the river bridge I thought of the Book of Genesis and Lot's wife, who turned into a pillar of salt when she looked back at Sodom and Gomorrah, and I avoided the rear-view mirror. I felt angry at myself, because I hadn't shaken off my Southern Baptist fear and trembling, which now left me to coddle my suffering friends, including Jack, who didn't seem to care about his newspaper job, much less writing as an art, and now needed to hurry back so—

A small thought—I hesitate to call it a plan—settled in my mind. A vision.

The first wave of nausea hit them just outside the city, and I pulled the car off the road under an overpass. "No, no," I said. "Take your time. Just let it go."

We dallied there in the shade for a long while, cleaning up the mess in fastidious detail. I insisted on waiting for their nausea to fade, every last murmur of it, before we carried on again. Once we resumed, I drove with a cautiousness, a slowness, usually reserved for school buses and hearses. When the second wave came, I eased again to the side and this time rolled down the windows, refusing to go farther until the last wisp of noxious gastric fumes had passed into the landscape.

In the fog of recovery, someone mentioned an older girl he knew at Southern Miss, and how nice it might be to see her again. "Sounds good to me," I said, and so we drove home to Vicksburg by way of Hattiesburg, zagging across most of the state for the unassailable cause of meeting college girls.

By the time we arrived home I had stretched a three-hour drive into an epic day-long tour of lower Mississippi. The next day I awoke and put on my church jacket and tie. I drove downtown, praying, looking for a sign. And there it was: *The Vicksburg Post.*

Inside I found the office of editor Charlie Mitchell, and told him I'd like to be a writer. Did he have any job openings?

*　　*　　*

The next day I returned unsure what exactly my new job was. Would I work in sports or features? Comics? Obituaries? The editor—a soft-spoken man who taught college courses in his spare time—gave me a tour of the building, starting with a framed sheet of newsprint hanging in the lobby. It was dated December 1953, when a tornado savaged the city and the newspaper staff won a Pulitzer Prize for documenting it.

That sounded good. I remembered that Faulkner had picked up a Pulitzer along the way. Or maybe two.

Mr. Mitchell introduced me to Pat Cashman, the paper's owner. His father's father's father's father had started the paper on the heels of the reconstruction after the Civil War. For five generations they had hung onto it, fending off competitors and corporate suitors. As we talked Mr. Cashman led us through the complex of buildings, to a sort of warehouse where he kept his car collection. He was partial to British makes that I had seen in pictures at the library: Jaguar, Healey, Lotus, row after row. I felt the heat rise in my face, and my teenaged brain shouted orders to run and touch them all, claim them, lick their steering wheels, use them to find girls, no, *women*—

"Nice cars," I said.

Later, as we re-entered the main building, Mr. Cashman complimented my Sunday jacket. I pulled back one side of it and slid a hand into my pocket in a comfortable, cosmopolitan manner. "Thanks."

Back inside we walked straight through the newsroom, just a blur of clicking keyboards and paper coffee cups. The news poured from a television on a bracket near the ceiling. I had never seen a television anywhere but the living room floor, sunk into the carpet like an immovable electronic boulder, so this struck me as the strangest, most delightful placement imaginable, like a bathtub porch swing, or a rooftop four-post bed. But we carried on toward the rear of the building, into a cavernous room where no keyboards clicked and no television chattered. Instead a wisp of old music floated from a little clock radio.

"Ladies," Mr. Mitchell said, and then waved toward me. "Your new helper."

Two older ladies smiled back. One stood holding a pair of scissors and the other sat peering over a set of reading glasses. And my job, it turned out, involved two steps: pulling long strips of newspaper copy from a printer and feeding it into a waxing machine, then cutting the waxed copy into newspaper-shaped bits and sticking them onto a template.

I wore my jacket every day, and showed up on time. When the writers and editors came in to review their stories at deadline, I pestered them about words, about great authors and literary derring-do. I kept it up for months, until one day the sports editor offered me a chance to write stories for twenty-five dollars each. My job description would mostly consist of covering girls' parochial softball games and fetching canned chewing tobacco for the real writers. My heart leapt.

Since then—thanks to the kindness of those people at the *Vicksburg Post*—writing carried me to bigger papers, then magazines, to *National Geographic*; to exotic, dreary, dangerous, boring, deadly, hot, and dusty places. I've met fascinating, murderous, brilliant, deceptive, and courageous people, and three kinds of terrorists. I've been blindfolded, starved, and nearly blown up, in dozens of countries. I've been shot at in China, interrogated in Sudan, and watched the sunrise from the summit of Mount Sinai. I've ridden motorcycles, planes, helicopters, the fender of an ancient tractor, and once tumbled from a bareback horse that I could swear laughed as it ran away. In Tonga I swam down to the sea floor and clung to volcanic rock that cut like glass, so I could hear the humpback whales sing for just a moment longer. Words did all that for me.

Something remains undone, though. When Faulkner delivered his Nobel acceptance speech in 1950, he might as well have been describing the condition of young writers now. "Our tragedy today is a general and universal physical fear so long sustained by now that we can even bear it," he said. "There are no longer problems of the spirit. There is only the question: When will I be blown up? Because of this, the young man or woman writing today has forgotten the problems of the human heart in conflict with itself which alone can make good writing because only that is worth writing about, worth the agony and the sweat."

I still feel the urgency, the compulsion toward fiction, because I've never shaken the fear and trembling long enough to embrace supreme vanity and try to beat the old writer and the dead mule he rode in on. True stories will never touch the conflicts of the human heart. Only literature can.

So sometimes when I visit New Orleans I still stop at the yellow house on Pirate's Alley. And I still make plans to someday move into Faulkner's place.

My Shit Job

by *Daniel Wallace*

I was the first one there every morning, so they gave me the keys to the place. There were at least twenty-five different keys on the ring—a collection of keys almost too big to fit in the pocket of my jeans—but most of them were to locks that had died long ago: widower keys. I only used four of them—two keys for the front door and two for the back—but having them in my possession served, at least during the first part of that long summer, to remediate the hour I had to get there in order to use them: seven AM. This meant I had to wake up at 6:15, and I'd never had to get up that early before for anything. The keys made me feel special, though, important, powerful. I showed them to my friends, who also had jobs but, unlike me, did not have the *keys* to their jobs. By July I realized all the keys meant was that I could lock and unlock a couple of doors so the other guys who worked with me could sleep in a little later. But I didn't get that at first.

The keys weren't all. They sweetened the deal by giving me a title: *vet tech*. Titles are important. Titles can make even the worst jobs—of which my job was undoubtedly one—appear to be positions you might need a special degree or advanced training for: think *sales associate, team member, administrative assistant, retail representative*. The truth is that anyone with a euphemistic job title (sanitation engineer!) has to have a pretty sorry-ass job. And of all the sorry-assed jobs I could find, mine was the sorriest.

I was in charge of the shit.

Even as a vet tech—or veterinary technician to you—I occupied the lowest rung on the hypothetical ladder—hypothetical because at the vet there was no ladder. The jobs I had, the jobs all of us had— from the two actual veterinarians, to the groomers, to me—were not going to be changing. I was not going to become a groomer, the groomer was never going to become a vet. So maybe it would be better to say that as vet tech I was at the bottom of a very deep hole from which there was no escape.

*　　*　　*

I love dogs. So far I've had nine of them, at least (ten if you count the four-year-old German Shepherd I brought home from the pound one day without asking my parents: he went back to the pound the next day, after destroying the carpet in our basement). Here's a picture of one of my dogs, Orsin, who died of an aneurysm when he was only three:

Orsin

Having a dog is better than having a kid, I think, for lots of reasons, among them being that when dogs grow up they don't resent you for never taking them to Disneyland, and if your dog gets pregnant, which she probably will, you can always give the offspring away and never have to think about them again. I don't love cats, but I like them well enough, and I've had a few of them too, but never on purpose. My sister had a cat before she went off to college, and when she went off to college it became mine. Stray cats—the homeless—have appeared at my house occasionally over the years and a bowl of cream later they never leave. And you can't just send them on their way. You have to take them into your home and your heart and patiently wait until they die.

At Jusco's Animal Clinic, there was life and there was death but more than anything else there was shit. Shit was omnipresent. There was no end to the shit and there will never be an end to it: it's part of the holy cycle of life. But no one wants to be in charge of that part of the holy cycle. I was, though, from June to August, 1976.

Ah, the summer of '76! How easy it is for me to remember it. While the summers of '75 and '77 have faded so in my memory that they're virtually interchangeable (which is weird because I'm sure I lost my virginity during one of them), '76 stands out the way 1492 and 1776 stand out: as a momentous, life-changing time.

As I said, I would get to the clinic at seven. Opened the doors, turned on the lights. I straightened up the waiting room, which meant sweeping the floor and arranging the magazines—*Cat Fancy, Dog Fancy, Pet World, Newsweek*—into neat little piles on the faux-wood coffee table. I'd take out the trash. Then I'd head back to the room our customers were never allowed to see: the cages where their pets were kept. The adage about not wanting to see how your sausage is made applies here as well, but times ten: No one wants to see the caged squalor little Buster endures before my arrival. When I left the night before, the small, stainless-steel cage that was, temporarily, Buster's home was immaculate, shining like a diamond, the classifieds section of yesterday's newspaper lining the bottom of it, his water fresh, his food luscious and crunchy. By morning the newspaper would be soaked in urine, browned with crap, his water dish murky, his food scattered everywhere. And since many of the animals there were sick (some were just boarding), more often than not Buster would have had a bad case of diarrhea, or he may have thrown up, and he was probably lying there in it. This is what I did that summer, two to three times a day: I made it all go away.

As a vet tech, however, I had other responsibilities as well, and once I was done with the cages I fulfilled them.

*　　*　　*

The anal sacs, or glands, of a dog are located on either side of the sphincter, at about five and seven o'clock. The sacs contain the glands that secrete an oily substance normally expressed with the feces: it's the aroma of this secretion that lends a unique scent to every dog's stool, and accounts for the tradition of butt-sniffing, a behavior that recognizes this aroma as peculiar to the individual, a kind of fecal perfume. The sacs are normally about the size of a green pea, but when impacted can become the size of the grape (or perhaps some other fruit or vegetable). You know when a dog's anal sacs are impacted: this is when he scoots his butt across the carpet.

Dog and cat glands are vestigial, like an appendix. They don't do anything except collect secretions and become infected, so when they're brought in to the vet to be groomed or for a check-up, this is one of the services performed. The anal glands are squeezed, or—in vet tech terminology—*expressed*. How is this done? It's not as difficult as it sounds. You just put a finger on each side of the rectum, on the outside edges of the anal sacs, then press upwards and inwards, until a thick – I'm sure you can imagine—stomach-turning liquid oozes out. It looks a little like the resin in a pipe.

This is another one of the services I performed. And enemas, of course. But I'm not going to go into that.

*   *   *

My mother got me the job. I didn't know it at the time, but now I think she might have been having an affair with the veterinarian. I don't have any proof, but if a man ever did my mother a favor it was a good bet they were having an affair then or were going to have an affair later. Don't judge my mother: that's the way it was in the mid-'70s in Birmingham, Alabama. The town was a hotbed of swingers. Ask anyone.

*   *   *

My father told me about his first job. He told me about it a lot. It was hawking newspapers in the New York City subway system. He was nine years old.

Nine years old. When I was nine I spent most of my time watching cartoons and kicking pinecones in a circle around the cul-de-sac where we lived. My father didn't have a cul-de-sac when he was nine; he probably didn't know what one was. I was a lucky kid.

Later, my father told me why that first job was the best job he ever had, and why I should think the same way about mine. "The first job you get should be the *worst* job you get: it's what you do to learn what it is you never want to do again." That's how you know it's the best, he said: It's the job that's waiting for you at the bottom of the hill if you ever slip down climbing up it.

* * *

Our family cat died there of feline leukemia. I don't remember the cat's name, but it was small and black, and they put her in a little glass cage, like an incubator, and I saw her every day I came in to work. When she died I buried her in the grassy lot behind the vet in an unmarked grave. I may have cried a little doing it.

* * *

MOSBY

The veterinarian, Dr. Jusco, bred black and tan coon hounds. One day I came into work and there were six of the handsomest coon hound puppies you've ever seen sucking like crazy on their mother's numerous nipples. He let me buy one from him for $100, and I named him Mosby, after a general in the Civil War. He was my first dog. After a couple of months I took him to obedience school, which was held every Thursday evening from six o'clock to seven. He was a smart dog and did very well. The day before he was supposed to graduate I came home from school and he was gone, and I imagined the worst, as I usually do. This time I was right: I found him in the tall grass on the side road, dead. He'd been run over, and even though he was wearing a tag the killer didn't call us, though he had clearly taken the time to move him out of the street and into the weeds, where I was lucky to have found him. I don't know if lucky is the right word there. Anyway, I buried him in the backyard. This time I cried a lot. My mother cried even more, and the next day gave me a sympathy card with $100 in it. That was supposed to assuage my grief; it didn't. Fifteen years later I decided to dig him up, to see what his bones would look like, but I couldn't find the shallow grave where I'd buried him. Which was just as well.

* * *

Sad, lonely, miserable, sick, old, forgotten, abused, abandoned: these are the dogs I spent my days with. The vet is not a day spa: it's a hospital. It's a place to leave your dogs while you go do something your dog can't do with you—something human and fun. There were dogs that were spending weeks there, in those little stainless steel cages, while their owners vacationed in Europe. I hated those people. Their dogs didn't hate them, though. Their dogs pined for them. I think of a beautiful white Corgi who practically lived at the vet all summer long: all he wanted was to once again look in his master's eyes, feel his hand kneading the back of his neck, sleep at his feet. He lived in a state of constant forgiveness.

* * *

I worked in the back room with two black men. One of them was a man of normal size, nondescript but for the scar running the length of his forehead, as if he'd had brain surgery; the other was huge. Not fat, but mammoth. His arms were bigger than my legs. Rosey Grier: that's who he looked like. Nothing that happened in the back room with the dogs ever surprised him, nothing. His face never changed expression. He'd seen it all. I bet a dog could have exploded on the table in front of him and he would have said something like *I hate it when that happens.*

One day I remember he had to groom a Scottish Terrier who growled and barked and tried to bite him. He held the dog up in the air, by its neck, choking him until it took a shit right there on the table, which, of course, I cleaned up. Afterwards the dog behaved beautifully, and we were able to bathe it, shave it, and even give it a manicure.

* * *

These are some of the things I remember from my summer at Jusco's Animal Clinic. This and the pervading sense of loneliness and loss. My father was proud of me for sticking with the job for almost the entire summer, only quitting two weeks before school started to vacation down in Florida with my friends, where we drank and smoked pot and sizzled on the sand. I wasn't a writer then, of course; I was just a kid. I wouldn't even begin writing for another eight years, after my father fired me from his own company for not sufficiently committing myself to the enterprise: I had always held open the possibility that if business turned out not to be for me, I could leave. When he asked for my allegiance I couldn't give it, so he fired me, or, probably more accurately (since our relationship suffered from the schism for the rest of his life), he let me go.

After that I wrote and I wrote and I wrote. Over the course of the next ten years I wrote five novels and two short story collections, all of which remain unpublished due to absence of qualities we usually associate with good writing. They were bad—or so I thought, anyway.

The problem, it turned out, is that I didn't have any dogs in these books. Not a single one. I had a lot of people but none of them had dogs and this was just wrong. I think that's why *Big Fish* was finally published: not only did it have a dog in it, but an important dog with a big part: he bit off people's fingers.

Since then I've written three more novels, and all of them are packed with dogs. I'm writing a fifth now and this one has more dogs in it than the first four combined; in this book there are more dogs than people and they're magical. What's better than a magical dog? I don't know if any other books have been written with magical dogs in them, but I bet there have been; there's nothing new under the sun.

So, yes. I love dogs. But when you spend a summer with dozens and dozens of them, keeping them alive, really, and taking care that they get fed and their cages cleaned and before leaving for the day taking the long-term boarders out for a walk around the gravel parking lot, it becomes more than love. It becomes a thing that seeps deep into your skin, through the muscle and the bones; a metamorphosis occurs, and a knowledge is exchanged, and for a split second both of you can remember what happened 10,000 years back to when some lone wolf took that big evolutionary step and became the very first dog. You can see this dog waiting outside the camp where the savages were, watching them, hiding behind a stand of trees. Every day she had come closer, but she'd never been this close before. The savages had built a fire, and all of them— there must have been a dozen—gathered around it, warming their hands, cooking some prehistoric rabbit. She took another step and broke a twig, and one of them, a boy, heard it, turned.

And he saw her.

It had taken this dog a long time to become a dog, and her wolfish family had left her here, alone. The boy—who was thin as a stick, you could count each and every rib on this boy—he walked toward her. And then she took her first steps out of the forest. There was a moment then when both of them stopped, froze, knowing that what came next could change their lives forever. And while the rest of the savages watched, the boy held out his hand—something no one in the history of the world had ever done before—and the dog licked it. From that moment on she was his and he was hers. The boy turned to his family, strong and tall and happy. He had changed. Everyone could tell he had changed.

The first dog made the first man.

"What Thou Lovest Well..."

by Brad Watson

The first job I ever wanted, the one I wanted more than any job since, I never got. I was nine years old, and I wanted to work in the salvage shop at my Uncle Aubrey's used auto parts business. It was summer, and I was spending a week with Uncle Aubrey, my Aunt Marjory, their daughter my cousin, and my grandmother in the big house my grandfather built after World War II. The house was long and deep and cool, a vast space to a nine-year-old, and far too quiet during the day, even though my grandmother Mimi's housekeeper, Velma, worked at cooking all morning and afternoon. At the far end of the house, you wouldn't even hear Velma clanking pots, singing gospel, cackling to herself about something funny, spitting snuff, or complaining to my grandmother that she was in the way.

The salvage shop, Engell's Used Parts, was an old high-roofed, concrete block building that sat beside the highway and did a half-ass job of hiding from the road a large junkyard of wrecked and scavenged vehicles that had supplied the business since its beginnings. In the blazing white, hazy-sky heat of the Mississippi summer, stacked in long rows a few feet apart and extending a good forty yards deep and at least that wide, bristling with tall weedy grass and twined over with snaking kudzu vines, was a graveyard of rusting cars and pickups and heavy trucks dating from the earliest days of the internal combustion automobile engine. The rows of wrecks were stacked two, three, even four upon one another, some crushed but not quite flattened, most fully formed and often doorless, seatless husks, their brittle steering wheels and gearshift rods oddly naked in their quiet, baking interiors. It was like a ruined city built of oxidized automobile steel and rotting rubber tires, with narrow sandy lanes between the rusted husks, and you walked the lanes through air suffused with the smells of old, solidifying axle grease, leaked motor oil, the dusty-sweet smell of the decaying rubber, and the dry odor of disintegrating upholstery—a scent like the hulls of desiccated insects—from the occasional bench seat that had not been removed and sold.

The first day of my visit that summer, Aubrey made the mistake of taking me over to the shop for a visit. After that, every morning and noon for the next several days, I begged him as he got ready to go to work in the morning, and before he returned there after lunch. I begged him to let me go to work with him, to give me some kind of job, no matter how simple or insignificant: I would sweep the garage floors with a push broom or even a sage broom. Anything. I would fetch the men bottles of Coke and packages of Nabs. I would run down to the general store (oddly enough owned by another man named Aubrey Engell, who may not have been related, I think maybe he wasn't, at best distantly—so people called him "Little Aubrey," because he was skinny and quiet) to fetch them Nehis or Dr. Peppers or Orange Crush, cigarettes and cigars. Anything. To which he repeatedly, and placidly, replied, "No."

I *did* want to be paid, because it wouldn't be a real job if I wasn't paid something. I thought a dime a day would be fine. Anything. It was just an amount I threw out there, although a dime a day would've been pretty good at age nine. Mainly, though, it would be something to legitimize the effort, to make it a real job. I thought it would be the coolest thing in the world to get up and go to work, to push or sweep a broom around in the grime on the shoproom floor.

Also, I loved the shop, where Uncle Aubrey and his employees did their honorably hard and dirty work. The concrete block walls were chipped and grimy as in an old factory. The air was ripely raw and edgy with engine exhaust, the senses tilted nicely with the barely controlled effects of carbon monoxide poisoning.

The shop's façade was fort-like, tall and square, unpainted (or with paint so chipped and grimy, worn and infused with dust and the particulate detritus of engine exhaust, motor oil, and axle grease as to seem unpainted) concrete block. There was a small office in the front, just to the right of the work bay, behind which was a warehouse full of the most commonly requested used parts. The bay, with large double doors that stayed swung open all day during warm weather, might once have had a discernible oak plank or concrete floor, but in my memory is just red clay mixed with spilled oil, grease, and gasoline so that over the years it had packed into a hard, slick black-orange surface that was unlike any other blend of natural and manmade materials on the earth. My uncle and his help could usually be found leaning into the maws of wrecked vehicles, evaluating and extracting the usable parts, cursing and grunting as they hoisted an engine, the manual winch and chain clanking and groaning, in order to strip the motor down to its essential self, clean it, and resell it to mechanic shops or people who rebuilt used engines for a living. There was an old Coca-Cola machine against the bay's south wall, the kind from which you could extract a 6 ½ ounce bottle of Coke by inserting a nickel and pushing down the little metal handle that released the bottle into the machine's chute. I have a memory of being given a nickel and allowed to purchase the occasional bottle, and how cold and delicious and bubbly it was. It was a small but gratifying mechanical pleasure to operate the machine, to put in the nickel and turn the little lever that sent the cold Co-Cola (as it was called by most grownups in that time and place) bumbling down the chute into the rectangular opening where it thumped to a stop, green glass glistening and waiting for your hand. And a memory of my uncle's father, whom everyone called Papa Fuel—not because of his business but because that was his name, Fuel Engell—sitting on an upended empty wooden Coca-Cola case, rolling and smoking Prince Albert tobacco, sipping from one of those little green bottles. Papa Fuel wore relatively clean clothing (since he did little labor at the shop anymore, being mostly an advisor— he had founded the business in the 1930s I think) that hung on his small, sparse frame as if he were carved and nailed together of sapling trunks and twined twigs, although he had a pleasant, ruddy, jowled face beneath the brim of a weathered old fedora. He had a sweet, soft, muttering voice that contrasted but could always be heard amidst the loud, hard-edged voices of the younger men. The smells of the bay were those of the axle grease, blackened motor oil, gasoline fumes, Prince Albert cigarette smoke, and the unmistakable particular pungent odor of perspiration from hard-working white men in the bay-shaded summer heat. (I knew the particular and unmistakable pungent odor of hard-working black men from visiting my maternal uncle's farm in the country, but that is in another story.) The light came from the open bay doors and a bank of heavy glass windows high up on the south and west walls, and it gave the bay a soft, natural light that needed aid only from a bulb hung from an open car or truck's hood when the men were bent deep in to work on the motor, or beneath the vehicle on a flat wooden dolly with the same bulb, inspecting or extracting transmissions, clutches, suspension parts or the like, the cantilevered metal dolly wheels squisselling as the man moved about beneath this car or that.

I wanted to be a part of this place, this world of work, this specific work, more than anything I had ever wanted in my brief life. I wanted entrance into the world of men, that being the world of worthy engagement, extracting workable and valuable parts from a sophisticated machine and hauling its eviscerated frame out back into the yard. It was important, to do work, to be paid for it, to have a purpose. As opposed to being a child to whom no one paid any real attention, for whom nothing was truly important, for whom the entire world was at best a mirror image of reality, where the essential qualities of understanding were reversed: responsibility was mere responsiveness to command; duty was the dull and stultified unremunerated chore; work was only play.

But my Uncle Aubrey placidly, intractably, refused.

He was a stout man, not tall, a little swarthy, with a husky voice and a rapid way of speaking that occasionally revealed itself to harbor an old stutter, a stutter so accommodated at this point that it was merely the occasional repetition of a first syllable that easily passed as simply idiosyncratic speech. He kept his dark hair in something between a flat-top and a crew cut, but his head was a good shape, slightly rounded, a good head for that hairstyle—although hair, or vanity in general, wasn't something that mattered much to him one way or another. He wore green cotton khaki work pants and shirts and low-cut work shoes, and when he walked across the dirt and gravel road separating shop and house for lunch, his hands and the skin beneath his fingernails would be black with engine grime. He would stand at the kitchen sink and sprinkle a palmful of Tide detergent into one hand and scrub himself clean up to the elbows. I loved the combined smells of the iron-rich well water, Tide, and the grease on his hands. I could smell it all on him when he dried them and came over to the dinner table to join us there, waiting, so he could mutter the hoarse, rapid syllables of a perfunctory grace and we could begin to eat.

I was very fond of him, as was my father, who called him "Colonel," though he'd been just a corporal, I think, as an aircraft mechanic in World War II. I never knew how that got started. Maybe it was just a Southern thing, or just as a joke about the uniform and a gesture of respect and familiarity. Everyone seemed to like Aubrey, in fact. He seemed to like people, he liked to banter, bullshit, and laugh. I was too young to know, but I imagine that if he was in a difficult situation, someone wanting too much for a car or a part, someone wanting to pay less for one, someone demanding something from him he couldn't reasonably give, then he would talk to them. He would tell them, straight-out, that here was the situation, he had this much money in the car, or the part, and he had to get this much for it or he was working for nothing, and then he would say, with genuine goodwill and humor in his voice, You see what I'm saying? Hell, I can't do it!" But the person usually, I suspect, got a good deal. Engell's Used Parts didn't seem to grow or prosper until Aubrey's son, my cousin

Mike, took over the business, brought in computers, erected a new, aluminum-sided building around the grimed-up womb of the old, got onto more parts networks, expanded the operation and modernized it, and started making some decent money out of it. But I was fascinated with the business before all that, when it was still the place Papa Fuel started up between the wars: a junkyard shop from which used car parts were sold, and behind which sat the junkyard, when it was still okay and honorable to call it just that, a junkyard, instead of whatever euphemistic sobriquet may be applied today when everyone seems sensitive to plain-spoken monikers, like janitor ("custodian") or garbage man ("sanitation engineer") or mechanic (think "automotive technician").

My first real jobs would turn out to be mostly construction, tire changer, wood shop, tender at a dive beer-in-the-can bar. I was working from some lingering, diluted ethic from the '60s, where the Man was the enemy, and the Man wore a suit. Before I moved to Wyoming and gave in to a lifelong desire to wear cowboy boots, my favorite shoes were lace-up work boots or Wellingtons. I still can hardly bear to wear any pants but jeans. I buy all my shirts second-hand, broken in, faded, as if worked in or at least lived hard in. I don't shave. I don't brush or comb my hair. It may have come from a '60s sensibility when I was in my teens. But something was there earlier on, and it came from Engell's Used Parts, that world. In high school, I begged to enroll in Auto Shop, but was turned away. I was on the college prep track, they informed me, though I hadn't known that. Must have been something my parents set up, behind my inattentive and lazy teenage back. Here in Laramie, there's a famous technical school, Wyotech, where young men and women spend up to two years and $30,000 in one of the most rigorous, comprehensive "automobile technical" training programs in the country. Don't think I haven't thought about taking a few months off from being a blue-collar dressing professor, dropping $7,500 on those guys, and learning every damn thing there is to learn about an automobile engine (oddly, they make everyone dress neatly, uniformly, and shave every day—it's kind of militaristic). I know people who've taught themselves to fix cars, but the truth is

I'm a terrible autodidact when it comes to machines. And I want to know. I still want to know. I still want a piece of it. It's a matter of very old pride, hanging on.

In family terms, this is ironic. My paternal great-grandfather, grandfather (he of the house I visited those summers)—all the Watson men—were committed white-collar risers. Philosophically committed to the dignity and sensibility and *higher calling* of white-collar work, usually in sales of some kind. Which from the *cradle* I felt was the most demeaning work I could do. I tried it, several times: photograph specials, fire alarms, newspaper ads, encyclopedias, others I forget or don't care to remember. I even belonged to the marketing club in high school. But I hated it, and I couldn't do it. My father said, "You have to believe in your product." Easy for you, I thought: You sell whiskey. How am I to "believe" in a bad studio portrait scam or a classified ad?

So it was also ironic that after my grandfather died, and my Uncle Aubrey's family moved into his big house to live with and take care of my grandmother, the junkyard began to spill over into the back property of my grandfather's house, the home with the three-car garage, because my grandfather was such a lover of *new* automobiles. He was a man who always had a new car, who somehow paid cash for them, and traded them in when they lost their newness—usually every year. He was a man for whom a new car signified status, and he often gave new cars not only to his wife, my grandmother, but also to young women who worked in his "ladies' shoe store" (but that is another story.) That the home of this white-collar businessman who revered the spanking new fancy automobile was gradually overrun—in its backlot which once was a long green lawn bordered by pasture and a small grove of apple trees—by a rabble of dilapidated junkers seemed to say something about the age of the automobile itself, about the hopes we invested in it, the importance we placed upon it as the *engine* (if you'll forgive me) of our commercial and private lives. Between the advent of the automobile and its demonization as an ozone-destroying, demoralizing, lazificationist symbol of modern industrial corruption, the beast beneath our present ecological disaster in the Gulf, there was the oddly ugly-beautiful purgatory of Engell's Used Parts.

There could not have been two men who more evenly and neatly personified the two main types of modern man in the middle of the twentieth century. Uncle Aubrey had served in World War II as an Army Air Force mechanic, returned home to work in his father's used parts business, marry his old sweetheart who lived across the road from the shop, dressed in shop clothes that resembled Army fatigues as much as anything, kept his hair clipped in a utilitarian cut that was barely even a flat-top, and seemed perfectly contented to live out his days as a businessman/shop mechanic, uninterested in expansion or modernization, whose only leisure activities involved working on the three adjoining small lakes owned by his parents, down the highway, constructing by himself with dozer and shade tree plumbing a sand-bottom, artesian spring-fed pond for a swimming hole for the children.

On the other hand, as I've said, my grandfather had long before eschewed anything but white-collar endeavors. He never served in the military. He started up an ice plant just after World War I, but never took another job that required him to perform physical labor. I'm not saying he was a dandy; he was one tough SOB and an outdoorsman who loved hunting and fishing, cut his own firewood, rode horses, was quick-tempered and prone to fistfights in public, downtown, often because of some insult unwisely let loose inside his shoe store. He once nearly strangled another man with that man's own necktie. But he believed in the middle class and laid claim to his stake in it.

Because my grandfather died before I was born, and my father ran the shoe store but didn't take me down there much at that age, the closest and most tangible sense of work I had was physical: the man who cut our yard and trimmed the shrubbery, sweating like a galley slave in the summer heat and smelling appropriately; the black women who worked as maids (we were *lower*-middle class white people, but maids were affordable then for reasons well known to just about everybody then and now), washing and ironing and mopping and cooking and flopping down into lawn chairs outside in the shade to rest when there was time to do it. I saw them work. I did not see my father work, nor my mother work after she went to work at a doctor's clinic. I did see Aubrey and his employees work, and like most boys I loved cars, and wanted to know how they worked, and so the job I wanted was in Aubrey's junkyard garage. Long before I had any sense of some idealized post-hippie version of the blue-collar life.

But it simply was not to be. I believe I even broke down into tears once or twice, hoping that would warm what seemed to me at the moment his icy heart (only in this case, in my experience—he was simply being pragmatic, because you can't let a dreamy kind of nine-year-old kid hang around a bunch of profane men working all day with potentially dangerous machines among toxic materials) concerning my pleas for employment. For a real job. But he would not give it. I spent my week or two out there, sometimes playing with my older cousin April when she had time and would let me, mostly wandering around in the cool rooms of the big house, bored and daydreaming, fingering musical gibberish on the grand piano or the electric organ. Finally, toward the end of my stay, Aubrey did let me help him mow the grass on the big house's two-acre property. Because the lot was so big, he had purchased an early version of a riding mower that resembled most remarkably a miniature version of the earliest, pyramidal Sherman tanks. He sat me on his lap and let me steer as we rode around and around, and back and forth, mowing the lawn. I can't say it wasn't a thrill, because of the machine and the noise and the excitement of handling the bar-like steering mechanism.

But it wasn't a real job. Even I knew that. It was a man amusing a boy by letting him think he was helping to do a job. It was a kind thing to do. But it wasn't what I'd really wanted. I couldn't get paid for it. I couldn't swagger around, proud of having done it. I couldn't feel as if I had entered into the world of men. I was a child, and there was nothing I could do about that.

These are my memories of that brief period of time and that place in it. My cousins may remember better, or just different. None of my memories is anything but fond. My grandmother, uncle, and aunt are long gone. My cousins and I are no longer, as they say, in touch. The business is still there, almost unrecognizable to me from the road. I don't know if the junkyard out back has been cleaned out or updated with stacks and rows of newer old cars and trucks. The old house I so loved is still there, and has been kept up, although someone cut down the towering water oaks and the magnolia near the road.

I did eventually get some real work out of that nice old place. I used the big house as a main character's house in my novel, *The Heaven of Mercury*, and some anecdotes I recalled my grandmother telling, and memories of her relationship with her housekeeper, Velma. The place became one of the most deeply imbedded rooms in my memory, informing imagination. Hanging around the shop, watching the men work on cars and engines, all the while telling stories on local characters conducting themselves in ways either honorably or disgracefully humorous or tragic—there is something to be said for the combination of oral storytelling with the breakdown and rebuilding of complex machines having some value for a boy who would become a storyteller who worked building stories on the page. I was given work. It was just work I wouldn't recognize as work until a long time later, after my interests and fascinations had turned to things less concrete, more abstract, in a sense—but in a sense not.

In the evenings when I lay in bed there, the swinging sussurant breeze of a heavy black oscillating fan calmed my frustrated mind, and the slapping sound of the tires of cars quietly whooshing by on the concrete slab highway at the far end of the long water oak-shaded front lawn seemed as right and regular as the coming and passing of some soothing thought or vague but pleasant memory. I didn't get what I wanted right then, but in the evenings all seemed right with the world. And more than I could really know or understand, it was.

So, You Want to Play
Some <u>Football</u>?

by Steve Yarbrough

Though you would not know it from looking at me today, there was a time when I carried 220 pounds on my six-foot, one-inch frame but had only a thirty-two inch waist. This period coincided with my last fall in high school, when—for a few glorious weeks—I was that prized species, "the sought-after athlete." Among the football schools that came calling were Tennessee, Ole Miss, Mississippi State, South Carolina and Southern Mississippi. In the end, none of them except Southern offered me a scholarship. I was an offensive lineman, and all they had to do was take one look at me in the flesh, as opposed to seeing me in a game film, to ascertain that the height and weight listed on my high school's game program—6'3", 235—represented a case of very wishful thinking. I'm relatively small-boned, and they must have figured that I was as big as I could be without becoming fat. By the time Southern made an offer, I'd already panicked and committed to play at a small Division II school within easy driving distance of my home in Indianola, Mississippi.

The two years I spent on that campus were, all things considered, the most difficult of my life. I say this with the full understanding that my life, in the main, has been incredibly easy. My wife and I and both of our daughters are healthy, and for almost twenty years now we've had more than enough money to live comfortably, and have been able to send our kids to good schools from which they will emerge debt-free. I've got a wonderful job in Boston at Emerson College, and I've been with the same great editor and publisher for more than a decade. In other words, it's been a long time since I got blindsided.

The years at that little Division II school were difficult, in large part, because even though I knew college athletes would be bigger, faster, and stronger than those I'd previously competed against, I foolishly assumed that the game I had enjoyed playing in high school and the one I'd play in college were, in essence, the same. In fact, college football is a business, and the players are all employees. Being a scholarship athlete was the first job I held as an adult, and it was far and away the worst.

*　　*　　*

It's been thirty-three years since I last saw the man I will henceforth refer to simply as "Coach," but I think about him every few days. When I met him, he must have been around forty years old. He was about my height, and he probably weighed no more than 190. He had a long, slack jaw that left him looking angry even on those rare occasions when he wasn't.

I made a recruiting trip to his campus fairly late in my senior season, when I had begun to fear that nobody would offer me a scholarship. Earlier, Ole Miss had informed me through the headmaster at my school that they were ready to make an offer; then the legendary Jake Gibbs came to see me play, in a game against North Sunflower Academy, and word filtered back to me, through one of my former high school coaches, that Gibbs was unimpressed. I'd flown up to Knoxville and stayed in a luxury hotel, and while there I'd had a private conference with Vols' coach Bill Battle; he was both personable and complimentary, but the entire time I was sitting across the desk from him I sensed that I was being downsized. So I was desperate when I walked into Coach's inner sanctum.

His office didn't look too much like the ones I'd seen at Ole Miss or Tennessee. If I recall correctly, the floor was bare concrete, and piles of discarded shoulder pads, helmets, and cleats were scattered about. A Styrofoam cup stood on his desk, and before rising and offering me his hand, he shot a stream of tobacco juice into it. "So," he said, "you want to play some *football?*"

"Yes, sir."

He grunted, we both sat down, and for the longest time he gazed out the window. After a while he turned back to me and asked, "Who all's been looking at you?"

I suspected, at the time, that it was probably not quite kosher for him to pose that question, but by then I knew that college football programs treated "the rules" as if they were made of Spandex. At Ole Miss, the athletic director had asked me to stand against a wall on which marks mysteriously appeared at one-inch intervals. At Tennessee, which was placed on probation a few years later, I was told that I could just sign for whatever I wanted at the hotel where I was staying, so I proceeded to rack up a hefty bar tab. Despite some misgivings, I answered Coach truthfully, figuring that if worse came to worst and nobody else made me an offer, it could only accrue to my advantage for him to know that larger schools had at least considered me.

After he heard my reply, a faint smile crossed his face. "What you got to do," he said, "is ask yourself if you can play at them places. You come in here saying you wanted to play some *football.* To do that, you got to be on the field. You can't play football riding the bench or perched in the stands wearing *street* clothes."

As I sat there trying to figure out an appropriate response, one of his assistants, a scholarly looking little man, stuck his head in and said, "Coach, it's less than an hour to kickoff."

He stood, so I did, too. "We'll keep an *eye* on you," he said.

I don't recall whether his team won that night or not, but I do know that as I watched the game unfold, I was wishing them only the worst luck. I drove back home that night in despair, hoping against hope that I'd receive an offer elsewhere. Though I was not religious, I think I probably even prayed over it. By the time my prayer was answered, I'd already signed on the dotted line.

STEVE YARBROUGH

* * *

I didn't just want the scholarship because I loved the game of football. I also wanted it because I did not know how I would go to college without it. My father, at that time in his life, might have been earning eight thousand dollars a year. Though he could not afford to send me to a private high school, he had done it, for the same reason that almost every other white parent in the Mississippi Delta did it: They all feared the effects of integration. Thus, a string of "segregation academies" had sprung up all over Mississippi, and by the time my dad got through paying for nine years at one of those, he had nothing left. I accepted it as a given that you couldn't go very far in life without a college degree, but I'd spent so much time lifting weights and focusing on football that my grades, while not atrocious, were nowhere near good enough for an academic scholarship.

I'm not sure the general public knows or cares just how poor many college athletes, including some of the best ones, really are. On my college team, I played with a center from another small Delta town, a young African American whom I'll call Robert. He weighed only 195 pounds, but he was jet-quick and had tremendous upper-body strength. One of the nicest guys I've ever known, he could not even afford a pair of tennis shoes, so during our winter workouts (which I'm guessing were probably illegal, since Coach made them mandatory, rather than voluntary), Robert ran sprints and agility drills in the only pair of street shoes he owned.

When I showed up for two-a-days my first year, there were only a few freshmen on scholarship. The rest of the guys in the locker room where all of us newbies dressed were there to try out, in hopes that Coach would think highly enough of them to help them acquire financial aid, through some mysterious process that I never fully understood. One such guy—a redhead with a sunny disposition, whose name I believe was Buddy—was married and in his late twenties or early thirties. As we dressed before our first practice, he cheerfully admitted that he knew next to nothing about football and hadn't played it since junior high. But he had

230

a couple of kids and even though he worked full time at a gas station, he couldn't go to school without some help, he said, so he meant to give it his best shot and see if anything came though.

For that first practice, all of us freshmen wore red jerseys, though red was not one of the team's colors. Coach was known for "redshirting" most of his incoming class, in order to give them an extra year to mature and also so they could be used as fodder for the starting teams. Thus, I found myself lined up at left defensive tackle, in a five-two defense, playing opposite a senior offensive lineman whom I will refer to as Chuck. He came from somewhere down in south Mississippi. He wore mutton-chop sideburns and cowboy boots and kept a pickup parked outside the athletic dorm. He was a little bigger than I was, somewhere in the neighborhood of 235 pounds, prohibitively tiny for a lineman at any level these days but by no means unusual back then in Division II.

On the first series the starting offense lined up, the backs set in an I. The quarterback called signals and, when the ball was snapped, he spun and handed off to the tailback. It was a straight-ahead run—what we called a "blast" play, since the fullback would isolate on the linebacker and attempt to blow him out of the hole.

I didn't know that Chuck was being hyped for all-conference that year, and if I had, it would not have impressed me. I was not prepared to be impressed by anyone on that team. I had expected to be playing someplace better and figured that while it was a mistake for me to be there, all the other guys were right where they belonged. But when Chuck slammed into me, I realized instantly that he was at least as strong as I was, if not stronger. Rather than shedding his block, as I'd been able to do back in high school on the rare occasions when I played defense, I could only manage a stalemate.

A stalemate, however, was enough to make the tailback veer outside, where the kid playing defensive end wrapped him up. It was also enough to draw Coach's attention. He strode over and, as the offense headed back to the huddle, bellowed, "Chuck!"

My opponent turned just in time to see Coach spit brown liquid on the ground. All the other coaches carried their cups during practice, but Coach himself sometimes didn't. Consequently, I would learn that it was not unusual to find yourself lying face-down in a puddle of spit, only a facemask between you and a little taste of North Carolina. "Yes, sir?" Chuck said, his cheeks suddenly bright red.

Coach stuck one long arm out in my direction. "What you mean, letting that little private school *dick* plug the hole like that?"

Chuck didn't answer. Those of us who didn't already know it would learn that on the practice field and in the locker room, Coach only posed rhetorical questions. You answered at your own peril.

Coach said, "Goddamn. Maybe all them big schools that didn't *want* him was making a mistake."

When the offense lined up again, I was feeling sorry for Chuck. I'd seen him around the dorm over the last couple of days, and he seemed like one of the friendlier guys. I remember that as I got down in my three-point stance, I hoped the play would be run to the other side, so that whatever happened between us would go unnoticed. I didn't want him to be insulted again.

Before I explain what happened next, I have to say something about the coaches I played for in high school. Though they relentlessly pushed us to excel and we lost only two games in three years and won a state championship, they also stressed the importance of good sportsmanship. One of them—a deeply religious man who never raised his voice and taught the defensive linemen such fine points as the importance of watching an opponent's fingertips to see how much pressure he was putting on them, since that could indicate whether he was going to fire out or set up to pass block—eventually gave up coaching to earn a Master's in applied math, after which he went to work as director of operations for a large Jackson bank. Another, whose knowledge of American history was vast, would coach at a number of Division I schools before moving on to the NFL, where he has earned three Super Bowl rings. They were fine coaches, smart, well-educated men, and they told us that we were representing not just ourselves but our town and our parents. One precept inculcated in us from day one was that you always play hard but you play by the rules. Getting flagged for unsportsmanlike conduct would have meant suspension from the team. Fighting one of your own teammates at practice would have been unthinkable.

Chuck crouched in his stance. The quarterback called signals and, after taking the snap, spun out to the opposite side and quick-pitched to the tailback. Just as I started to slide to my right in pursuit, something that felt like a sledgehammer smashed into my face, right under the chin. Then the wind whooshed out of me as Chuck buried his other fist in my solar plexus.

I think I was on my knees, though I can't really say, for I lost a little bit of my life. Whether it was a couple of minutes, or only a few seconds, I will never know for sure. Nor did I know that when I finally rose, to stand gasping on wobbly legs, I was losing something else—namely, Coach's respect. The only appropriate response, in his eyes and in the eyes of most, though not all, of my teammates, would have been for me to run after Chuck, who was just bending over in the huddle, and attack him while he had his back turned.

I became aware that Coach was standing nearby, observing me. "Welcome to college football, Yarbrough," he said.

By the end of two-a-days, I was black and blue all over. Every time I managed to stand my ground against Chuck, I'd pay for it on the next play, when I'd take a forearm under the chin, a punch in the gut, a knee in the nuts. To compensate, I began to line up a few inches offside, in an effort to make contact before he got his arms up. Though his strength, as I have said, was at least equal to mine, if not greater, he wasn't very quick and didn't move that well, and if I'd wanted to, I think I could have beaten him on almost every pass play. What kept me from doing that was the knowledge that if I did get by him, my back would be exposed, and the few times that happened he slammed into me from behind after the whistle had blown, driving me to the ground and rooting around on top of me until the assistants pulled him off.

In time, somewhere around the middle of October, I would learn to behave like virtually everybody else on that team. If someone hit me late or took a swing at me, I and whoever had done it would roll around on the ground for thirty or forty seconds, pummeling each other's helmets and shoulder pads and doing no damage except for skinning our own knuckles. Eventually, a couple of assistants would pull us apart, and practice would resume as if nothing untoward had happened.

In the Ur-world of Coach, instant retaliation was a prized commodity. That may have had something to do with the high number of penalties we'd draw that season for unsportsmanlike conduct.

*   *   *

The beginning of school would mean a single afternoon practice, with full-speed hitting only on Tuesdays and Wednesdays, so I was immensely grateful when Coach called us all together on the last afternoon of pre-season workouts. I assumed things would get a little easier, that I'd survived the worst. Twenty or thirty guys, including Buddy, had already disappeared—some because Coach told them he couldn't help them with financial aid, others because they couldn't take the pounding, the insults, or the torturous wind sprints we ran at the end of each practice, in heat that sometimes exceeded 100 degrees. I myself had even thought of quitting. "Quit," however, was an ugly word, and in my case, it might spell the end of college; the most I could hope for would be to go get a job at a gas station, like Buddy, or try to get on as a tractor driver somewhere and see if I could save enough over a few years to re-enroll.

"Men," Coach said, "tomorrow morning y'all'll register for *classes*." All of us had taken a knee, forming a ragged circle with him in the middle and the assistants off to one side. "Now some of these courses like English composition and *mathematics* are hard. And some of y'all are *dumb* sons of bitches." That produced a loud laugh from most of my teammates. Coach actually grinned, one of only a handful of times I saw him do that. "Now if your ass is *smart* enough to know you not smart, what I recommend doing is getting over yonder to see Coach and let him *hep* you with your schedule. You got to pass three classes a semester to stay *eligible*, and you can't make up but six units in summer school." He switched the topic then, talking about our opening game, and after he dismissed us, the vast majority of my teammates lined up before the designated assistant coach to make an appointment with him to get their course schedules filled out. Most of them would take a stream of classes like "Fundamentals of Coaching Football," "Fundamentals of Coaching Basketball" and so on. A great many would make it all the way to their final semester and discover they still hadn't passed more than a handful of basic degree requirements. We were primarily there to do a job, not to receive an education.

I was one of the few who didn't line up to get the assistant coach's help. But as I turned toward the locker room, I heard Coach holler, "Yarbrough, I need to have a *word* with you."

Rumor had it that sometimes, if Coach decided you didn't fit into his plans, he would strip you of your scholarship. I feared that might be about to happen. I imagined the sense of loss I would experience in my hometown, where everybody who'd hailed me as one of the best players our school had ever produced would ignore me when I walked down the street. In fact, that was precisely what did happen when I finally quit and, after earning a few thousand dollars working my tail off stocking groceries, transferred to another school to study literature. Almost everybody forgot who I was until I began to publish novels. Then they learned my name again and began to show up at various bookstores, where they waited in line to get their copies signed.

That day, to my surprise, Coach put his hand on my shoulder. I'd seen him cuff guys upside the head after they blew an assignment, but he'd never touched me until now, and he did it in a surprisingly gentle manner, nudging me away from the crowd seeking help with their schedules. "Son," he said quietly, "you been dragging since you got here, and if you're not careful, you're not gonna get invited back. I don't know how bad you *want* to be here. You don't look to me like you want to play football. Ain't no law says everybody's got to."

I swallowed hard, and all these years later, when I have about as much security as anyone who began life like I did could ever hope for, it shames me to recall this encounter. On the verge of tears, in a voice that could only be called whiny, I said, "I want to play, Coach."

"Well," he said, "I don't believe you got what it takes. If somebody did to me what Chuck's been doing to you, I'd take a two-by-four to him. I had my doubts about you on the front end. That ain't to say there's not something else in the world you may prove to be real good at."

There's an infinitive phrase Southerners of my generation used to employ, to describe what happened when one was sent slinking ignominiously away: *to be run off*. A minister might get run off for having an affair with a member of his congregation, a cashier might get run off for stealing spare change, and a football coach might get run off for losing too many games. I said, "You're not going to run me off."

If you'd applied a layer of lacquer to his face, it could not have looked any harder than it did in that moment. "I'm gonna do my dead-level *best* to run your ass off," he said before he turned and walked away.

* * *

What his best would consist of, I could only imagine. But he didn't leave me wondering long. That evening, as I sat at a table in the athletic cafeteria with a couple other freshmen who'd fallen into disfavor, his gaze lit on me—he'd just left the serving line and was carrying his tray. We were having chicken fried steak that night, and I had a good-sized piece of it on my plate, along with a mound of mashed potatoes and gravy, some stewed carrots, a piece of cornbread and for dessert, on a smaller plate, a slab of apple pie. Some guys ate a lot more.

He walked over to our table and, for what seemed like five minutes but was probably just a few seconds, stood looking at my dinner. The cafeteria had gotten very quiet. "Yarbrough," he said, "I been watching what you eat. You love them fucking *'taters*. You need to stay away from that shit. You don't have but one *asshole*, and everything that goes in your mouth has got to come out it, and right now there's a logjam. That's why you move in slow *motion*."

To the credit of my teammates, only three or four of whom I remember with any fondness, nobody laughed. Coach walked on past and took a space at a table with two assistants. My cheeks on fire, I sat there for a few more seconds, then got up and carried my tray to the window where we returned our dishes.

The mind-fucking continued the following day. After I ran the first windsprint, Coach called a halt to the proceedings. "Yarbrough," he said, "I'm tired of your complaining, telling everybody we ain't good enough for you."

"I haven't been complaining," I said. Big mistake.

"The hell you haven't. You been complaining about our *food*, saying it don't *taste* good. Been complaining about our *girls*, saying they ain't *purty*. I reckon you think you belong up at Ole Miss. Well, far as I'm concerned, if they want you, they can have you." Then he blew the whistle, and we ran some more.

It was one thing after another. He accused me of sneaking out of the dorm after curfew. He said my hair was too long, that it made me look like a girl, and he ordered me to go have it cut by his own personal barber. He made fun of me, calling me "professor," when he saw me sitting on a bench in the quad reading a Walker Percy novel. This in turn led one of my teammates to post a "poem" on the door to my room:

> *Roses are red.*
> *Violets are blue.*
> *I love to read.*
> *Do you?*

Coach directed that I be assigned a new roommate, a student trainer whose job was evidently to let him know if I made any misstep, like sleeping late and missing class, criticizing him or any of the other coaches, failing to make my bed properly or vacuum the carpet. A few times I could tell that the "spy" had gone through my desk, opening letters and looking through them for any incriminating evidence. Apparently, nothing turned up, because after a few weeks, he was moved to yet another player's room, and I was paired with the second-team kicker, one of the few guys on the team that I liked.

Only two things kept my life from becoming absolute hell. First of all, there was another freshman he held in equally low esteem—a running back from east Mississippi who today is an extremely successful physician—and his desire to give him equal time necessarily distracted some of his attention from me. (He once decreed that for an entire practice, this young man would carry the ball on every single play against the first-team defense. When the session ended, he could hardly walk, and when I tried to talk to him, all he could say was "Huh?") Secondly, and more importantly, our season began to go badly awry: though expected to be the top team in the conference, we started losing games, which had the effect of diluting his anger, forcing him to spread it around. While none of us knew it at the time, he was under a fair amount of pressure himself. The previous head coach, who'd amassed a huge number of wins during his career, was the athletic director, and he could not have been happy with what he saw on the field. By the mid-point of the season, Coach was leaving me alone, directing his ire at the starters, calling them dicks, questioning their urge to win and threatening them, as he had once threatened me.

I recall walking off the practice field one day near the end of the season and seeing him trudge toward me. For the last several minutes he'd stood off to one side with the school president and the athletic director. I have no idea what they were talking about, but as we neared each other, Coach's face was unusually drawn, and he had his head down. For whatever reason, he looked up just as I passed and, for perhaps the only time during the two years I knew him, he called me by my first name. "Hey, Steve," he said.

I don't know what prompted him to greet me that way. Nor can I identify the particular form of madness that made me reply as I did. For the better part of three months, I'd done everything I could to avoid him, even skipping dinner many days since it was the one meal he always ate with the team. "Hey, Coach," I said. "I'm still here."

My response stopped him dead. Jesus Christ, I thought, why did I do that?

"Yeah," he finally said, "I know you are." Then he walked on by.

*　*　*

I lasted one more year. Coach himself survived for two.

In spring practice I was moved to right offensive tackle—Chuck's old position—where I performed well enough to win an occasional word of praise, despite having lost close to twenty pounds the previous fall, partly because of all those skipped meals. I did not expect to start the following season, but coming out of spring I was on the second team.

Coach never called me a dick again, nor did he give me the impression that he still hoped to run me off. When two-a-days rolled around, bringing a new group of freshmen, he directed his wrath at an overweight scholarship fullback. He called him various names—fat-ass being a favorite—and he made it plain that he wanted the scholarship back. It would make me feel a lot better about the young man I was if I could tell you that I aligned myself with the unfortunate freshman, gave him sage advice, helped him buck up and withstand the abuse, but that would be giving myself more credit than I deserve. I didn't do anything to make his life harder, but I didn't do anything to make it easier, either. Mostly, I was glad Coach had focused on someone else.

My own lot, however, was not what I'd expected. In desperation, Coach had brought in a number of junior-college transfers, and one of them played right tackle. Suddenly, I found myself demoted. Hoping to avoid being exiled to the scout team again, I approached Coach after practice on the third or fourth day of fall camp and asked if he would let me try to play center. Robert, the guy who'd run all those windsprints in street shoes during winter workouts, was now the starter, but we didn't have an experienced backup. After mulling over my request for a minute or two, Coach agreed.

The next morning it was raining. The first few times I tried to snap the ball, it went between the quarterback's legs. After about the third or fourth muffed exchange, Coach came running over and told me to hold out my hands. I thought he intended to whack me, but instead he stood there looking at them with the oddest expression. "Goddam, Yarbrough," he soon said. "You can't play center with hands as small and soft as that." He paused for a moment, then smiled and added: "I bet the women love 'em, though."

*　*　*

He quit under pressure after the 1977 season. I don't know what he did in the immediate aftermath of his resignation, but he resurfaced some years later as an assistant at a Division I program. While there, he was implicated in one of the more sensational recruiting scandals in college football history, and once again he lost his job. The last time I heard anything about him, he was coaching at a community college.

As strange as this may sound, I'm glad I played for him. Had I played at a different school, for a different kind of coach, my life might have worked out very differently. I still love football, and back then I loved it enough that I might well have become a coach myself. I don't think I would have been a good one, though, because football is, above all else, about imposing your will on another, and I lack the mindset to do that.

I didn't let him run me off. I simply quit at the end of my sophomore season, informing him of my decision in a meeting in his office, at which he was perfectly polite. "You're majoring in English, aren't you?" he asked. I told him I was. "Well," he said, "I hope that works out for you. I never was much good at it myself." We shook hands, just as we had the day I met him, and he wished me the best and I left.

I suspect that Coach, wherever he is, would not disagree with my opening assessment that playing football at the college level is a job. I was not a good employee, and I don't think he was a very good boss. But back during my freshman year, when he told me he didn't think I had what it took to play college football, he'd also observed that I might one day prove to be very good at something else. He was the first person to tell me that, and for a long time I was driven by the urge to prove him right.

Contributors

HOWARD BAHR, a native of Meridian, Mississippi, is the author of *The Black Flower* and three other novels. He teaches at Belhaven University in Jackson, Miss.

RICK BRAGG is the author of the bestselling *All Over but the Shoutin'*, *Ava's Man* and *The Prince of Frogtown*, among other books. He lives in Alabama with his family.

SONNY BREWER is the author of four novels, including *The Poet of Tolstoy Park* and *The Widow and the Tree*. He edited the anthology series *Stories from the Blue Moon Café*, and is working on a memoir about the day jobs in his life.

LARRY BROWN was a lifelong resident of Oxford, Mississippi. He authored two short story collections, *Facing the Music* and *Big Bad Love*; and six novels: *Dirty Work*, *Joe*, *Father and Son*, *Fay*, *The Rabbit Factory*, *and A Miracle of Catfish*; as well as an autobiography, *On Fire*, and a collection of essays, *Billy Ray's Farm: Essays from a Place Called Tula*. His work won many prizes and awards, including two Southern Book Critics Circle Awards for fiction; the Mississippi Institute of Arts and Letters Award for Literature; and the Lila Wallace-Reader's Digest Writer's Award. He died in 2004. In 2005 he was posthumously inducted into the Fellowship of Southern Writers.

PAT CONROY is the author of nine books, four of which were made into award-winning motion pictures, including *The Prince of Tides*. He lives in the area his works praise, the low country of South Carolina.

CONNIE MAY FOWLER is the author of one memoir and six novels, including *How Clarissa Burden Learned to Fly* and *Before Women had Wings*, which was the recipient of the 1996 Southern Book Critics Circle Award for Fiction. A Visiting Faculty member of The Vermont College of Fine Arts, Connie May lives on a sandbar in the Gulf of Mexico with her husband and four dogs.

TOM FRANKLIN is the author of *Poachers: Stories, Hell at the Breech, Smonk,* and *Crooked Letter, Crooked Letter*, all published by William Morrow. He lives in Oxford, Mississippi, and teaches at Ole Miss.

TIM GAUTREAUX's latest novel is *The Missing* (Knopf). He has published two other novels and two collections of short stories. His fiction has appeared in the *New Yorker, Atlantic,* and *Harper's*. He lives in Louisiana and North Carolina.

WILLIAM GAY is the author of three novels, including *Provinces of Night*, as well as *I Hate to See That Evening Sun Go Down*, a collection of short stories. He lives in Hohenwald, Tennessee, where he is at work on a new novel.

JOHN GRISHAM is the author of a bunch of legal thrillers, two books about football, a collection of long stories, and a kids' book.

WINSTON GROOM writes novels and histories. One of the novels was *Forrest Gump*. He lives with his wife, Anne-Clinton, and daughter, Carolina, in Point Clear, Alabama.

SILAS HOUSE is the bestselling author of four novels, two plays, and a work of nonfiction. He is the winner of the Appalachian Book of the Year, the Storylines Prize, two Kentucky Novel of the Year awards, the Appalachian Writer of the Year Award, and many others. He is Chair of Appalachian Studies at Berea College in Berea, Kentucky.

SUZANNE HUDSON is the author of a collection of short stories; two novels; and, under the pen name Ruby Pearl Saffire, a book of humor and social commentary, *Second Sluthood: A Manifesto for the Post-Menopausal, Pre-Senilic Matriarch*. She lives near Fairhope, Alabama, with author Joe Formichella.

JOSHILYN JACKSON is the *New York Times* bestselling author of *gods in Alabama, Between, Georgia, The Girl Who Stopped Swimming*, and *Backseat Saints*. She lives in Georgia with her husband and their children.

BARB JOHNSON's work has appeared in such magazines as *Glimmer Train, Washington Square*, the *Greensboro Review, Guernica* and *Oxford American*. Her debut collection of short stories is *More of This World or Maybe Another* (Harper Perennial, 2009). Johnson is the recipient of a grant from A Room of Her Own Foundation, which will support the writing of her first novel. She lives and writes in New Orleans.

CASSANDRA KING is the author of four novels, *Making Waves, The Sunday Wife, The Same Sweet Girls*, and *Queen of Broken Hearts*, as well as numerous short stories and articles. A native of L. A. (Lower Alabama), she now lives in South Carolina.

BARRY MOSER won the American Book Award for design in 1983. He has designed and/or illustrated nearly 400 books in his forty-year career. He teaches at Smith College.

JANIS OWENS is a native of West Florida, born in Marianna in 1960, and was a student of Harry Crews' Creative Writing Workshop at the University of West Florida. She is an essayist, folklorist, and novelist; the author of four books: *My Brother Michael, Myra Sims, The Schooling of Claybird Catts*, and most recently, a memoir/cookbook, *The Cracker Kitchen*.

MICHELLE RICHMOND is the author of *The Year of Fog, No One You Know, Dream of the Blue Room*, and *The Girl in the Fall-Away Dress*. She grew up in Mobile, Alabama, and now lives in northern California.

CLAY RISEN is a staff editor at the *New York Times* op-ed page and the author of *A Nation on Fire: America in the Wake of the King Assassination*. He is also a regular contributor to Chapter16.org, the literary website of the Tennessee Humanities Council. Clay grew up in Nashville and lives in New York City.

GEORGE SINGLETON has published four collections of stories, two novels, and a book of advice. He lives in South Carolina.

MATTHEW TEAGUE is a native of the Mississippi Delta and now lives with his wife, Nicole, and two children in Fairhope, Alabama. He has written from places as diverse as Algeria, Sri Lanka, New Zealand and more for *National Geographic*. His work has been included in several anthologies, and he was named by the *Columbia Journalism Review* as one of America's Top Ten Young Writers.

DANIEL WALLACE is the author of four novels. He lives in Chapel Hill, North Carolina, with his wife Laura, and teaches at the University of North Carolina.

BRAD WATSON is the author of *Last Days of the Dog-Men, The Heaven of Mercury*, and *Aliens in the Prime of Their Lives*. Originally from Mississippi, and having lived most of his adult life in Alabama, he currently maintains in Wyoming.

STEVE YARBROUGH is the author of three story collections and five novels, the most recent of which is *Safe from the Neighbors*. He lives in Massachusetts and teaches at Emerson College.

Contributors'
Works

Also by Howard Bahr

The Black Flower
The Year of Jubilo
The Judas Field
Pelican Road
Home for Christmas

Also by Rick Bragg

All Over but the Shoutin'
Wooden Churches: A Celebration
Somebody Told Me: The Newspaper Stories of Rick Bragg
Ava's Man
I Am a Soldier, Too: The Jessica Lynch Story
The Prince of Frogtown
The Most They Ever Had

Also by Sonny Brewer

Rembrandt the Rocker
A Yin for Change
The Poet of Tolstoy Park
A Sound Like Thunder
Cormac: The Tale of a Dog Gone Missing
The Widow and the Tree
(Ed.) Stories from the Blue Moon Café Volumes I-IV
(Ed.) A Cast of Characters and Other Stories

Also by Larry Brown

Facing the Music
Big Bad Love
Dirty Work
Father and Son
Joe
Fay
The Rabbit Factory
A Miracle of Catfish
On Fire
Billy Ray's Farm

Also by William Gay

The Long Home
Provinces of Night
I Hate To See That Evening Sun Go Down
Wittgenstein's Lolita/The Iceman
Twilight
The Lost Country

Also by John Grisham

Theodore Boone: Kid Lawyer
The Confession
Ford County
The Associate
The Appeal
Playing for Pizza
The Innocent Man
The Broker
The Last Juror
Bleachers
The King of Torts
The Summons
Skipping Christmas
A Painted House
The Brethren
The Testament
The Street Lawyer
The Partner
The Runaway Jury
The Rainmaker
The Chamber
The Client
The Pelican Brief
The Firm
A Time to Kill

Also by Winston Groom

Vicksburg 1863
Patriotic Fire
1942
A Storm in Flanders
The Crimson Tide
Such a Pretty, Pretty Girl
Forrest Gump
Gump & Co.
Gumpisms
Shrouds of Glory
Only
Conversations With the Enemy
As Summers Die
Better Times Than These

Also by Silas House

Eli the Good
Something's Rising: Appalachians Fighting Mountaintop Removal
The Hurting Part
A Parchment of Leaves
Clay's Quilt
The Coal Tattoo

Also by Suzanne Hudson

Opposable Thumbs
In a Temple of Trees
In the Dark of the Moon
*Second Sluthood: A Manifesto for the post-Menopausal, pre-Senilic
Matriarch*

Also by Joshilyn Jackson

Backseat Saints
Between, Georgia
gods in Alabama
The Girl Who Stopped Swimming

Also by Barb Johnson
More of This World or Maybe Another

Also by Cassandra King
Queen of Broken Hearts
The Same Sweet Girls
The Sunday Wife
Making Waves

Also by Janis Owens
My Brother Michael
Myra Sims
The Schooling of Claybird Catts
The Cracker Kitchen

Also by Michelle Richmond
The Year of Fog
No-One You Know
Dream of the Blue Room
The Girl in the Fall-Away Dress: Stories

Also by Clay Risen
A Nation on Fire: America in the Wake of the King Assassination

Also by George Singleton
These People Are Us
The Half-Mammals of Dixie
Why Dogs Chase Cars
Drowning in Gruel
Novel
Work Shirts for Madmen

Also by Matthew Teague
Matthew Teague's work has appeared in National Geographic,
The Atlantic, Philadelphia, Men's Journal, GQ, Esquire,
Popular Science, Sports Illustrated and many others.

Also by Daniel Wallace
Mr. Sebastian and the Negro Musician
Big Fish
Ray in Reverse
The Watermelon King

Also by Brad Watson
Last Days of the Dog Men
The Heaven of Mercury
Aliens in the Prime of Their Lives

Also by Steve Yarbrough
Family Men
Mississippi History
Veneer
The Oxygen Man
Visible Spirits
Prisoners of War
The End of California
Safe from the Neighbors